Beginning Entity Framework Core 5

From Novice to Professional

Eric Vogel

Apress®

Beginning Entity Framework Core 5: From Novice to Professional

Eric Vogel
Okemos, MI, USA

ISBN-13 (pbk): 978-1-4842-6881-0 ISBN-13 (electronic): 978-1-4842-6882-7
https://doi.org/10.1007/978-1-4842-6882-7

Managing Director, Apress Media LLC: Welmoed Spahr
Acquisitions Editor: Jonathan Gennick
Development Editor: Laura Berendson
Coordinating Editor: Jill Balzano

Cover image designed by Freepik (www.freepik.com)

Distributed to the book trade worldwide by Springer Science+Business Media LLC, 1 New York Plaza, Suite 4600, New York, NY 10004. Phone 1-800-SPRINGER, fax (201) 348-4505, e-mail orders-ny@springer-sbm.com, or visit www.springeronline.com. Apress Media, LLC is a California LLC and the sole member (owner) is Springer Science + Business Media Finance Inc (SSBM Finance Inc). SSBM Finance Inc is a **Delaware** corporation.

For information on translations, please e-mail booktranslations@springernature.com; for reprint, paperback, or audio rights, please e-mail bookpermissions@springernature.com.

Apress titles may be purchased in bulk for academic, corporate, or promotional use. eBook versions and licenses are also available for most titles. For more information, reference our Print and eBook Bulk Sales web page at http://www.apress.com/bulk-sales.

Any source code or other supplementary material referenced by the author in this book is available to readers on GitHub via the book's product page, located at www.apress.com/9781484268810. For more detailed information, please visit http://www.apress.com/source-code.

Printed on acid-free paper

Table of Contents

About the Author

Eric Vogel is a seasoned contributor to *Visual Studio Magazine* and Senior Software Developer at Red Cedar Solutions Group. He has been developing .NET Framework web and desktop solutions for 13 years. He holds a Bachelor of Science degree in computer science from Michigan State University. He is Acting President of the Greater Lansing User Group for .NET.

About the Technical Reviewer

Pieter Nijs is a Belgian .NET architect with a passion for mobile and cloud development. He has played a key role in several projects ranging from large consumer-facing healthcare, telecom, and media apps to smaller LOB applications. As a mobile development expert at Xpirit Belgium, he loves helping customers implement mobile-first and cloud-first applications. Pieter is primarily interested in the Microsoft stack, so his interest and expertise translate to technologies like .NET, C#, XAML, Xamarin, UWP, Azure, Azure DevOps, and so on. Both at work and in his spare time, Pieter is constantly working and playing with these and other new technologies. He likes to tell everybody about the things he does, sharing his knowledge. Hence, you can find him speaking at conferences, giving trainings, and blogging at blog.pieeatingninjas.be. Since 2017, Pieter has been receiving the Microsoft MVP Award in the Windows Development category for sharing his passion and expertise with the community.

Introduction

This book is aimed at readers who have a beginner's knowledge of the .NET Framework who are looking to use Entity Framework (EF) Core 5 for a side project or business application. No prior knowledge of Entity Framework Core 5 is required. The book guides the user through the basics of Entity Framework Core 5 up to some more advanced concepts and culminates in creating an ASP.NET Core Razor Pages web application that has full create, read, update, and delete (CRUD) capability.

We will be using the NUnit Framework to test Entity Framework Core 5 behavior before using it in a full web application. You will first go over how to query data and then how to insert, update, and delete data. Later in the book, we will go over more advanced techniques like how to aggregate data, use navigation properties to get related data, and call custom raw SQL and stored procedures.

The later chapters also cover basic authentication, authorization, and reporting in an ASP.NET Core Razor Pages web application. You will learn how to query and manipulate a SQL Server database by testing each facet through NUnit integration tests.

PART I

Getting Started

CHAPTER 1

Installation

In order to use Entity Framework Core 5, you will need some tools. These tools include Visual Studio (VS) 2019 and some NuGet packages for your solution.

Install Visual Studio

The first step is getting a version of Visual Studio 2019. The Community Edition of Visual Studio 2019 for Windows can be used for all code in this book. If you are running macOS, you can also opt to install Visual Studio for Mac. I'll be using Windows for the remainder of the book, but the steps are about the same for macOS.

You can download Visual Studio 2019 from `https://visualstudio.microsoft.com/downloads/` as seen in Figure 1-1.

E. Vogel, *Beginning Entity Framework Core 5*, https://doi.org/10.1007/978-1-4842-6882-7_1

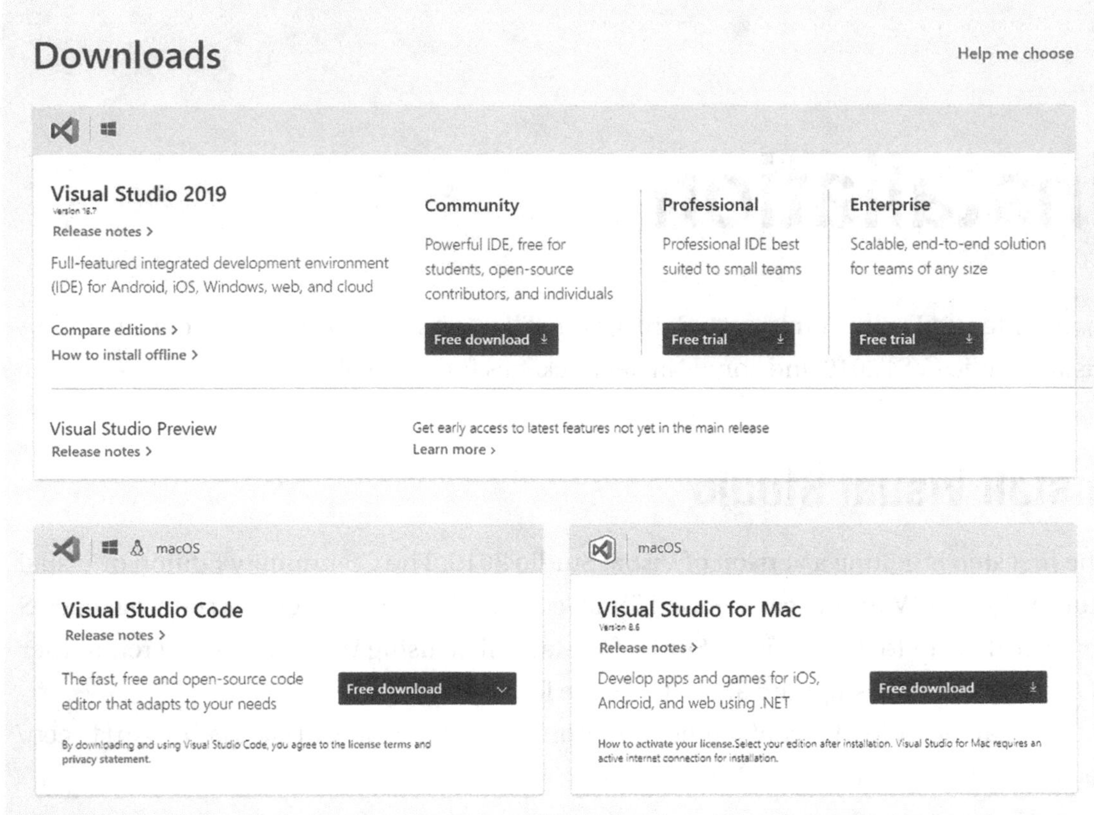

Figure 1-1. *Download VS 2019*

Next, install the latest Visual Studio 2019 and select the .NET Core option as seen in Figure 1-2.

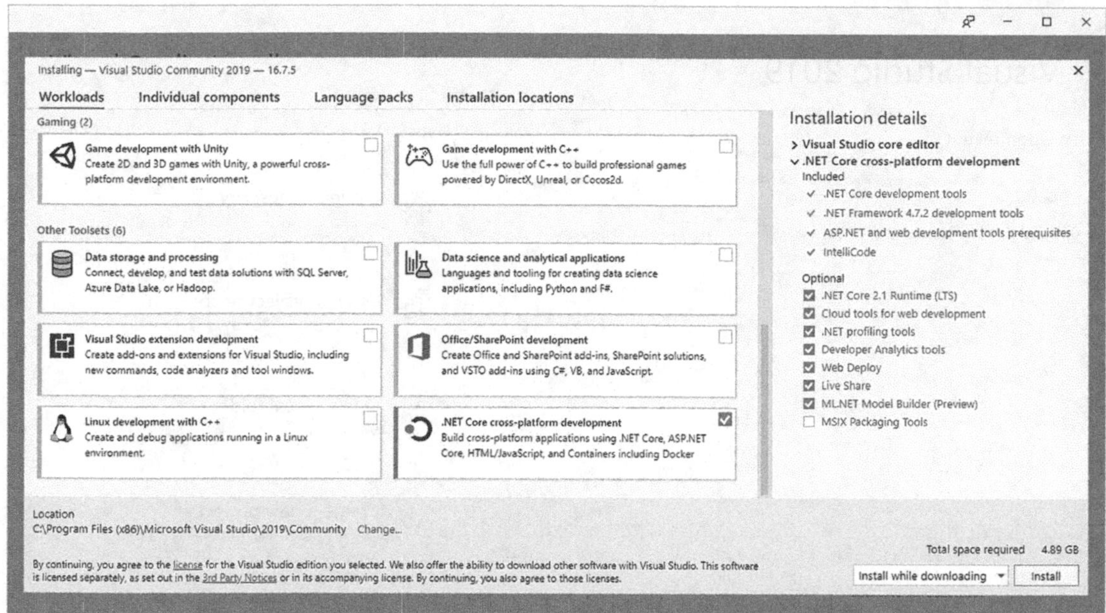

Figure 1-2. *Install .NET Core Support*

Entity Framework Core 5 will run on both .NET Core 3.1 and .NET 5. For this book, we will be using .NET Core 3.1.

Create a Project

Entity Framework Core 5 works on a variety of application types from console apps, desktop apps, and web apps. For this book, we will be creating an ASP.NET Core MVC (Model-View-Controller) app.

We will now create the project in Visual Studio and install all the required tools to use Entity Framework Core 5. First, create a new project in Visual Studio as seen in Figure 1-3.

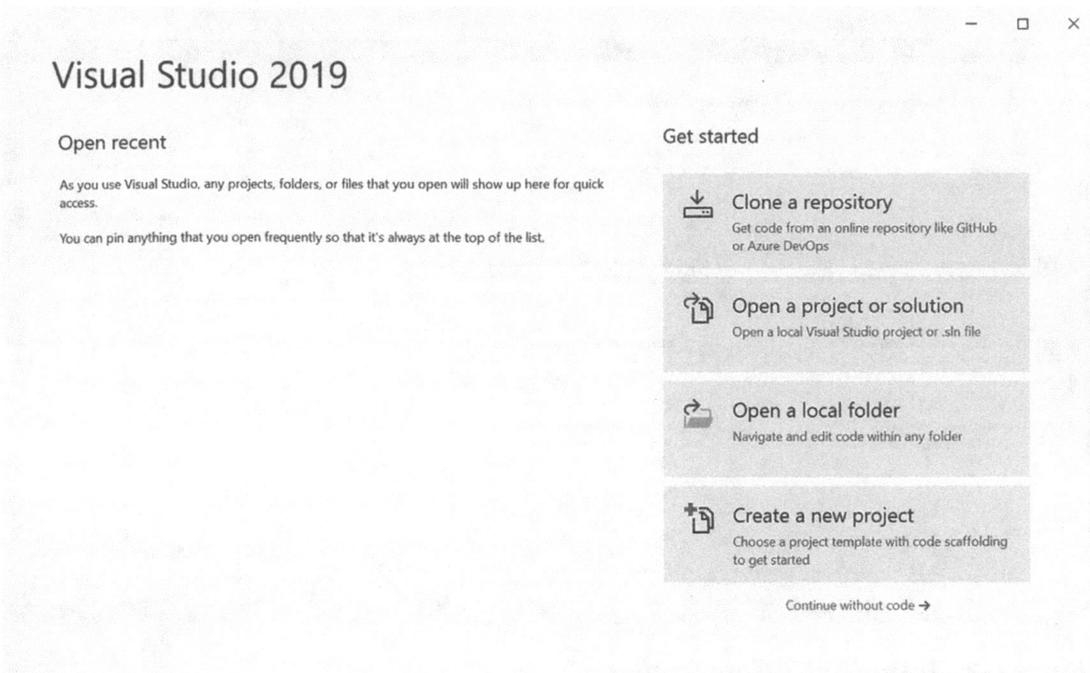

Figure 1-3. *Create a New Visual Studio 2019 Project*

Then create a new ASP.NET Core web application as seen in Figure 1-4.

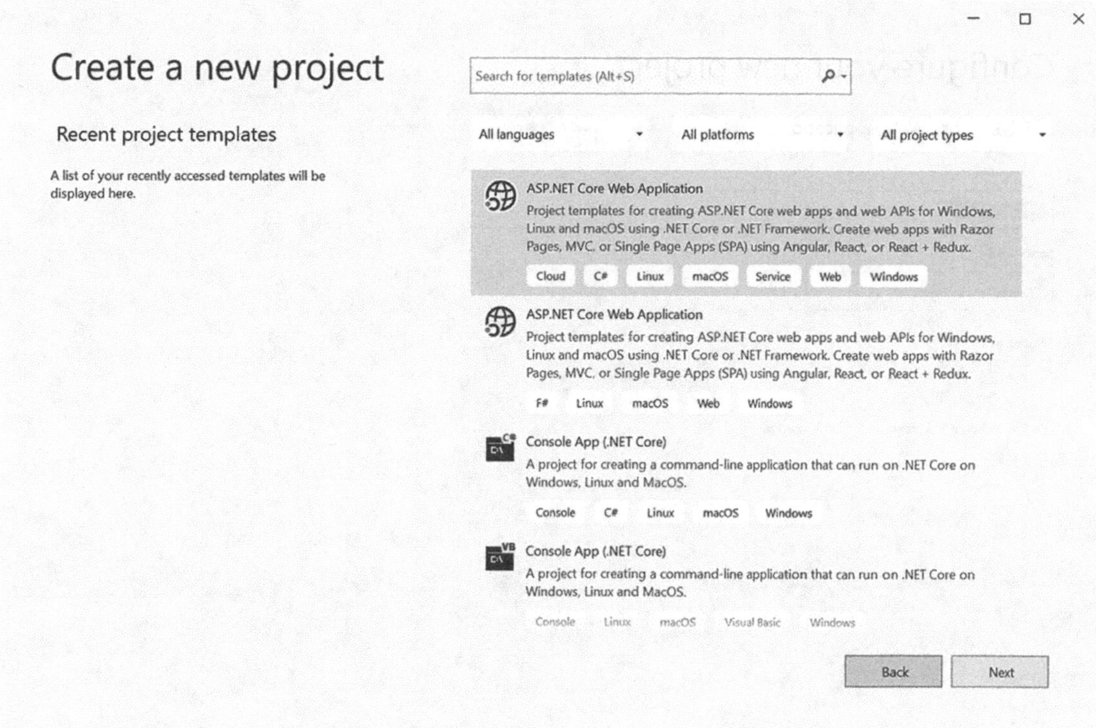

Figure 1-4. *New ASP.NET Core Web App*

Next, name your ASP.NET Core web application. I named my app EFCore5WebApp as seen in Figure 1-5.

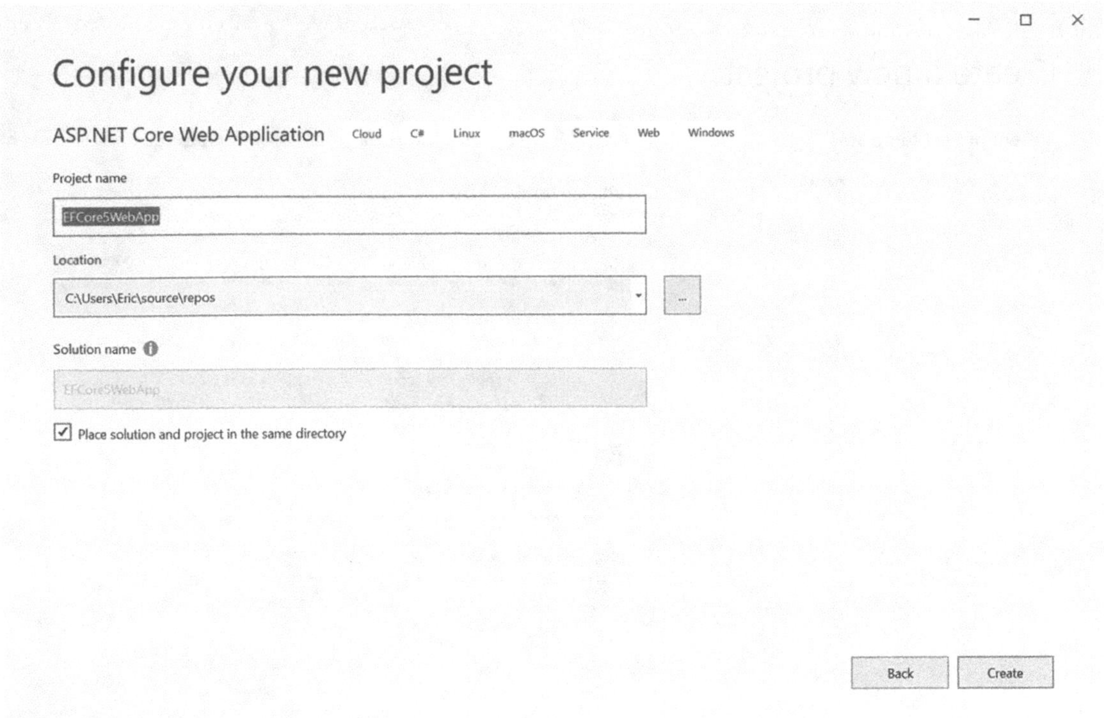

Figure 1-5. Naming the Web App

After that, select ASP.NET Core 3.1 as the target framework and select the Model-View-Controller template as seen in Figure 1-6.

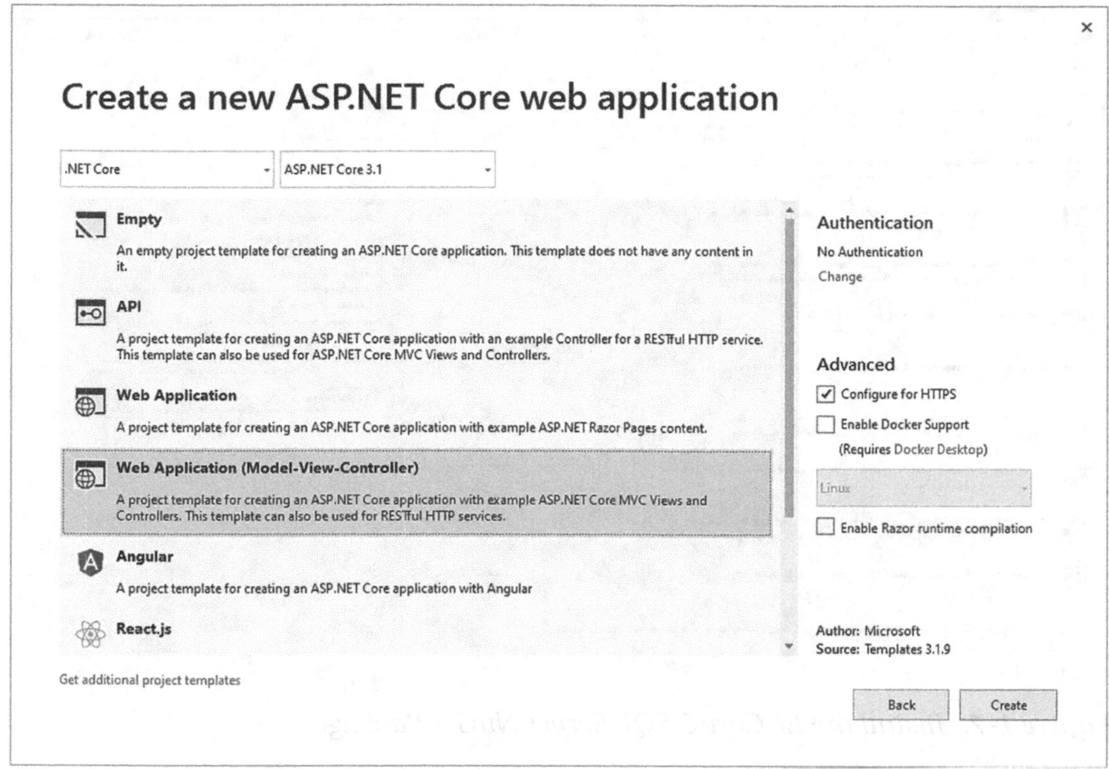

Figure 1-6. *Creating an ASP.NET Core 5.0 MVC App*

Then click the "Create" button to create the project and solution. After this, you will see the generated project opened in Visual Studio.

Install Entity Framework

Entity Framework Core 5 has providers for Microsoft SQL Server, SQLite, Cosmos, and in-memory databases. For this book, we will be using the SQL Server provider.

Entity Framework is installed through the NuGet Package Manager. We will be installing the Entity Framework Core 5 SQL Server NuGet package, which will allow us to interact with a Microsoft SQL Server instance.

Now it is time to install the Entity Framework Core 5 SQL Server NuGet package into the web app. Open the NuGet installer and search for "Entity Framework" and click the "Include prerelease" checkbox as shown in Figure 1-7.

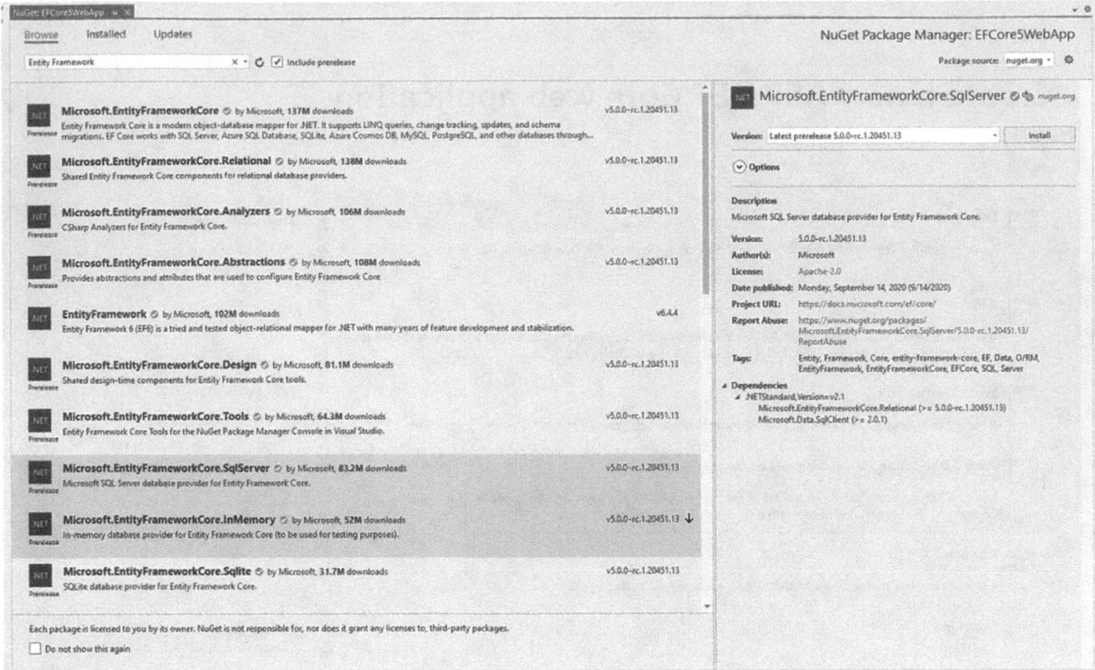

Figure 1-7. *Install the EF Core 5 SQL Server NuGet Package*

Click the Install button, and you should be prompted to confirm your installation as seen in Figure 1-8. Make sure the version is 5.* and that the package name is Microsoft. EntityFrameworkCore.SqlServer, which will install Entity Framework Core 5 with SQL Server support.

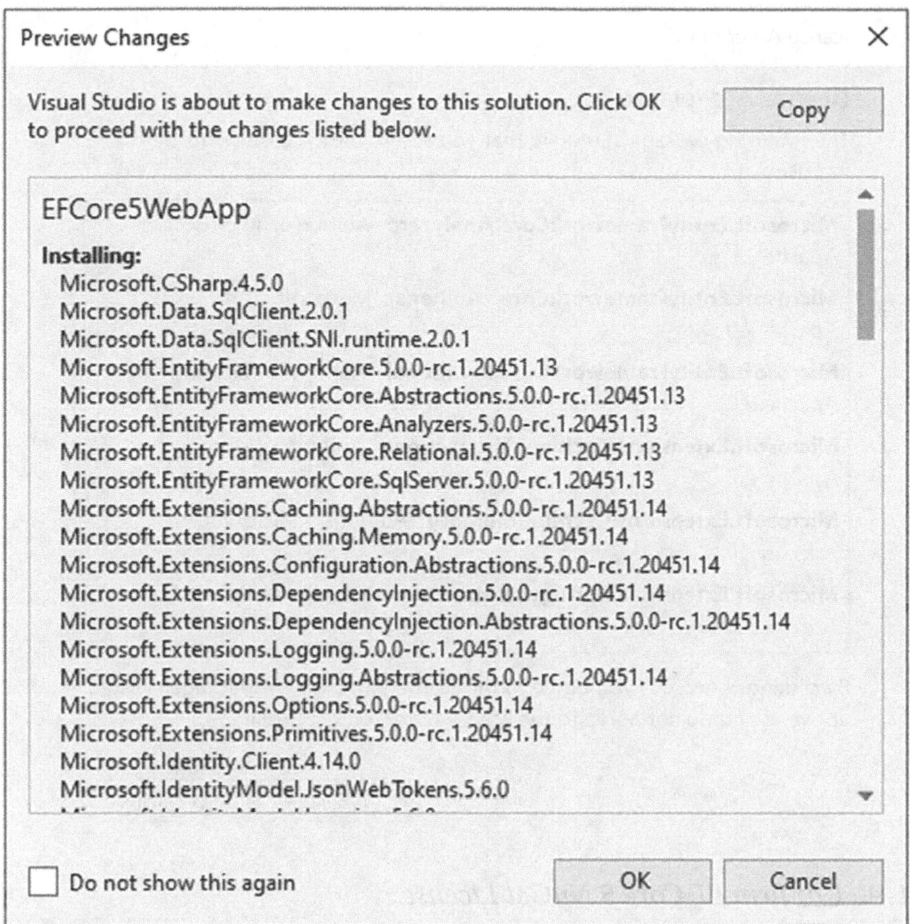

***Figure 1-8.** Confirm EF Core SQL Server NuGet Installation*

Lastly, you'll be prompted to accept the license to install the EF Core 5 NuGet package as seen in Figure 1-9.

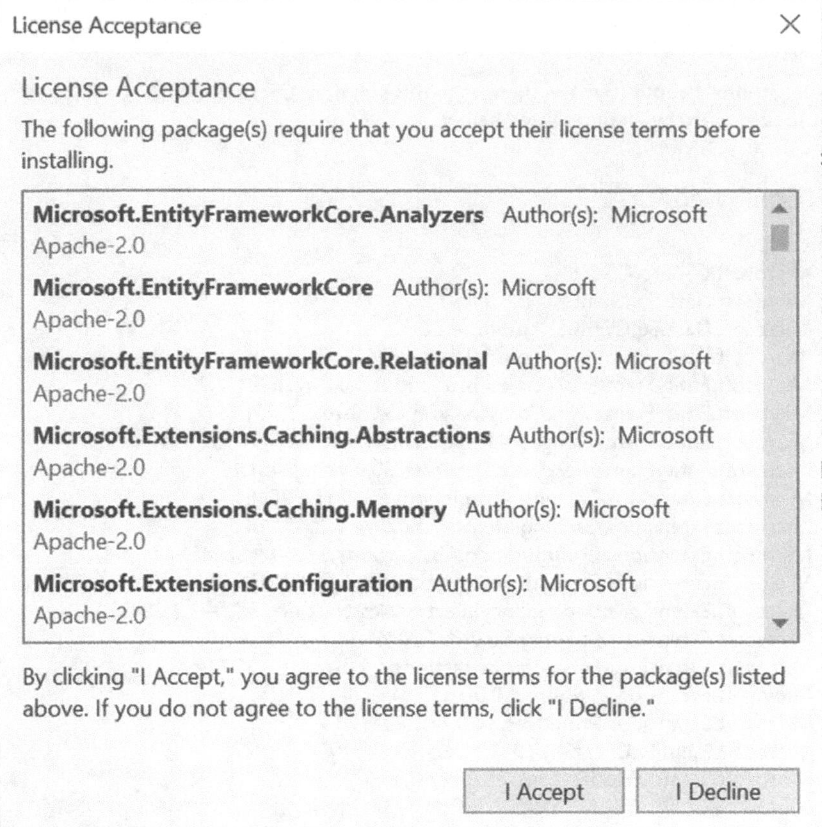

Figure 1-9. *Confirm EF Core 5 NuGet License*

Click the I Accept button, and the package will be installed.

Install the Core Tools Package

Finally, you'll need to install the Entity Framework 5 Core Tools package, which will allow you to create and update your database from the NuGet Package Manager Console. Open up the NuGet Package Manager and search for "Entity Framework Tools" and install the package as seen in Figure 1-10. Make sure to install the package named "Microsoft.EntityFrameworkCore.Tools" and that the version is 5.*.

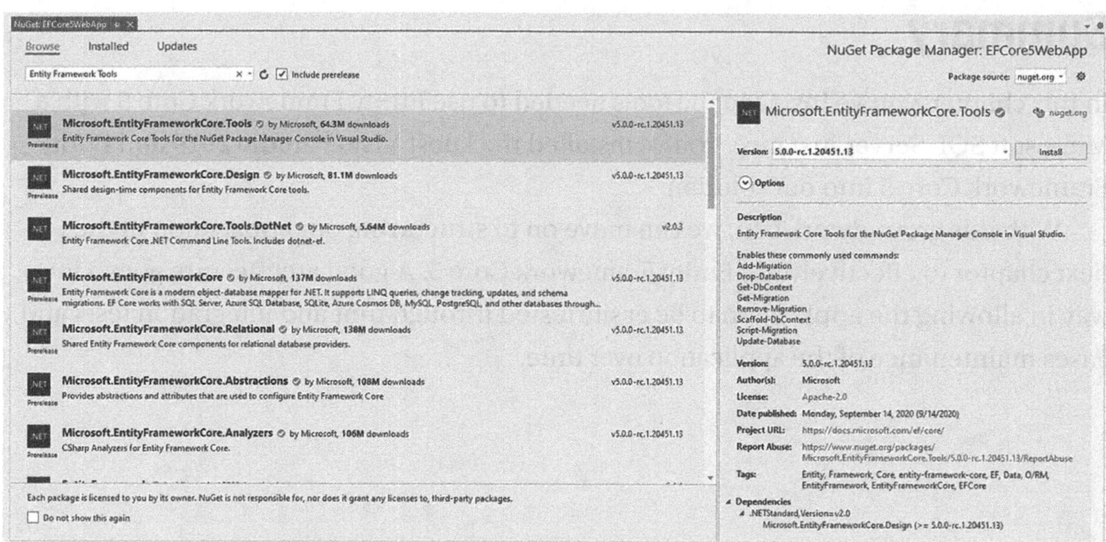

Figure 1-10. *Install the EF Core 5 Tools NuGet Package*

You have now successfully installed the needed tools to use Entity Framework Core 5. In the next chapter, we will cover how to move the Entity Framework 5 NuGet installation to a data access layer (DAL) project and how to structure your application using an N-tier architecture. You are well on your way to learning how to effectively use Entity Framework Core 5.

SQL Server Database

For this book, we will be using SQL Server Express LocalDb that is installed automatically by Visual Studio 2019 Preview as part of the .NET Core workload. Feel free to use your own full SQL Server instance. I will cover how to set the database connection string and create the database from code in Chapter 5.

Summary

In this chapter, you've installed the tools needed to use Entity Framework Core 5 with a Microsoft SQL Server instance. You've installed the latest Visual Studio 2019 and Entity Framework Core 5 into our solution.

With this groundwork lain, we can move on to structuring our application in the next chapter to effectively use Entity Framework Core 5. A good architecture goes a long way in allowing the application to be easily tested through unit and integration tests and eases maintenance of the application over time.

CHAPTER 2

Project Structure

Creating the structure of your application is an important step. In this chapter, I will detail how to use a multilayered architecture to separate concerns in the application. This will make your application easier to maintain and extend.

Core Project

The Core project is where the commonly used code shared across the entire application will reside. This is where the entity classes used by Entity Framework will live. This is also where common interfaces and utility code will exist.

To get started, open the solution you created in Chapter 1. Then add a new .NET Standard C# class library project named "EFCore5WebApp.Core" to the solution as seen in Figure 2-1.

E. Vogel, *Beginning Entity Framework Core 5*, https://doi.org/10.1007/978-1-4842-6882-7_2

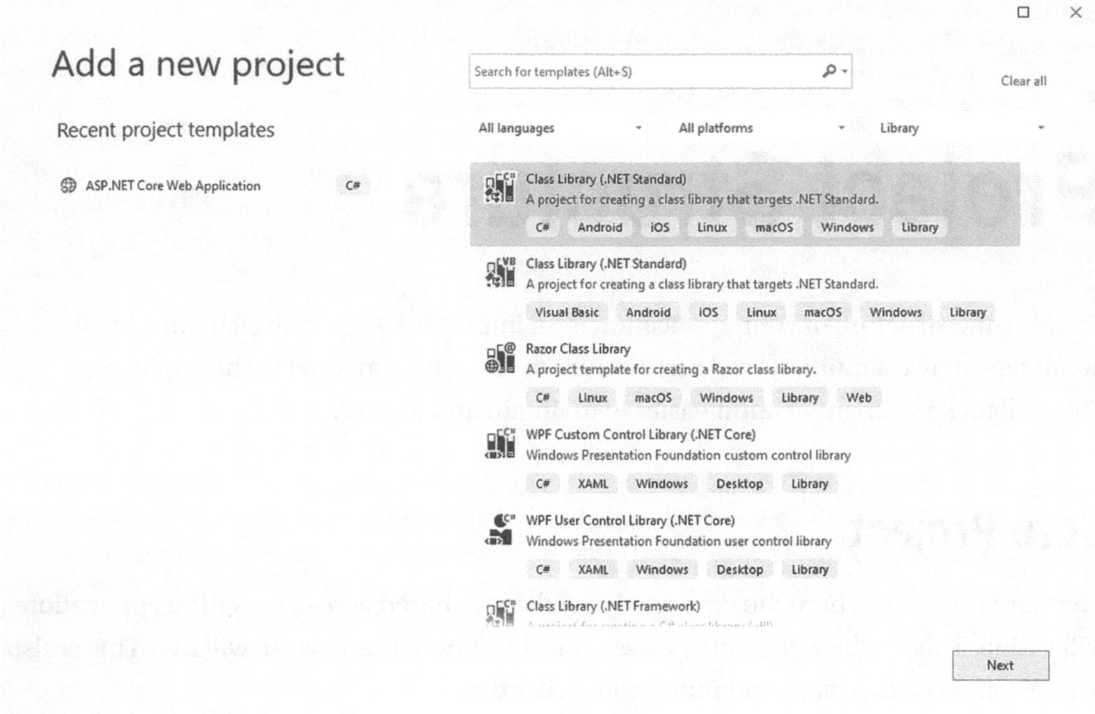

Figure 2-1. *New Class Library*

On the next screen, name your project “EFCore5WebApp.Core” as seen in Figure 2-2.

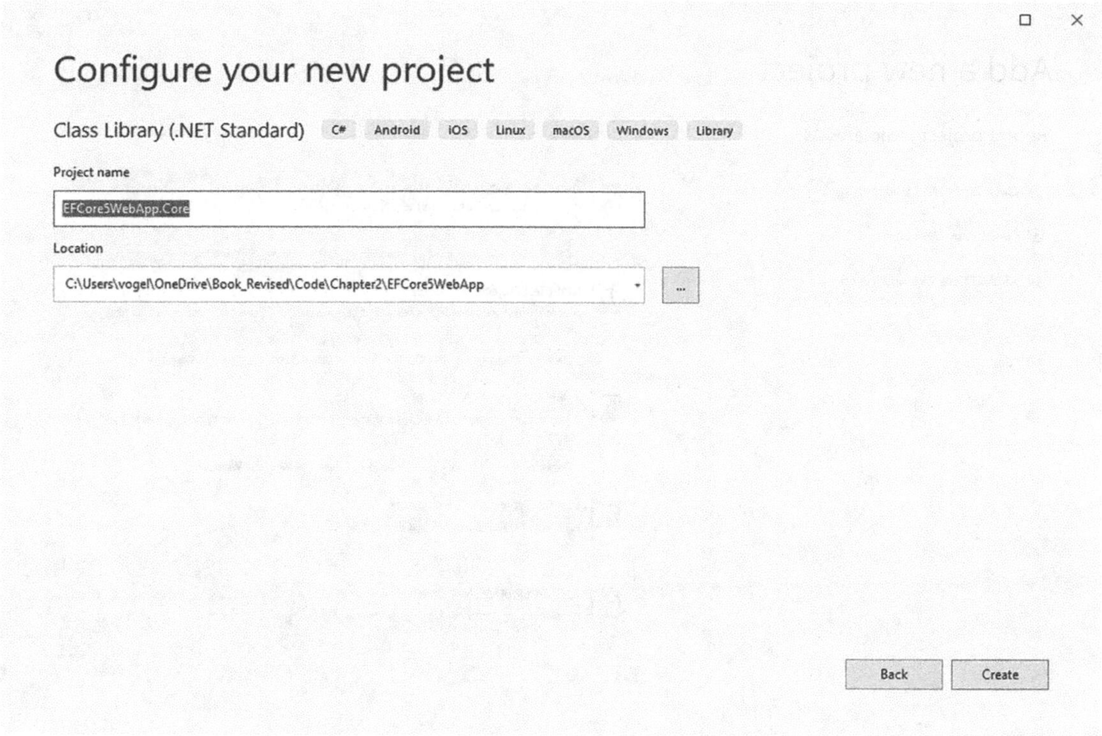

Configure your new project

Class Library (.NET Standard) C# Android iOS Linux macOS Windows Library

Project name

EFCore5WebApp.Core

Location

C:\Users\vogel\OneDrive\Book_Revised\Code\Chapter2\EFCore5WebApp

Back Create

Figure 2-2. *Naming the Core Project*

Next, create a new NUnit Test Project (.NET Core) template project named "EFCore5WebApp.Core.Tests". This project will be where we'll create any needed unit tests for shared application code. You can easily find the correct template by searching for "NUnit" in the template dialog as seen in Figure 2-3.

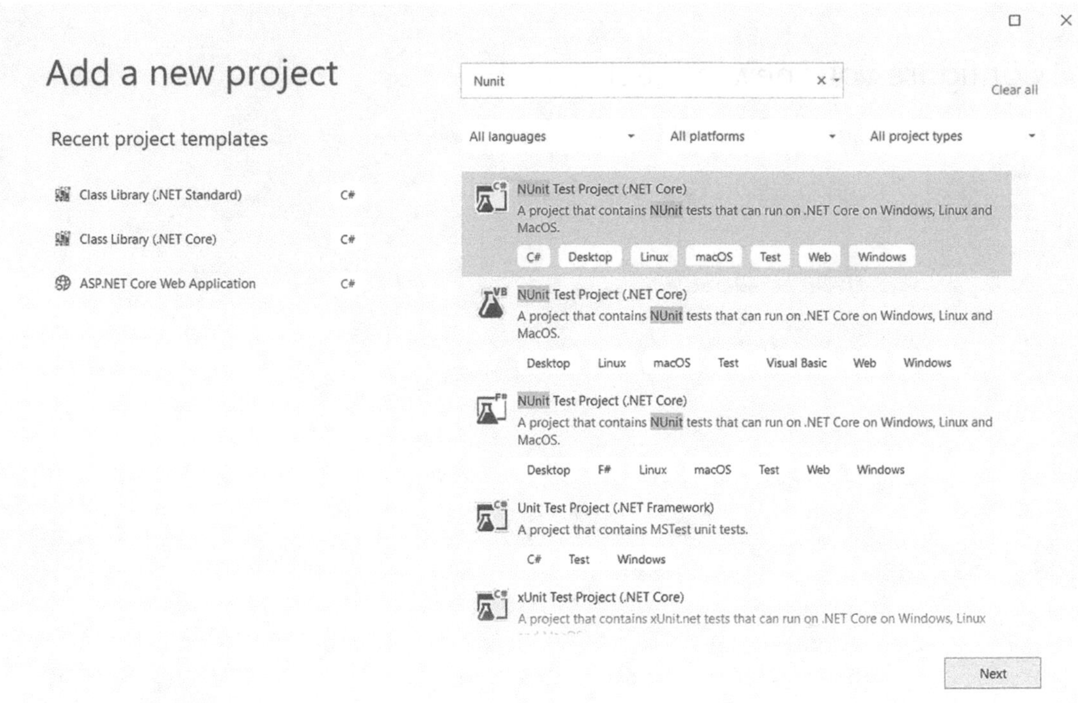

Figure 2-3. *Adding a NUnit Project*

After adding the Core.Tests project, add a project reference to the Core project to it.

Unit Testing Overview

NUnit is a commonly used unit testing framework. Unit tests have become popular with the whole Test-Driven Development (TDD) movement, in which you create unit tests first and then write the code to make the tests pass. Later in the book, we'll be testing that our Entity Framework Core 5 code works correctly before integrating it into our web project.

A unit test tests a small set of code, usually at the method level. You test the happy path as well as potential edge cases to make sure your code is solid before it becomes integrated into the rest of the solution.

Data Access Layer Project

Next, we'll create the data access layer project, or DAL project for short. Create a new .NET Core C# class library as seen in Figure 2-4 called "EFCore5WebApp.DAL".

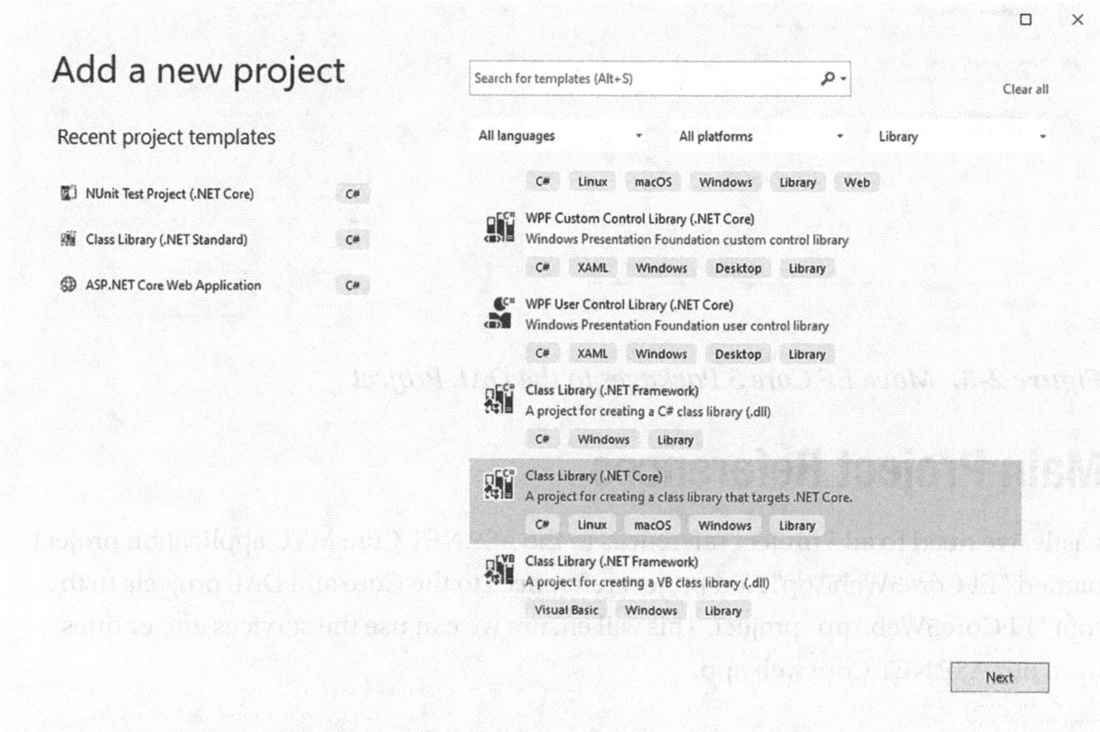

Figure 2-4. *New .NET Core Class Library*

Then add a project reference to the Core project to the DAL project. After that, add a NUnit Test Project to the solution named "EFCore5WebApp.DAL.Tests". Add references to the DAL and Core projects to the DAL.Tests project. After that, add Core project reference to the DAL and DAL.Tests projects. The DAL.Tests project will be where we test all of our Entity Framework Core 5 code before putting it to use in the web project.

Next, we'll move the EF Core 5 NuGet packages into the DAL projects. Right-click the solution node and click the Manage NuGet Packages for Solution option. Then select the Microsoft.EntityFramewrokCore.SqlServer project and select the DAL and DAL.Tests projects and click the Install button as seen in Figure 2-5.

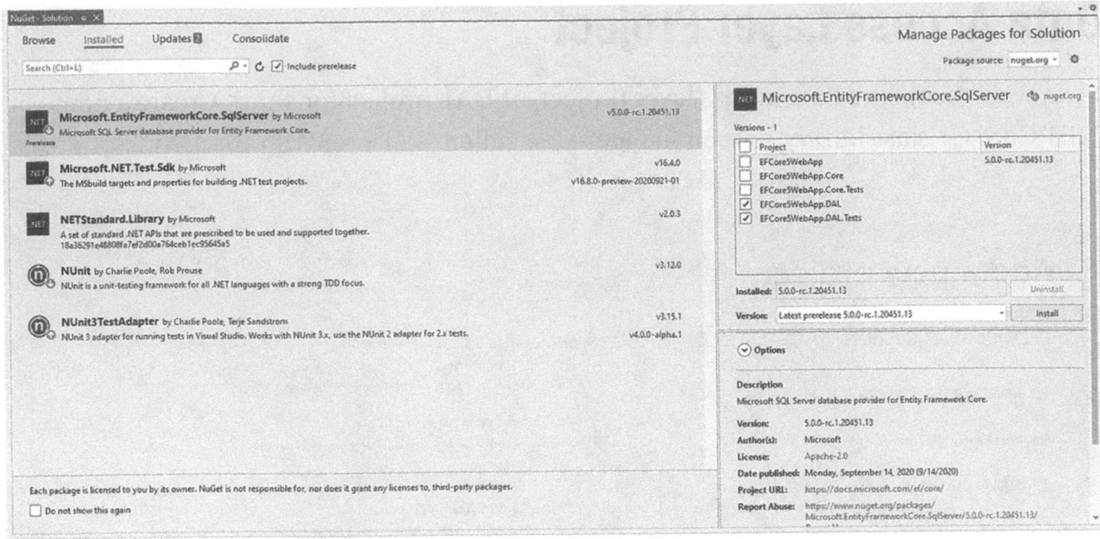

Figure 2-5. Move EF Core 5 Packages to the DAL Project

Main Project References

Lastly, we need to add project references to the ASP.NET Core MVC application project named "EFCore5WebApp". Add project references to the Core and DAL projects to the root "EFCore5WebApp" project. This will ensure we can use the services and entities from our ASP.NET Core web app.

Summary

In this chapter, we've set ourselves up for success by creating a multilayered project structure. The Core project contains our entities that will be used by Entity Framework in the DAL project. The DAL project is where our Entity Framework Core 5 code will reside. Our web project will make use of the Core and DAL projects. Your project structure should now look like Figure 2-6.

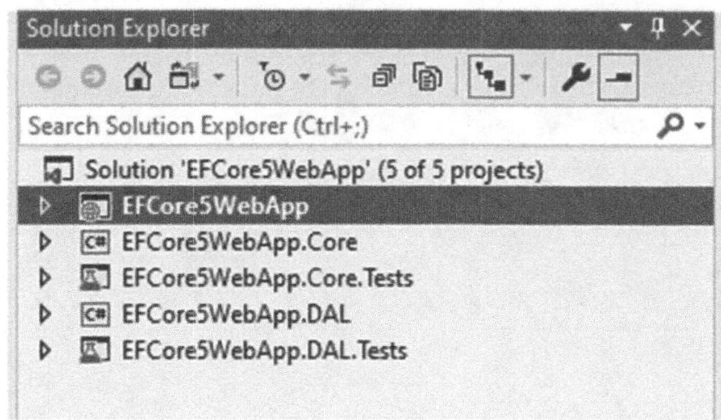

Figure 2-6. *Project Structure*

By separating your projects by application concerns, the project will be easier to maintain and extend over time. We've also architected the solution with unit testing support. This will speed up development time by making it easier to safely make changes to the application without worrying about introducing new side effect bugs, and functionality will be regression tested during development time.

In the next chapter, I'll cover how to create the entity classes that will later be used by Entity Framework Core 5 in Chapter 4. Entity classes are used by Entity Framework Core 5 to map to tables in your database.

PART II

Core Features

CHAPTER 3

Entities

Entities are the focus of Entity Framework Core 5. An entity is an object that maps to one or more tables in a database. Entity Framework Core 5 uses a code-first approach. This means that you create your entities and Entity Framework will generate the database schema to store your entity data.

Person Entity

Our first entity is going to be a Person entity that will have an Id, first name, last name, and one-to-many addresses. The address will be its own entity. First, let's make the Person entity without any addresses.

To get started, create an Entities folder in the Core project. Next, add a Person class to the Entities folder. Then add an integer Id property and FirstName, LastName, and EmailAddress string properties as seen in Listing 3-1.

Listing 3-1. Initial Person Class

```
namespace EFCore5WebApp.Core.Entities
{
    public class Person
    {
        public int Id { get; set; }
        public string FirstName { get; set; }
        public string LastName { get; set; }
        public string EmailAddress { get; set; }
    }
}
```


E. Vogel, *Beginning Entity Framework Core 5*, https://doi.org/10.1007/978-1-4842-6882-7_3

Address Entity

Now it is time to create the Address class. The Address class will have Id, line 1, line 2, city, state, country, person Id, and zip code properties as seen in Listing 3-2.

Listing 3-2. Initial Address Class

```
namespace EFCore5WebApp.Core.Entities
{
    public class Address
    {
        public int Id { get; set; }
        public string AddressLine1 { get; set; }
        public string AddressLine2 { get; set; }
        public string City { get; set; }
        public string State { get; set; }
        public string Country { get; set; }
        public string ZipCode { get; set; }
        public int PersonId { get; set; }
    }
}
```

Simple Navigation Property

Now we add the Addresses navigation property to the Person class. This will allow a person to have one-to-many address records associated with them as seen in Listing 3-3.

Listing 3-3. Person Class with Addresses

```
using System.Collections.Generic;

namespace EFCore5WebApp.Core.Entities
{
    public class Person
    {
        public int Id { get; set; }
        public string FirstName { get; set; }
```

```
        public string LastName { get; set; }
        public string EmailAddress { get; set; }
        public List<Address> Addresses { get; set; } = new List<Address>();
    }
}
```

Navigation properties are covered in more detail in Chapter 11. Their purpose is to link one entity to another entity. In the case of Listing 3-3, the Addresses property is a list of Address values, and each Address value will be an Id value of an object in the Address class.

In our example, we are defining a one-to-many relationship between a Person entity and its collection of mapped Address entities. Navigation properties can also be in one-to-one relationships in which case the navigation property would not be a collection but just the type of the mapped entity.

Entity Property Constraints

Entity Framework supports two ways to configure entities beyond the default column and relationship settings. For this chapter, I'll cover how to use data annotations to add constraints to entity properties. In the next chapter, I'll cover the fluent API configuration path. Both are valid ways of containing entities and have their pros and cons.

In order to use these attributes with our .NET Standard "Core" project, we need to install the "System.ComponentModel.DataAnnotations" NuGet package as seen in Figure 3-1.

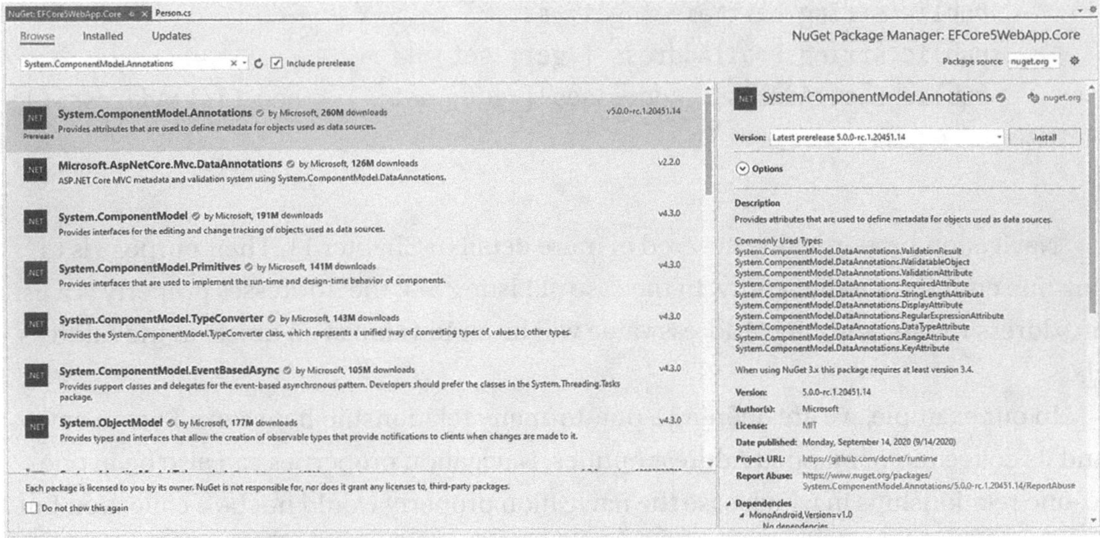

Figure 3-1. *Installing the System.ComponentModel.DataAnnotations NuGet Package*

Let's make the first name, last name, and email address columns required by decorating them with the Required attribute as seen in Listing 3-4.

Listing 3-4. Person Class with Required Fields

```
using System.Collections.Generic;
using System.ComponentModel.DataAnnotations;

namespace EFCore5WebApp.Core.Entities
{
    public class Person
    {
        public int Id { get; set; }
        [Required]
        public string FirstName { get; set; }
        [Required]
        public string LastName { get; set; }
        [Required]
        public string EmailAddress { get; set; }
        public List<Address> Addresses { get; set; } = new List<Address>();
    }
}
```

Furthermore, we can also limit the maximum length of string properties by decorating class properties with the MaxLength property. Let's make the first and last names be limited to 255 characters as seen in Listing 3-5.

Listing 3-5. Person with Limited-Length Fields

```
using System.Collections.Generic;
using System.ComponentModel.DataAnnotations;

namespace EFCore5WebApp.Core.Entities
{
    public class Person
    {
        public int Id { get; set; }
        [Required]
        [MaxLength(255)]
        public string FirstName { get; set; }
        [Required]
        [MaxLength(255)]
        public string LastName { get; set; }
        [Required]
        public string EmailAddress { get; set; }
        public List<Address> Addresses { get; set; } = new List<Address>();
    }
}
```

When it comes time for Entity Framework Core to create the database schema, the FirstName and LastName fields will be created as nvarchar(255) columns, and both columns will not allow nulls because they are required.

Entity Schema Attributes

Entity schema class-level attributes can be used to define settings for the entire entity. A quite common setting is the Table annotation, in which you can define the table and schema that are used for an entity in the database.

For example, if we wanted the Person entity to be stored in a table called Persons, we would decorate the class with the Table annotation and pass in "Persons" as seen in Listing 3-6.

Listing 3-6. Person Class Mapped to Persons Table

```
using System.Collections.Generic;
using System.ComponentModel.DataAnnotations;
using System.ComponentModel.DataAnnotations.Schema;

namespace EFCore5WebApp.Core.Entities
{
    [Table("Persons")]
    public class Person
    {
        public int Id { get; set; }
        [Required]
        [MaxLength(255)]
        public string FirstName { get; set; }
        [Required]
        [MaxLength(255)]
        public string LastName { get; set; }
        [Required]
        public string EmailAddress { get; set; }
        public List<Address> Addresses { get; set; } = new List<Address>();
    }
}
```

Furthermore, you can create an entity in a given database schema by specifying the Schema property in the Table attribute. For example, to place the person records in the dbo schema, you would use

```
[Table("Persons", Schema ="dbo")]
public class Person
```

The Person class will now be stored in the dbo schema, in a table named Persons.

More Entity Schema Attributes

Another commonly used entity schema attribute is the NotMapped attribute, which as the name suggests will not store the associated property in the database. Choosing to not store a property is useful for calculated fields. For example, we could add a full name property that is the concatenation of the first and last names like this:

```
[NotMapped]
public string FullName => $"{FirstName} {LastName}";
```

If you want to have a database column be named something other than the property name, you can use the Column property attribute. You pass in the name of the column into the attribute like this:

```
[Column("Person_Id")]
public int Id { get; set; }
```

This is particularly useful if you have a database administrator on your team who wants the columns to use a different naming convention than you want your entities to be in code.

The Column attribute also has a TypeName property that as the name suggests allows you to force the database column type to use. For example, if you wanted to use varchar instead of nvarchar for the FirstName property, you could tell Entity Framework to map the first name to a varchar(255) like this:

```
[Column(TypeName = "varchar(255)")]
public string FirstName { get; set; }
```

Mapping of the Primary Key Column

Entity Framework by default will mark a property that is named either Id or EntityNameId as the primary key. This means that for our Person class, Entity Framework will make the Id property the primary key in the database.

If you want to break this naming convention, you can simply use the Key property like this:

```
[Key]
public int Person_Id { get; set; }
```

The Key annotation can come in handy if you have, for example, a lookup table that contains a character code, a description, and a lookup type and you want to make the Code column be the primary key as seen in Listing 3-7.

Listing 3-7. LookUp Entity Class

```
using System.ComponentModel.DataAnnotations;

namespace EFCore5WebApp.Core.Entities
{
    public class LookUp
    {
        [Key]
        public string Code { get; set; }
        public string Description { get; set; }
        public int LookUpType { get; set; }
    }
}
```

Enum Mapping

A handy feature of Entity Framework is that you can map an enum to an integer in the database and use the enum in your entity. For our code, we'll be using a generic lookup table to store states and countries and will store the type as an enum in the entity. Look at Listing 3-8 to see this in action.

Listing 3-8. LookUp Entity with Enum Type

```
using System.ComponentModel.DataAnnotations;

namespace EFCore5WebApp.Core.Entities
{
    public enum LookUpType
    {
        State = 0,
        Country = 1
    }
```

```
    public class LookUp
    {
        [Key]
        public string Code { get; set; }
        public string Description { get; set; }
        public LookUpType LookUpType { get; set; }
    }
}
```

Entity Inheritance Mapping

There are two types of inheritance trees in Entity Framework Core 5, table-per-hierarchy and table-per-type. The default is table-per-hierarchy inheritance where if you have derived classes, they will roll into the hierarchy into a single table. If you want to use table-per-type, you can use the [Table()] attribute on the derived type to instruct Entity Framework Core 5 to map the derived type to its own table. Let's now go over both approaches in more detail.

Table-per-Hierarchy

With table-per-hierarchy, you define a base class and a derived class and specify a discriminator column that determines what rows match to which type (base/derived). You can only have one subclass that will be included using table-per-hierarchy inheritance. For example, if we have a Shape entity that has Width and Height properties and we want to add a Cube entity that extends Shape and adds a Length property, our code would look like Listing 3-9.

Listing 3-9. Table-per-Hierarchy Code Example

```
public class Shape
{
    public int Width { get; set; }
    public int Height { get; set; }
}
```

```
public class Cube : Shape
{
    public int Length { get; set; }
}

class MyContext : DbContext
{
    public DbSet<Shape> Shapes { get; set; }
    public DbSet<Cube> Cube { get; set; }
}
```

In our code, Entity Framework will create a shadow property called "Discriminator" for use that stores the name of the entity as its value. You can explicitly map this shadow property using the OnModelCreating() method on your DbContext class like this:

```
protected override void OnModelCreating(ModelBuilder modelBuilder)
{
    modelBuilder.Entity<Shape>()
        .HasDiscriminator<string>("ShapeType")
        .HasValue<Shape>("S")
        .HasValue<Cube>("C");
}
```

In the preceding example, we named our discriminator column "ShapeType" and store the value "S" for Shape rows and "C" for Cube rows.

Table-per-Type

Table-per-type inheritance mapping allows us to store derived entities in their own tables. This is a new feature to Entity Framework Core 5. We have two ways to explicitly tell Entity Framework Core 5 what table names we want to use. The two options are the Table attribute and the model builder API using OnModelCreating().

Let's look over using the Table attribute first. We would change our code to look like Listing 3-10.

Listing 3-10. Table-per-Type Table Attribute Approach

```
[Table("Shape")]
public class Shape
{
    public int Width { get; set; }
    public int Height { get; set; }
}

[Table("Cube")]
public class Cube : Shape
{
    public int Length { get; set; }
}

class MyContext : DbContext
{
    public DbSet<Shape> Shapes { get; set; }
    public DbSet<Cube> Cube { get; set; }
}
```

The second approach is to use OnModelCreating() in our DbContext, and we can avoid using any annotations. To do this, we use the ToTable() method on the model builder API in OnModelCreating() as seen in Listing 3-11.

Listing 3-11. Table Mapping using OnModelCreating

```
public class Shape
{
    public int Width { get; set; }
    public int Height { get; set; }
}

public class Cube : Shape
{
    public int Length { get; set; }
}
```

```
class MyContext : DbContext
{
    public DbSet<Shape> Shapes { get; set; }
    public DbSet<Cube> Cube { get; set; }

    protected override void OnModelCreating(ModelBuilder modelBuilder)
    {
        modelBuilder.Entity<Shape>().ToTable("Shape");
        modelBuilder.Entity<Cube>().ToTable("Cube");
    }
}
```

Summary

We have covered a lot of ground in this chapter. You have learned how to create a simple Person entity object with an Addresses navigation property. Furthermore, we covered how to change the Entity Framework Core mapping to the destination database table with the Table class attribute. Then we went over how to further customize the entity property mappings through property attributes to provide instructions to Entity Framework Core on how to construct its mapped database column when it will be generated in Chapters 4 and 5.

The next chapter will cover the Entity Framework Core database context class in detail. The database context class will be used to interface our entities with the target database to perform create, read, update, delete, and aggregation operations. All of these topics will be covered in detail in later chapters.

CHAPTER 4

Database Context

In this chapter, I will cover what an Entity Framework Core 5 database context is and how to configure it. The database context implemented in the DbContext class allows you to interface with your database store. Through DbContext, you can perform create, read, update, and delete operations. In addition, you can perform aggregations such as sum, max, average, and count.

Creating a Simple Database Context

To get started, create a class named AppDbContext that inherits from DbContext as seen in Listing 4-1.

Listing 4-1. Our Initial DbContext Class

```
using Microsoft.EntityFrameworkCore;

namespace EFCOre5WebApp.DAL
{
    public class AppDbContext : DbContext
    {
    }
}
```

Connecting to Our Database

Entity Framework Core 5 can have many database providers, and the provider you want to use is built using the DbContextOptions fluent API class. To enable this functionality for us, we will define a constructor as seen in Listing 4-2.

E. Vogel, *Beginning Entity Framework Core 5*, https://doi.org/10.1007/978-1-4842-6882-7_4

Listing 4-2. AppDbContext Class That Allows Database Options

```
using Microsoft.EntityFrameworkCore;

namespace EFCOre5WebApp.DAL
{
    public class AppDbContext : DbContext
    {
        public AppDbContext() : base()
        {

        }

        public AppDbContext(DbContextOptions options) : base(options)
        {

        }
    }
}
```

For example, to connect to a SQL Express LocalDb instance named DemoDb, we would create AppDbContext like this:

```
var context = new AppDbContext(
                new DbContextOptionsBuilder<AppDbContext>()
                    .UseSqlServer(
                        "Server=(localdb)\\mssqllocaldb;Database=DemoDb;
                        Trusted_Connection=True;MultipleActiveResultSets=
                        true")
                    .Options);
```

You can use other database providers like SQLite by installing their database providers for Entity Framework Core 5 through NuGet. To use the SQLite provider, you just pass in the filename for the database into the DbContextOptionsBuilder class like this:

```
var context = new AppDbContext(
                new DbContextOptionsBuilder<AppDbContext>()
                    .UseSqlLite(
                        "Filename=Demo.db")
                    .Options);
```

We will be installing and using the SQLite provider for unit testing purposes later in the book.

Accessing Entities in a Database Context

A database context is not very useful if you don't have any entities accessible. The DbSet class is used to access entities stored in your database of choice. To access our Person, Address, and LookUp entities, we will add them to our database context class as DbSet type properties as seen in Listing 4-3.

Listing 4-3. AppDbContext Updated to Access Entities

```
using EFCore5WebApp.Core.Entities;
using Microsoft.EntityFrameworkCore;

namespace EFCOre5WebApp.DAL
{
    public class AppDbContext : DbContext
    {
        public DbSet<Person> Persons { get; set; }
        public DbSet<Address> Addresses { get; set; }
        public DbSet<LookUp> LookUps { get; set; }
        public AppDbContext() : base()
        {

        }
        public AppDbContext(DbContextOptions options) : base(options)
        {

        }
    }
}
```

The DbSet class provides access to create, read, update, and delete entity records and will be covered in detail in Chapters 7–10.

Saving Entity Changes

Entity Framework Core 5 uses the SaveChanges method to persist data to your database. Nothing is persisted to your database store until you call the SaveChanges or SaveChangesAsync method on your DbContext instance; in this case, AppDbContext exposes the SaveChanges and SaveChangesAsync methods from the base DbContext class. This means you can add, update, and remove data and then commit all of those changes by calling SaveChanges or SaveChangesAsync. The SaveChangesAsync method is the asynchronous counterpart to SaveChanges, and you call it like this:

```
private async Task SaveDemo()
{
    var context = new AppDbContext();
    await context.SaveChangesAsync();
}
```

You would perform your database operations after creating AppDbContext and prior to the SaveChangesAsync call.

Configuring a Database Context

In Chapter 3, we covered how to use data annotations to configure your entity mapping to the source database schema that will be generated. Instead of specifying the same attributes on all your entities, you can use the OnModelCreating method to apply these changes to all mapped entities. The OnModelCreating method is called when DbContext is created and is used to further configure DbContext. There are also certain mappings that must currently use the OnModelCreating method to wire up like composite keys.

Most configurations can be done either using attributes or the OnModelCreating event. Let us now go over some of these configurations.

Set a Database Schema for All Entities

You can set a default mapped schema for all of your entities by using the HasDefaultSchema fluent API method on the model builder in the OnModelCreating method. For example, to set the default schema to be “Custom” for all of your entities, you would use this:

```
protected override void OnModelCreating(ModelBuilder modelBuilder)
{
    modelBuilder.HasDefaultSchema("Custom");
}
```

Composite Key Constraint

A composite primary key is a primary key constraint that specifies an entity record is uniquely identified by more than one entity property. For example, if we wanted to say the primary key of a person is their first and last names combined, we could define the composite key in the OnModelCreating method like so:

```
protected override void OnModelCreating(ModelBuilder modelBuilder)
{
     modelBuilder.Entity<Person>()
         .HasKey(c => new { c.FirstName, c.LastName });
}
```

Primary Key Constraint

If you prefer to use the fluent syntax over using data attributes, you can also specify a single-column primary key by using the HasKey method. For example, to define the “Code” LookUp entity column as a primary key, we would use this code:

```
protected override void OnModelCreating(ModelBuilder modelBuilder)
{
    modelBuilder.Entity<LookUp>().HasKey(c => c.Code);
}
```

Furthermore, you can use the fluent model builder API to specify the name of the primary key constraint in the target database. The default name of the constraint is PK_EntityName. For example, to change the lookup primary key constraint name to “PK_LookUp_Code”, you would do this:

```
protected override void OnModelCreating(ModelBuilder modelBuilder)
{
     modelBuilder.Entity<LookUp>().HasKey(c => c.Code)
         .HasName("PK_LookUp_Code");
}
```

Default Property Value

You can use the model builder API in the OnModelCreating method to set a default property value. This value can either be a hardcoded value or a database construct like the getdate() SQL Server method.

Hardcoded Default Value

For example, to set the default country on an address record to "USA", you could set that up like this:

```
modelBuilder.Entity<Address>()
    .Property(b => b.Country)
    .HasDefaultValue("USA");
```

SQL Computer Default Value

You can use the HasDefaultValueSql model builder API method to specify that the default value should be computed by the database server. For example, to have the CreatedOn value on the Person entity be set to a default value of the "getdate()" SQL Server method, you would code it this way:

```
protected override void OnModelCreating(ModelBuilder modelBuilder)
{
    modelBuilder.Entity<Person>()
        .Property(b => b.CreatedOn)
        .HasDefaultValueSql("getdate()");
}
```

Foreign Key Relationships

You can also use the model builder fluent API to have full control over how foreign key relationships are defined. I will cover the most common cases in Chapter 11.

Summary

We have covered a lot of ground in this chapter on creating and configuring a database context. We covered how to create a simple database context class. Then we covered how to set the connection properties of a database context to connect it to your target database. Then we covered how to add your entities to the database context. Next, we covered how to persist changes made through a database context. We then finished with how to configure a database context by the use of the OnModelCreating method with the model builder API.

As you can see, Entity Framework Core 5 gives you a lot of configuration settings to allow you to map your entity model to your target database. In the next chapter, I will cover how to create and run the initial database migration that will actually create our database from code!

CHAPTER 5

Creating a Database from Code

So far we have created our entities and their metadata to instruct Entity Framework Core 5 what to create. As you will soon see, the process of taking those instructions and having them be interpreted by Entity Framework Core 5 to create your database is as simple as creating an initial migration and running that migration using Visual Studio. We will primarily be using the Microsoft SQL Server provider for Entity Framework Core in this book and thus will be creating a SQL Server database.

Setting the Connection String

The first step in creating a database from code in Entity Framework Core 5 is to define the connection string for your application. Open the appsettings.json file in your ASP. NET Core web app. Next, we add the connection string that will be used by our app by defining the "ConnectionStrings" property. For our app, we will be calling the name of the connection string "connection", and it will point to a SQL database named "EfCore5WebApp" as seen in Listing 5-1.

Listing 5-1. Adding a Connection String to appsettings.json

```
{
  "Logging": {
    "LogLevel": {
      "Default": "Information",
      "Microsoft": "Warning",
      "Microsoft.Hosting.Lifetime": "Information"
    }
  },
```


E. Vogel, *Beginning Entity Framework Core 5*, https://doi.org/10.1007/978-1-4842-6882-7_5

```
  "AllowedHosts": "*",
  "ConnectionStrings": {
    "connection": "Server=(localdb)\\mssqllocaldb;Database=EfCore5WebApp;
    Trusted_Connection=True;MultipleActiveResultSets=true"
  }
}
```

The example in Listing 5-1 is connecting to a local SQL Server database. You can see that from the connection string which includes the text "(localdb)". Now that the connection string is set, we need to tell our web app to use that connection string. Open up the Startup.cs class file. In the ConfigureServices method, we use the AddDbContext() method to connect to our SQL Server as seen in the following code example:

```
public void ConfigureServices(IServiceCollection services)
{
    services.AddControllersWithViews();

    services.AddDbContext<AppDbContext>(options =>
        options.UseSqlServer(Configuration.GetConnectionString(
        "connection")));
}
```

We are using the "UseSqlServer" extension method that was included in the Entity Framework Core 5 SQL NuGet package. Your Startup.cs class file should now look like Listing 5-2.

Listing 5-2. Startup Class That Points to the SQL Server Database

```
using System;
using System.Collections.Generic;
using System.Linq;
using System.Threading.Tasks;
using EFCOre5WebApp.DAL;
using Microsoft.AspNetCore.Builder;
using Microsoft.AspNetCore.Hosting;
using Microsoft.AspNetCore.HttpsPolicy;
using Microsoft.EntityFrameworkCore;
```

```
using Microsoft.Extensions.Configuration;
using Microsoft.Extensions.DependencyInjection;
using Microsoft.Extensions.Hosting;

namespace EFCore5WebApp
{
    public class Startup
    {
        public Startup(IConfiguration configuration)
        {
            Configuration = configuration;
        }

        public IConfiguration Configuration { get; }

        // This method gets called by the runtime. Use this method to add
        services to the container.
        public void ConfigureServices(IServiceCollection services)
        {
            services.AddControllersWithViews();

            services.AddDbContext<AppDbContext>(options =>
                options.UseSqlServer(Configuration.GetConnectionString(
                "connection")));
        }

        // This method gets called by the runtime. Use this method to
        configure the HTTP request pipeline.
        public void Configure(IApplicationBuilder app, IWebHostEnvironment env)
        {
            if (env.IsDevelopment())
            {
                app.UseDeveloperExceptionPage();
            }
```

```
            else
            {
                app.UseExceptionHandler("/Home/Error");
                // The default HSTS value is 30 days. You may want to
                change this for production scenarios, see https://aka.ms/
                aspnetcore-hsts.
                app.UseHsts();
            }
            app.UseHttpsRedirection();
            app.UseStaticFiles();

            app.UseRouting();

            app.UseAuthorization();

            app.UseEndpoints(endpoints =>
            {
                endpoints.MapControllerRoute(
                    name: "default",
                    pattern: "{controller=Home}/{action=Index}/{id?}");
            });
        }
    }
}
```

Now that our application is pointed to the database, we can actually create the database through adding a migration.

Creating the Initial Migration

The next step in creating a database through code in Entity Framework Core 5 is to create an initial migration.

To create the initial migration, we can use the NuGet Package Manager Console and run the "Add-Migration" command passing in the name of our migration as the second parameter.

Let us now create the initial migration and name it "InitialCreate". Open the NuGet Package Manager Console and change the Default project dropdown to your DAL project and run this command: "Add-Migration InitialCreate". Also make sure your web project is set as the Startup project in your solution.

See Figure 5-1 as a reference.

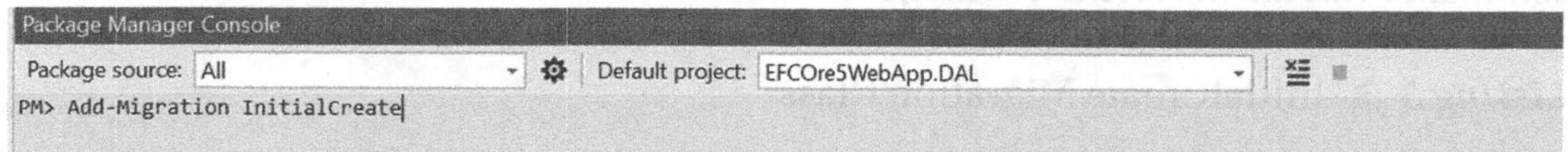

Figure 5-1. *Creating Initial Migration*

You will now see a Migrations folder added to your DAL project with a class file created for the actual migration as seen in Figure 5-2.

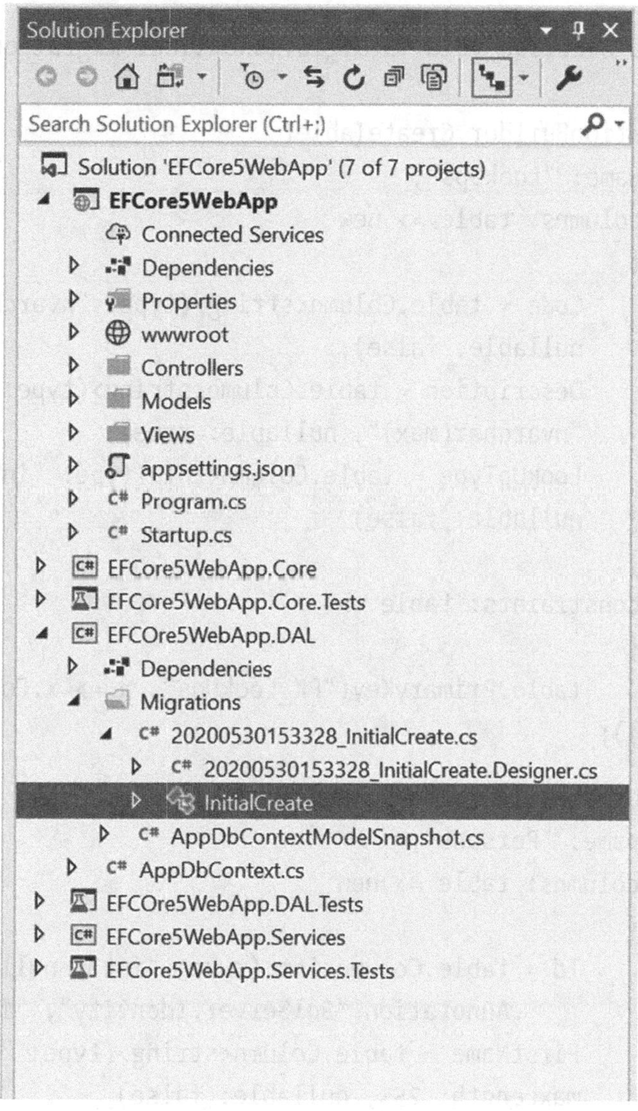

Figure 5-2. *Migrations Folder and Class File Created*

You will now see a class file named InitialCreate that was created by the "Add-Migration" command. This file will look like Listing 5-3.

Listing 5-3. InitialCreate Migration Class

```
using Microsoft.EntityFrameworkCore.Migrations;

namespace EFCore5WebApp.DAL.Migrations
{
    public partial class InitialCreate : Migration
    {
        protected override void Up(MigrationBuilder migrationBuilder)
        {
            migrationBuilder.CreateTable(
                name: "LookUps",
                columns: table => new
                {
                    Code = table.Column<string>(type: "nvarchar(450)",
                    nullable: false),
                    Description = table.Column<string>(type:
                    "nvarchar(max)", nullable: true),
                    LookUpType = table.Column<int>(type: "int",
                    nullable: false)
                },
                constraints: table =>
                {
                    table.PrimaryKey("PK_LookUps", x => x.Code);
                });

            migrationBuilder.CreateTable(
                name: "Persons",
                columns: table => new
                {
                    Id = table.Column<int>(type: "int", nullable: false)
                        .Annotation("SqlServer:Identity", "1, 1"),
                    FirstName = table.Column<string>(type: "nvarchar(255)",
                    maxLength: 255, nullable: false),
```

```
            LastName = table.Column<string>(type: "nvarchar(255)",
            maxLength: 255, nullable: false),
            EmailAddress = table.Column<string>(type:
            "nvarchar(max)", nullable: false)
        },
        constraints: table =>
        {
            table.PrimaryKey("PK_Persons", x => x.Id);
        });

    migrationBuilder.CreateTable(
        name: "Addresses",
        columns: table => new
        {
            Id = table.Column<int>(type: "int", nullable: false)
                .Annotation("SqlServer:Identity", "1, 1"),
            AddressLine1 = table.Column<string>(type:
            "nvarchar(max)", nullable: true),
            AddressLine2 = table.Column<string>(type:
            "nvarchar(max)", nullable: true),
            City = table.Column<string>(type: "nvarchar(max)",
            nullable: true),
            State = table.Column<string>(type: "nvarchar(max)",
            nullable: true),
            Country = table.Column<string>(type: "nvarchar(max)",
            nullable: true),
            ZipCode = table.Column<string>(type: "nvarchar(max)",
            nullable: true),
            PersonId = table.Column<int>(type: "int",
            nullable: false)
        },
        constraints: table =>
        {
            table.PrimaryKey("PK_Addresses", x => x.Id);
            table.ForeignKey(
                name: "FK_Addresses_Persons_PersonId",
```

```
                        column: x => x.PersonId,
                        principalTable: "Persons",
                        principalColumn: "Id",
                        onDelete: ReferentialAction.Cascade);
                });

            migrationBuilder.CreateIndex(
                name: "IX_Addresses_PersonId",
                table: "Addresses",
                column: "PersonId");
        }

        protected override void Down(MigrationBuilder migrationBuilder)
        {
            migrationBuilder.DropTable(
                name: "Addresses");

            migrationBuilder.DropTable(
                name: "LookUps");

            migrationBuilder.DropTable(
                name: "Persons");
        }
    }
}
```

I will go over how to decipher this file and delve deeper into migrations in Chapter 14. Now that the migration is created, let's run it to create our "EfCore5WebApp" database in the SQL Server instance defined in our appSettings.config file in our web project.

Creating the Database from the Migration

Lastly, we will create the database from the "InitialCreate" migration that we just created. Open the NuGet Package Manager Console and run the "Update-Database" command as seen in Figure 5-3.

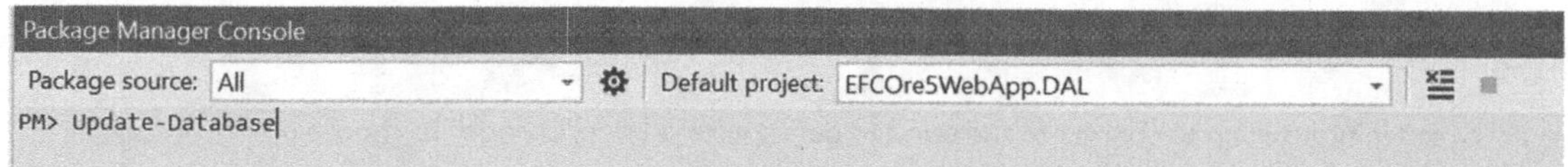

Figure 5-3. *Running Our Migration*

The "Update-Database" command is what we will use to update the database whenever we add a new migration to our project.

Connect to the New Database from Visual Studio

We are using LocalDb as our database, so we need to follow the steps in this section to connect to the database via Visual Studio. First, verify that the database was created. Open up a Command Prompt and run "SqlLocalDB.exe start" to start the LocalDb instance as seen in Figure 5-4.

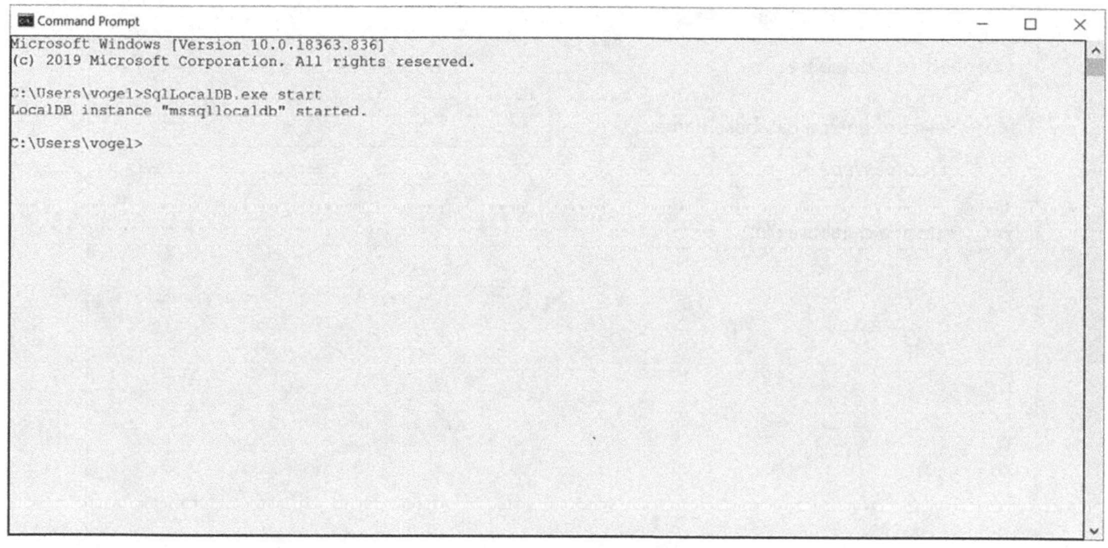

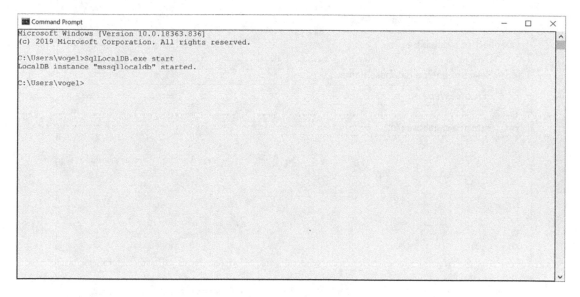

Figure 5-4. *Starting a LocalDb SQL Server Instance*

Next, we add a connection to our LocalDb instance through Visual Studio. Go to Tools ➤ Connect to Database. If you are using SQL Server or SQL Server Express, use that connection instead. To connect to our LocalDb, add a new SQL Server connection as seen in Figure 5-5.

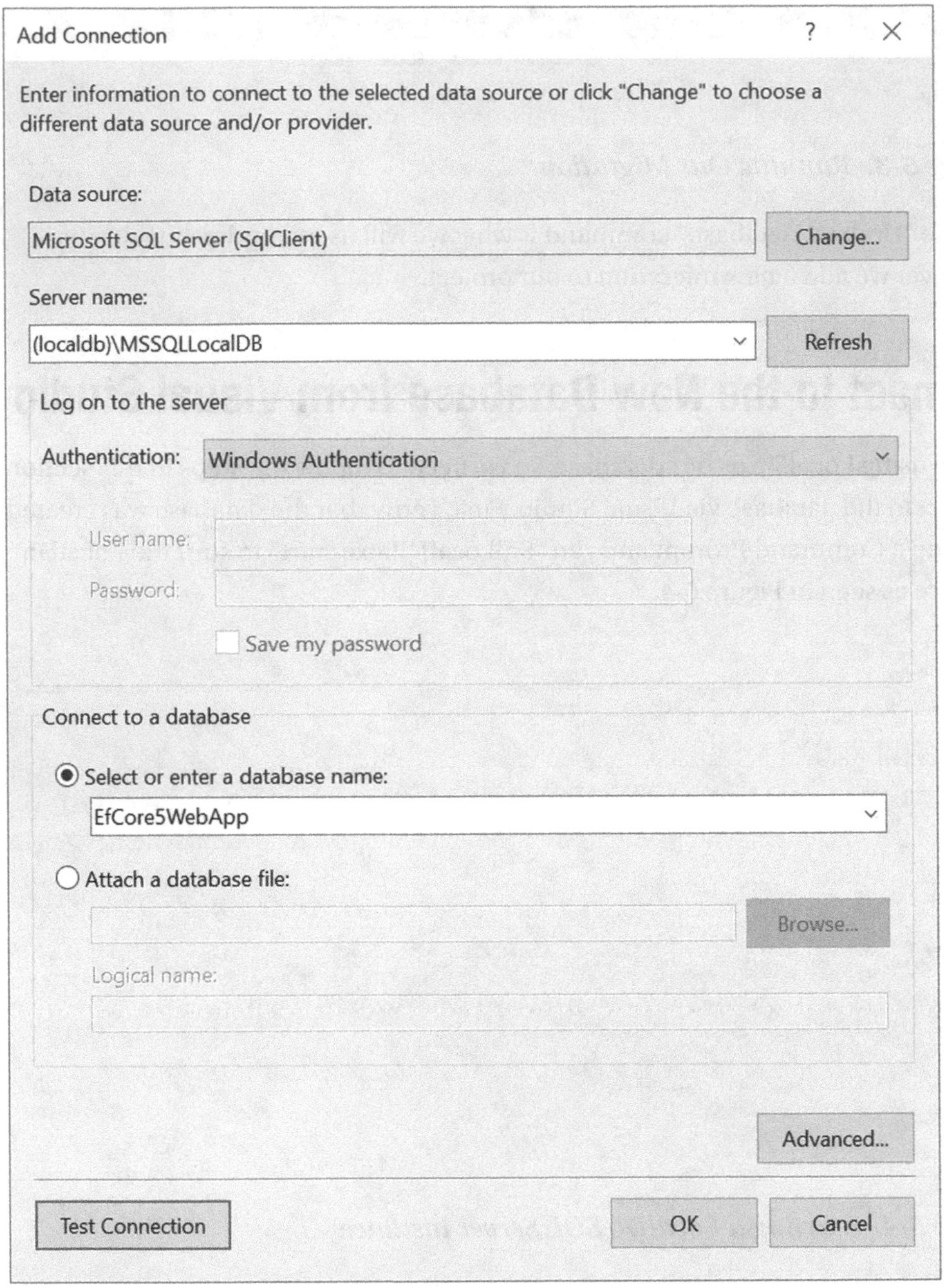

Figure 5-5. Adding a Database Connection

Then click the "OK" button. You should now be able to browse and query your newly created database as seen in Figure 5-6.

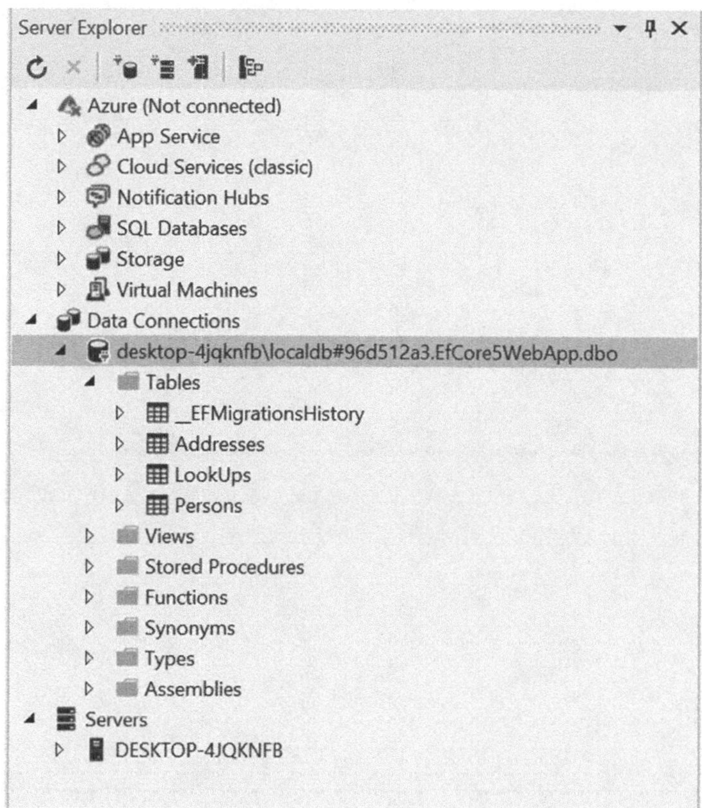

***Figure 5-6.** Browsing Our Database*

Summary

In this chapter, we have gone through the journey of creating a database using Entity Framework Core 5. First, we created the connection string that tells our app how to connect to a SQL Server database. Then we used Entity Framework tooling to create a migration by using the "Add-Migration" command that generated all the code to create our database schema. After that, we used Entity Framework tooling through the "Update-Database" command to run the migration code. Lastly, we started and connected to our created database. In the next chapter, we will see how to seed our newly created database with data.

CHAPTER 6

Seeding Data

In the last chapter, we finally created our database using Entity Framework Core 5. In this chapter, we will seed our database with some data. We will add a few sample persons and addresses and load up our lookup tables with some states and countries.

Populating Lookup Data

We will start out by populating some lookup records for states and countries. To get started, open the AppDbContext class file. To seed data, we override the OnModelCreating method like this:

```
protected override void OnModelCreating(ModelBuilder modelBuilder)
{
}
```

The OnModelCreating event can also be used to configure the database schema, and that should be done prior to seeding data. You've seen this other use of overriding the method earlier, in Chapter 4.

The next step is to use the ModelBuilder instance to specify the data to seed using the Entity<T>.HasData() method. For example, to seed the LookUp table with a single LookUp record for the state of Alabama, we would use the following code:

```
protected override void OnModelCreating(ModelBuilder modelBuilder)
{
    modelBuilder.Entity<LookUp>().HasData(new List<LookUp>()
    {
        new LookUp() { Code = "AL", Description = "Alabama", LookUpType =
        LookUpType.State}
    });
}
```


E. Vogel, *Beginning Entity Framework Core 5*, https://doi.org/10.1007/978-1-4842-6882-7_6

After we have the data set up to be seeded, we create a migration to actually perform the needed insert, update, and delete statements that will be run on the database. Let us see that in action by creating a new migration to insert the single Alabama state lookup record. Open the NuGet Package Manager Console and run

"Add-Migration AddStateAL"

You will now see a new class file with the suffix "AddStateAL" was added under the Migrations folder. The generated migration code should look like Listing 6-1.

Listing 6-1. Test Migration to Add a Single State Lookup Item

```
using Microsoft.EntityFrameworkCore.Migrations;

namespace EFCore5WebApp.DAL.Migrations
{
    public partial class AddStateAL : Migration
    {
        protected override void Up(MigrationBuilder migrationBuilder)
        {
            migrationBuilder.InsertData(
                table: "LookUps",
                columns: new[] { "Code", "Description", "LookUpType" },
                values: new object[] { "AL", "Alabama", 0 });
        }

        protected override void Down(MigrationBuilder migrationBuilder)
        {
            migrationBuilder.DeleteData(
                table: "LookUps",
                keyColumn: "Code",
                keyValue: "AL");
        }
    }
}
```

Now we will run the migration by running the "Update-Database" command in the NuGet Package Manager Console. After that, let us query the LookUps table to see our newly added record as seen in Figure 6-1.

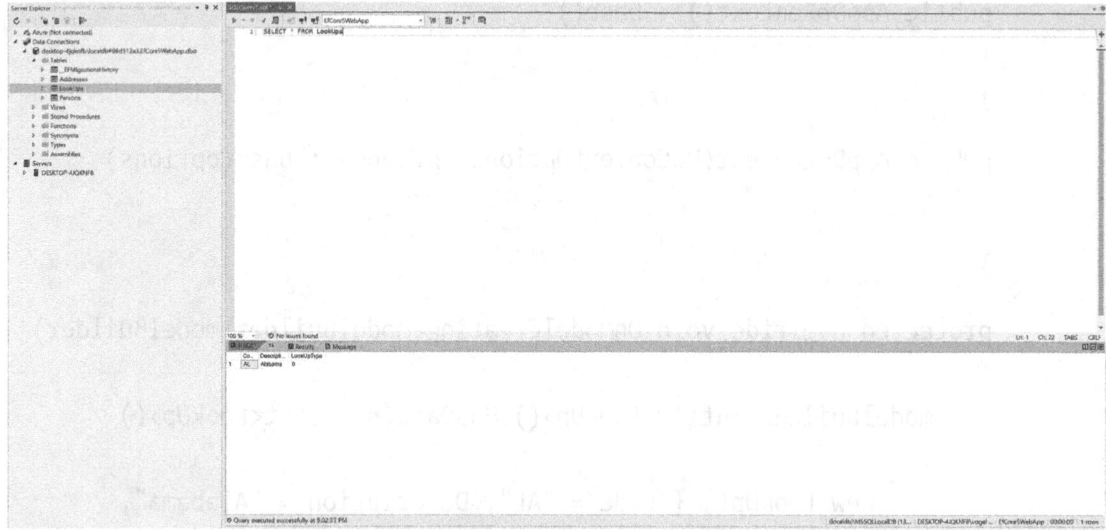

Figure 6-1. *Seeing the Seeded Data in Server Explorer*

Now that you've seen how to seed a single record, let us now seed the LookUps table with all of the states in the United States as well as Puerto Rico. We will also add the United States as a country lookup item as seen in Listing 6-2.

Listing 6-2. AppDbContext That Seeds Lookup Records

```
using System.Collections.Generic;
using System.Runtime.CompilerServices;
using System.Threading.Tasks;
using EFCore5WebApp.Core.Entities;
using Microsoft.EntityFrameworkCore;
using Microsoft.VisualBasic;

namespace EFCOre5WebApp.DAL
{
    public class AppDbContext : DbContext
    {
        public DbSet<Person> Persons { get; set; }
        public DbSet<Address> Addresses { get; set; }
        public DbSet<LookUp> LookUps { get; set; }
```

```
        public AppDbContext() : base()
        {
        }

        public AppDbContext(DbContextOptions options) : base(options)
        {

        }

        protected override void OnModelCreating(ModelBuilder modelBuilder)
        {
            modelBuilder.Entity<LookUp>().HasData(new List<LookUp>()
            {
                new LookUp() { Code = "AL", Description = "Alabama",
                LookUpType = LookUpType.State},
                new LookUp() { Code = "AK", Description = "Alaska",
                LookUpType = LookUpType.State},
                new LookUp() { Code = "AZ", Description = "Arizona",
                LookUpType = LookUpType.State},
                new LookUp() { Code = "AR", Description = "Arkansas",
                LookUpType = LookUpType.State},
                new LookUp() { Code = "CA", Description = "California",
                LookUpType = LookUpType.State},
                new LookUp() { Code = "CO", Description = "Colorado",
                LookUpType = LookUpType.State},
                new LookUp() { Code = "CT", Description = "Connecticut",
                LookUpType = LookUpType.State},
                new LookUp() { Code = "DE", Description = "Delaware",
                LookUpType = LookUpType.State},
                new LookUp() { Code = "DC", Description = "District of
                Columbia", LookUpType = LookUpType.State},
                new LookUp() { Code = "FL", Description = "Florida",
                LookUpType = LookUpType.State},
                new LookUp() { Code = "GA", Description = "Georgia",
                LookUpType = LookUpType.State},
                new LookUp() { Code = "ID", Description = "Hawaii",
                LookUpType = LookUpType.State},
```

```
new LookUp() { Code = "IL", Description = "Idaho",
LookUpType = LookUpType.State},
new LookUp() { Code = "IN", Description = "Illinois",
LookUpType = LookUpType.State},
new LookUp() { Code = "IA", Description = "Indiana",
LookUpType = LookUpType.State},
new LookUp() { Code = "KS", Description = "Iowa",
LookUpType = LookUpType.State},
new LookUp() { Code = "KY", Description = "Kansas",
LookUpType = LookUpType.State},
new LookUp() { Code = "LA", Description = "Kentucky",
LookUpType = LookUpType.State},
new LookUp() { Code = "ME", Description = "Louisiana",
LookUpType = LookUpType.State},
new LookUp() { Code = "MD", Description = "Maine",
LookUpType = LookUpType.State},
new LookUp() { Code = "MA", Description = "Maryland",
LookUpType = LookUpType.State},
new LookUp() { Code = "MI", Description = "Massachusetts",
LookUpType = LookUpType.State},
new LookUp() { Code = "MN", Description = "Michigan",
LookUpType = LookUpType.State},
new LookUp() { Code = "MS", Description = "Minnesota",
LookUpType = LookUpType.State},
new LookUp() { Code = "MO", Description = "Mississippi",
LookUpType = LookUpType.State},
new LookUp() { Code = "MT", Description = "Missouri",
LookUpType = LookUpType.State},
new LookUp() { Code = "NE", Description = "Montana",
LookUpType = LookUpType.State},
new LookUp() { Code = "NV", Description = "Nevada",
LookUpType = LookUpType.State},
new LookUp() { Code = "NH", Description = "New Hampshire",
LookUpType = LookUpType.State},
```

```
new LookUp() { Code = "NJ", Description = "New Jersey",
LookUpType = LookUpType.State},
new LookUp() { Code = "NM", Description = "New Mexico",
LookUpType = LookUpType.State},
new LookUp() { Code = "NY", Description = "New York",
LookUpType = LookUpType.State},
new LookUp() { Code = "NC", Description = "New Carolina",
LookUpType = LookUpType.State},
new LookUp() { Code = "ND", Description = "North Dakota",
LookUpType = LookUpType.State},
new LookUp() { Code = "OH", Description = "Ohio",
LookUpType = LookUpType.State},
new LookUp() { Code = "OK", Description = "Oklahoma",
LookUpType = LookUpType.State},
new LookUp() { Code = "OR", Description = "Oregon",
LookUpType = LookUpType.State},
new LookUp() { Code = "PA", Description = "Pennsylvania",
LookUpType = LookUpType.State},
new LookUp() { Code = "RI", Description = "Rhode Island",
LookUpType = LookUpType.State},
new LookUp() { Code = "SC", Description = "South Carolina",
LookUpType = LookUpType.State},
new LookUp() { Code = "SD", Description = "South Dakota",
LookUpType = LookUpType.State},
new LookUp() { Code = "TN", Description = "Tennessee",
LookUpType = LookUpType.State},
new LookUp() { Code = "TX", Description = "Texas",
LookUpType = LookUpType.State},
new LookUp() { Code = "UT", Description = "Utah",
LookUpType = LookUpType.State},
new LookUp() { Code = "VT", Description = "Vermont",
LookUpType = LookUpType.State},
new LookUp() { Code = "VA", Description = "Virginia",
LookUpType = LookUpType.State},
new LookUp() { Code = "WA", Description = "Washington",
LookUpType = LookUpType.State},
```

```
                new LookUp() { Code = "WV", Description = "West Virginia",
                LookUpType = LookUpType.State},
                new LookUp() { Code = "WI", Description = "Wisconsis",
                LookUpType = LookUpType.State},
                new LookUp() { Code = "WY", Description = "Wyoming",
                LookUpType = LookUpType.State},
                new LookUp() { Code = "PR", Description = "Puerto Rico",
                LookUpType = LookUpType.State},
                new LookUp() { Code = "USA", Description = "United States
                of America", LookUpType = LookUpType.Country}
            });
        }
    }
}
```

Now we will repeat the process of creating a migration and running that migration. To create the migration, run "Add-Migration AddLookUps" from the NuGet Package Manager Console. Then run "Update-Database" to actually insert the lookup records from the NuGet Package Manager Console. Now that we have seeded the lookup items, let us add some person and address records.

Seeding Test Persons

Let us now seed some test person records. We will add on to the end of the OnModelCreating method in the AppDbContext class to accomplish that. We will add two person records, one that has a single address and one that has two addresses. See Listing 6-3 for the code block to add the test person records.

Listing 6-3. AppDbContext with Sample Person Seeding

```
modelBuilder.Entity<Person>().HasData(new List<Person>()
{
    new Person(){ Id = 1, FirstName = "John", LastName = "Smith",
    EmailAddress = "john@smith.com"},
    new Person(){ Id = 2, FirstName = "Susan", LastName = "Jones",
    EmailAddress = "john@smith.com" }
});
```

The next step is to create a migration for the person records. To do this, run "Add-Migration AddTestPersons" from the NuGet Package Manager Console. Lastly, run "Update-Database" to add the actual records to the target database.

Seeding Addresses

Now we can add the address records and associate them to their person records through the PersonId property value as seen in Listing 6-4.

Listing 6-4. Add Seeded Addresses

```
modelBuilder.Entity<Address>().HasData(new List<Address>()
{
    new Address() { Id = 1, AddressLine1 = "123 Test St", AddressLine2 = "",
    City = "Beverly Hills", State = "CA", ZipCode = "90210", PersonId = 1,
    Country = "USA"},
    new Address() { Id = 2, AddressLine1 = "123 Michigan Ave",
    AddressLine2 = "", City = "Chicago", State = "IL", ZipCode = "60612",
    PersonId = 2, Country = "USA"},
    new Address() { Id = 3, AddressLine1 = "100 1St St", AddressLine2 = "",
    City = "Chicago", State = "IL", ZipCode = "60612", PersonId = 2,
    Country = "USA"}
});
```

The next step is to create a migration for the address records. To do this, run "Add-Migration AddTestAddresses" from the NuGet Package Manager Console. Lastly, run "Update-Database" to add the actual records to the target database.

Summary

In this chapter, I have covered how to seed the lookup records for states and countries as well as persons and addresses. To seed data, we first added the test data in the OnModelCreating method in our application database context class. After that we created a migration for each entity type and ran the migrations in sequence. You can feel free to create one migration to seed all your data as well. I did it as separate migrations to focus on one entity at a time. In the next chapter, I will cover how to query data in depth.

CHAPTER 7

Getting Data

Now that we have loaded some sample data into our database, let us learn how to retrieve and filter it using Entity Framework Core 5. To filter data, we use LINQ either through its Query syntax or the Method syntax. I tend to use a mix of the two syntaxes to get my desired data. I will first cover the Query syntax and then explain the Method syntax. After we go over the basics of LINQ, I will show you how to test Entity Framework Core against our database through some NUnit integration tests.

LINQ Queries

I will explain the Query syntax first as I find it easier to understand. A LINQ query looks a lot like a SQL query except the "from" clause comes before the "select" clause. For example, to get all person records with the first name of "Susan", we could use the Query syntax like this:

```
var persons = from p in Persons
    where p.FirstName == "Susan"
    select p;
```

The query will not be executed on the database until we materialize it through a Method syntax method like ToList() as will be discussed later. Let us break down the parts of the LINQ query. The "from" clause tells us what collection we are querying, in this case "Persons" from our AppDbContext. The "where" clause is where we specify any filter criteria; in this case, we want to get all person records where the "FirstName" property value is "Susan". The "where" clause takes any predicate so you can have much more complex filters on your collection. Lastly, "select" specifies what we want to retrieve from the collection; this can be an entire entity like in our sample query, or you can choose to select a single property value and create an instance of a defined or even an anonymous type.

E. Vogel, *Beginning Entity Framework Core 5*, https://doi.org/10.1007/978-1-4842-6882-7_7

For example, we can modify our query to only retrieve the "Id" property values from all persons with the first name of "Susan" like this:

```
var persons = from p in Persons
    where p.FirstName == "Susan"
    select p.Id;
```

In this case, we will get back a collection of integer values instead of the entire Person entity. The collection type is IQueryable<T> where T is the data type you specify in your select clause. In the preceding query, T would be int because that is the data type of the Id property.

Select Anonymous Types

If you do not want to bother creating a full class just to get a subset of data from your database, you can specify an anonymous type instead of a full class. For example, we can select only the first and last names of our person records like this:

```
var persons = from p in Persons
    where p.FirstName == "Susan"
    select new {p.FirstName, p.LastName};
```

In this case, you will get an IQueryable<T> where T is an anonymous type. An anonymous class is one that you have not already defined in your application and is handled by the compiler. If you are wondering how this really works, .NET is creating a class that you never see. Selecting an anonymous type can be useful if you are creating an intermediate query or only need a subset of the data that will not be exposed to other areas of your code. In most cases, I prefer to create a Data Transfer Object (DTO) class if the data will be consumed by another part of the code such as a public API.

Select Object Transformation

Following our last example where we got an anonymous type with FirstName and LastName properties, if we want to expose this data to another part of our codebase, we can use a DTO. To do this, first, create the DTO class like this:

```
public class PersonDto
{
    public string FirstName { get; set; }
    public string LastName { get; set; }
}
```

Next, we create a method to demonstrate selecting this DTO transformation from our LINQ query like this:

```
public IQueryable<PersonDto> GetDisplayPersons()
{
     return from p in Persons
         where p.FirstName == "Susan"
         select new PersonDto
         {
             FirstName = p.FirstName,
             LastName = p.LastName
         };
}
```

In the end, we get the same data, but now the rest of your application will get a known strongly typed object to consume.

Joins in LINQ

If you are familiar with SQL, you know that in some cases you need to get data from multiple entities that usually have a one-to-many relationship linked through a foreign key constraint. In our case, we have person and address records where a person has one-to-many addresses linked through the PersonId property in the Address entity. In our example, there are two ways we can get addresses for a person: we can use a LINQ join to relate the two entities, or we can use our navigation property. I'll explain how to use a join first and then show you how to use the navigation property to simplify the query.

For example, to get all of the addresses for Susan, we would use the following LINQ query:

```
var personAddresses = from p in Persons
    join a in Addresses on p.Id equals a.PersonId
                        where p.FirstName == "Susan"
    select a;
```

As you can see, the "join" clause links two entities through a shared property value. Usually, this will be the foreign key column in the database. In our case, the common property is the Person entity's Id property.

Select the Navigation Property

We can simplify the query from the join example by leveraging the Addresses navigation property on our Person entity like this:

```
var personAddresses = (from p in Persons
    where p.FirstName == "Susan"
    select p.Addresses).SelectMany(a => a);
```

This result will match the join example through the use of the SelectMany Method syntax method.

Sorting Data

It is easy to order data in a LINQ query by using the "order by" clause. You are able to sort by one or many columns either ascending or descending per column. For example, to sort person records by last name descending and then first name ascending, you would run this query:

```
var personAddresses = from p in Persons
    orderby p.LastName descending, p.FirstName
                        select p
```

Method Syntax Queries

The fluent LINQ syntax uses method chaining to get your data. You can filter a collection of data through the Where() extension method, which accepts a predicate as its argument. The predicate defines the criteria for the filter. For example, to get all persons with the last name of Smith from our Persons collection, we would use

```
var persons = Persons.Where(x => x.LastName == "Smith").ToList();
```

The ToList() method used in the preceding code will run the query against our database. To get a single record, we can use the Single(), First(), or Last() method, all of which do exactly what they say. The Single() method will throw an exception if there is no matching record found. There are also SingleOrDefault(), FirstOrDefault(), and LastOrDefault(). The difference between the two is that Single(), First(), and Last() methods will throw an exception if a matching record doesn't exist. The OrDefault variants will return null if no matching record was found.

The Select method is used if you want to only get a subset of the data or to transform the data into a new type. For example, to select only the first name of a person, you could call the Select method like this:

```
var persons = Persons.Select(x => x.FirstName);
```

To order the data, you can use the OrderBy() or OrderByDescending() method. If you need to sort on multiple properties, you follow the OrderBy() or OrderByDescending() method by a ThenBy() or ThenByDescending() method call. For example, to sort all person records by last name descending and then first name ascending, you could do this:

```
var persons = Persons.OrderByDescending(x => x.LastName).ThenBy(x =>
x.FirstName);
```

If you only need a specified range of data, you can use the Skip() and Take() methods. These are commonly used to implement server-side paging logic. For example, if you could implement a generic paging method like this

```
public IEnumerable<T> GetPagedData<T>(IQueryable<T> data, int pageSize,
int page)
    where T: class, new()
{
    return data.Skip((page - 1) * pageSize).Take(pageSize).ToList();
}
```

you could then call the method to get the first page of ten records like this:

```
var persons = GetPagedData(Persons, 10, 1);
```

We can also easily filter our address records by using the Method syntax. For example, to get all addresses in the state of IL, we could use the following query:

```
var addresses = Addresses.Where(x => x.State == "IL").ToList();
```

As you can see, the fluent syntax is very concise and to the point. I often use the Method syntax unless I need to join or group data.

Testing Our Data

Now that we have a basic understanding of how to query our data, it is time to test that Entity Framework Core 5 is correctly connecting to our SQL Server database by using some NUnit tests. These are more commonly called integration tests as we are testing directly against our SQL Server database.

Start out by renaming the UnitTest1 class in your DAL.Tests project to SelectTests. Remove the test code in the class and get it to match Listing 7-1.

Listing 7-1. Empty the SelectTests Class

```
using NUnit.Framework;

namespace EFCOre5WebApp.DAL.Tests
{
    [TestFixture]
    public class SelectTests
    {
    }
}
```

In order to connect to our SQL Server database, we have to create an instance of our AppDbContext class and pass in our database connection string. We will do that in our SetUp method, which will be called only once for all of our tests in the SelectTests class fixture. Doing this will create a private variable named _context and initialize it in our SetUp method like this:

```
private AppDbContext _context;

[SetUp]
public void SetUp()
{
    _context = new AppDbContext(new DbContextOptionsBuilder<AppDbContext>()
.UseSqlServer("Server=(localdb)\\mssqllocaldb;Database=EfCore5WebApp;
Trusted_Connection=True;MultipleActiveResultSets=true")
        .Options);
}
```

Now that we have a connection to our database, we can verify that our seeded data was correctly inserted through an NUnit integration test. As a simple first test, we will ensure that only two person records were created. The simple blueprint of a unit or integration test is arrange, act, and assert (AAA). For our first integration test, we are combining the arrange and act steps by getting all of the records in one call. Then we assert that we have two person records like this:

```
[Test]
 public void GetAllPersons()
 {
     IEnumerable<Person> persons = _context.Persons.ToList();
     Assert.AreEqual(2, persons.Count());
 }
```

Your SelectTests class file should now look like Listing 7-2.

Listing 7-2. Our First Unit Test

```
using EFCore5WebApp.Core.Entities;
using Microsoft.EntityFrameworkCore;
using NUnit.Framework;
using System.Collections.Generic;
using System.Linq;

namespace EFCOre5WebApp.DAL.Tests
{
    [TestFixture]
    public class SelectTests
```

```
    {
        private AppDbContext _context;

        [SetUp]
        public void SetUp()
        {
            _context = new AppDbContext(new DbContextOptionsBuilder
            <AppDbContext>()
    .UseSqlServer("Server=(localdb)\\mssqllocaldb;Database=
    EfCore5WebApp;Trusted_Connection=True;MultipleActiveResult
    Sets=true")
                  .Options);
        }

        [Test]
        public void GetAllPersons()
        {
            IEnumerable<Person> persons = _context.Persons.ToList();
            Assert.AreEqual(2, persons.Count());
        }
    }
}
```

We will now verify that our first person record has one address and our second person record has two addresses through a unit test like this:

```
[Test]
 public void PersonsHaveAddresses()
 {
     List<Person> persons = _context.Persons.Include("Addresses").ToList();
     Assert.AreEqual(1, persons[0].Addresses.Count);
     Assert.AreEqual(2, persons[1].Addresses.Count);
 }
```

Lastly, let us test that our seeded LookUp records were created successfully by creating a unit test. We will verify that we have one country record and 51 states like in Listing 7-3. Your SelectTests class should now look like Listing 7-3.

Listing 7-3. Updated SelectTests Class

```
[Test]
public void HaveLookUpRecords()
{
    var lookUps = _context.LookUps.ToList();
    var countries = lookUps.Where(x => x.LookUpType == LookUpType.Country).
    ToList();
    var states = lookUps.Where(x => x.LookUpType == LookUpType.State).ToList();

    Assert.AreEqual(1, countries.Count);
    Assert.AreEqual(51, states.Count);
}

using EFCore5WebApp.Core.Entities;
using Microsoft.EntityFrameworkCore;
using NUnit.Framework;
using System.Collections.Generic;
using System.Linq;

namespace EFCOre5WebApp.DAL.Tests
{
    [TestFixture]
    public class SelectTests
    {
        private AppDbContext _context;
        [SetUp]
        public void SetUp()
        {
            _context = new AppDbContext(new DbContextOptionsBuilder
            <AppDbContext>()
```

```
.UseSqlServer("Server=(localdb)\\mssqllocaldb;Database=
EfCore5WebApp;Trusted_Connection=True;MultipleActiveResult
Sets=true")
                .Options);
        }

        [Test]
        public void GetAllPersons()
        {
            IEnumerable<Person> persons = _context.Persons.ToList();
            Assert.AreEqual(2, persons.Count());
        }

        [Test]
        public void PersonsHaveAddresses()
        {
            List<Person> persons = _context.Persons.Include("Addresses").
            ToList();
            Assert.AreEqual(1, persons[0].Addresses.Count);
            Assert.AreEqual(2, persons[1].Addresses.Count);
        }

        [Test]
        public void HaveLookUpRecords()
        {
            var lookUps = _context.LookUps.ToList();
            var countries = lookUps.Where(x => x.LookUpType == LookUpType.
            Country).ToList();
            var states = lookUps.Where(x => x.LookUpType == LookUpType.
            State).ToList();

            Assert.AreEqual(1, countries.Count);
            Assert.AreEqual(51, states.Count);
        }
    }
}
```

Summary

In this chapter, I covered how to use the Query syntax. Then I covered some of the basics of the Method syntax. We used both syntaxes to retrieve, filter, and sort our data. We also explored how to implement paging by using the Skip() and Take() methods. We ended by testing that our seeded data was correctly inserted by verifying its presence though some NUnit integration tests. These integration tests are useful for testing our data created in our migrations. In the next chapter, I'll cover how you can insert new data into a database using Entity Framework Core 5.

Summary

CHAPTER 8

Inserting Data

Now that we learned how to retrieve data from our database using Entity Framework Core 5, let us look at how to insert new data into our database. I will cover how to insert into a table and its child tables by the use of its navigation properties.

Inserting the Root Entity

The code to insert a root into a database using Entity Framework Core 5 is simple. New records are added via the DbSet<T>.Add method. For example, to add a new person record without any addresses to our database using EF Core, you could use the following code:

```
using (var context = new AppDbContext())
{
    context.Persons.Add(new Person
    {
        FirstName = "Clarke",
        LastName = "Kent",
        CreatedOn = DateTime.Now,
        EmailAddress = "clark@daileybugel.com",
    });

    context.SaveChanges();
}
```

The first step is creating a new DbContext. Then we call the Add method on the Persons DbSet property and pass in a new Person class instance with our property values set. Finally, call SaveChanges on DbContext to commit the record to the database. If you want to add multiple records, you can wait to call SaveChanges after adding all of the records with the Add method.

E. Vogel, *Beginning Entity Framework Core 5*, https://doi.org/10.1007/978-1-4842-6882-7_8

Inserting Child Records

Child records can easily be added through use of a navigation property. Our Person class has a navigation property named Addresses. For example, to add the same person record but also add an address, you could use the following code:

```
using (var context = new AppDbContext())
{
    context.Persons.Add(new Person()
    {
        FirstName = "Clarke",
        LastName = "Kent",
        CreatedOn = DateTime.Now,
        EmailAddress = "clark@daileybugel.com",
        Addresses = new List<Address>
        {
            new Address
            {
                AddressLine1 = "1234 Fake Street",
                AddressLine2 = "Suite 1",
                City = "Chicago",
                State = "IL",
                ZipCode = "60652",
                Country = "United States"
            }
        }
    });

    context.SaveChanges();
}
```

You can add multiple child records if the navigation property has a one-to-many relationship with its parent record like our Addresses navigation property. For example, to add two addresses to our person when adding the record, you could use the following code:

```
using (var context = new AppDbContext())
{
    context.Persons.Add(new Person()
    {
        FirstName = "Clarke",
        LastName = "Kent",
        CreatedOn = DateTime.Now,
        EmailAddress = "clark@daileybugel.com",
        Addresses = new List<Address>
        {
            new Address
            {
                AddressLine1 = "1234 Fake Street",
                AddressLine2 = "Suite 1",
                City = "Chicago",
                State = "IL",
                ZipCode = "60652",
                Country = "United States"
            },
            new Address
            {
                AddressLine1 = "555 Waverly Street",
                AddressLine2 = "APT B2",
                City = "Mt. Pleasant",
                State = "MI",
                ZipCode = "48858",
                Country = "USA"
            }
        }
    });

    context.SaveChanges();
}
```

Primary Key Values

A primary key is a unique identifier for a record in a database table. It is most often a single column but can also be a compound key comprised of multiple columns. You can specify that primary key values be generated automatically, or you can supply them yourself from the application.

Identity Seeded Primary Key

Entity Framework Core 5 uses identity seeded primary keys by default. This means that whenever a new record is inserted, its key value will be one value greater than the last inserted record. The data type of your key can be any integer data type such as short, int, or long.

Guid Primary Key

If you specify the data type of a property named Id to be a Guid, then Entity Framework Core 5 will instruct your database to generate a globally unique identifier value when the record is inserted for you.

Non-computed Primary Key

If you prefer to have your application explicitly set the primary key value, then you can specify the DatabaseGenerated property attribute on your primary key column, for example:

```
[DatabaseGenerated(DatabaseGeneratedOption.None)]
public int Id { get; set; }
```

By specifying the value DatabaseGeneratedOption.None, you are telling Entity Framework that your application will supply the key values.

Foreign Key Values

If you add a child entity to your parent record like adding an address through the Addresses navigation property, then Entity Framework Core 5 will automatically generate the primary key of the child entity and set the foreign key value appropriately.

Default Values

If you prefer to have a hardcoded or database-generated value when a record is inserted, you can use the HasDefaultValue or the HasDefaultValueSql method in the OnModelCreating method of your DbContext. For example, to have the CreatedOn DateTime value on our Person class be set to a default value of "getdate()", we would use the following code:

```
protected override void OnModelCreating(ModelBuilder modelBuilder)
{
    modelBuilder.Entity<Person>().Property(x => x.CreatedOn).HasDefault
    ValueSql("getdate()");
}
```

Similarly, if we wanted to default the Country property value on the Address entity to be "USA", we would add the following code to the OnModelCreating method:

```
protected override void OnModelCreating(ModelBuilder modelBuilder)
{
    modelBuilder.Entity<Address>().Property(x => x.Country).
    HasDefaultValue("USA");
}
```

Record Insertion Integration Tests

Now that we have a grasp of the basics of inserting a record into a database using Entity Framework Core 5, let us see it in action through some unit tests. Create a new class named AddTests into the EFCOre5WebApp.DAL.Tests project.

Then add the code from Listing 8 1 into your AddTests class.

Listing 8-1. AddTests Unit Test Class

```
using EFCore5WebApp.Core.Entities;
using Microsoft.EntityFrameworkCore;
using NUnit.Framework;
using System;
using System.Collections.Generic;
using System.Linq;
```

```
namespace EFCOre5WebApp.DAL.Tests
{
    [TestFixture]
    public class AddTests
    {
        private AppDbContext _context;

        [SetUp]
        public void SetUp()
        {
            _context = new AppDbContext(new DbContextOptionsBuilder
            <AppDbContext>()
    .UseSqlServer("Server=(localdb)\\mssqllocaldb;Database=
    EfCore5WebApp;Trusted_Connection=True;MultipleActiveResult
    Sets=true")
                .Options);
        }

        [Test]
        public void InsertPersonWithAddresses()
        {
            var record = new Person()
            {
                FirstName = "Clarke",
                LastName = "Kent",
                EmailAddress = "clark@daileybugel.com",
                Addresses = new List<Address>
                {
                    new Address
                    {
                        AddressLine1 = "1234 Fake Street",
                        AddressLine2 = "Suite 1",
                        City = "Chicago",
                        State = "IL",
                        ZipCode = "60652",
                        Country = "United States"
                    },
```

```
                new Address
                {
                    AddressLine1 = "555 Waverly Street",
                    AddressLine2 = "APT B2",
                    City = "Mt. Pleasant",
                    State = "MI",
                    ZipCode = "48858",
                    Country = "USA"
                }
            }
        };

        _context.Persons.Add(record);

        _context.SaveChanges();

        var addedPerson = _context.Persons.Single(X => X.FirstName ==
        "Clarke" && X.LastName == "Kent");
        Assert.Greater(addedPerson.Id, 0);
        Assert.AreEqual(2, addedPerson.Addresses.Count);
        Assert.AreEqual(record.FirstName, addedPerson.FirstName);
        Assert.AreEqual(record.LastName, addedPerson.LastName);
        Assert.AreEqual(record.EmailAddress, addedPerson.EmailAddress);

        for (int i = 0; i < record.Addresses.Count; i++)
        {
            Assert.AreEqual(record.Addresses[i].AddressLine1,
            addedPerson.Addresses[i].AddressLine1);
            Assert.AreEqual(record.Addresses[i].AddressLine2,
            addedPerson.Addresses[i].AddressLine2);
            Assert.AreEqual(record.Addresses[i].City, addedPerson.
            Addresses[i].City);
            Assert.AreEqual(record.Addresses[i].State, addedPerson.
            Addresses[i].State);
            Assert.AreEqual(record.Addresses[i].ZipCode, addedPerson.
            Addresses[i].ZipCode);
```

```
                Assert.AreEqual(record.Addresses[i].Country, addedPerson.
                Addresses[i].Country);
            }
        }

        [TearDown]
        public void TearDown()
        {
            var person = _context.Persons.Single(X => X.FirstName ==
            "Clarke" && X.LastName == "Kent");
            _context.Persons.Remove(person);
            _context.SaveChanges();
        }
    }
}
```

The first thing I do in the AddTests class is declare a member variable for DbContext just like in the SelectTests class. Next, I initialize DbContext to open our SQL Server database in the SetUp method. The SetUp method will get called before every unit test in the class.

Then in the InsertPersonWithAddresses method, I create a new Person entity that has two child address records. Then I add that record through the DbSet<T>.Add method. Lastly, in the method, I call SaveChanges on the context to persist the record to the database. Once the record is saved, I then retrieve it using Entity Framework Core 5 and verify the data through my Assert calls. First, I verify that the Id value of the added person is not 0; then, I verify that the person has two addresses. Then I verify that the fields on the person were set correctly. Lastly, I verify that the addresses have the same values that we passed into the Add method to insert them into the SQL Server database.

The TearDown method will find the newly added person record and delete it from the database so that our test record gets cleaned up for the next run of the unit test.

This method of unit testing is often referred to as AAA, which stands for arrange, act, and assert. This is the typical flow of a unit test.

Summary

We have covered a lot of ground in this chapter. First, I went over how to insert a root entity using EF Core 5. Next, I went over how to add child records to the root entity with the root record insert. After that, we saw how to set primary key values for entities. Then we saw how to set default values on non-key entity properties. Lastly, I covered how to test adding a new root entity with its child records using NUnit. In the next chapter, I will cover how to update records in a database using EF Core 5 and test it with unit tests.

Summary

CHAPTER 9

Updating Data

In this chapter, I will cover how to update existing data using Entity Framework Core 5. I will cover how to update the root entity and its associated child entities as well.

Updating the Root Entity

A simple way to update an entity is to first retrieve it and then modify the needed properties and commit the change through SaveChanges. For example, to update a record by Id, you would first retrieve the record by its Id, then change any property values, and commit the change through the context as follows:

```
using (var context = new AppDbContext())
{
    var person = context.Persons.Single(x => x.Id == 1);
    person.FirstName = "Kent";
    person.LastName = "Jones";
    context.SaveChanges();
}
```

If you are unsure if the record will still exist, you can use SingleOrDefault instead of Single to retrieve the record. You should always check for null when using this approach, or you might get a null reference exception. The new code would look like

```
using (var context = new AppDbContext())
{
    var person = context.Persons.SingleOrDefault(x => x.Id == 1);
    if (person != null)
    {
        person.FirstName = "Kent";
        person.LastName = "Jones";
```


E. Vogel, *Beginning Entity Framework Core 5*, https://doi.org/10.1007/978-1-4842-6882-7_9

```
        context.SaveChanges();
    }
}
```

In the preceding example, we first try to get a person record with an Id of 1. If the person exists, we then update the FirstName and LastName properties and save the changes.

Updating a Child Entity

You can update a child entity either directly in the same manner as a root entity or by using a navigation property on the root entity. For example, to update the AddressLine1 property value on the person's first address, you would get the person record, then modify the first address through a navigation property, and then call SaveChanges as follows:

```
using (var context = new AppDbContext())
{
    var person = context.Persons.SingleOrDefault(x => x.Id == 1);
    if (person != null)
    {
        person.Addresses.First().AddressLine1 = "1234 New Street";
        context.SaveChanges();
    }
}
```

If you already know the primary key value of the child entity, you can update the child entity just like a root entity like this:

```
using (var context = new AppDbContext())
{
    var address = context.Addresses.SingleOrDefault(x => x.Id == 1);
    if (address != null)
    {
        address.AddressLine1 = "1234 New Street";
        context.SaveChanges();
    }
}
```

In the preceding code, we try to get an address record by an Id value of 1. If the address record exists, we then update the AddressLine1 value and save the changes.

Integration Test

Now that you know the basics on how to update data, let us create an integration test to see it in action. Create a new class named UpdateTests in the DAL.Tests project. The first step we are going to do is create the SetUp method, which will add a new test record for the update test as seen in Listing 9-1.

Listing 9-1. SetUp Method in UpdateTests.cs

```
private AppDbContext _context;
 private int _personId;

 [SetUp]
 public void SetUp()
 {
     _context = new AppDbContext(new DbContextOptionsBuilder
     <AppDbContext>()
  .UseSqlServer("Server=(localdb)\\mssqllocaldb;Database=EfCore5WebApp;Trust
  ed_Connection=True;MultipleActiveResultSets=true")
        .Options);

     var record = new Person()
     {
         FirstName = "Clarke",
         LastName = "Kent",
         CreatedOn = DateTime.Now,
         EmailAddress = "clark@daileybugel.com",
         Addresses = new List<Address>
         {
             new Address
             {
                 AddressLine1 = "1234 Fake Street",
                 AddressLine2 = "Suite 1",
                 City = "Chicago",
```

```
                State = "IL",
                ZipCode = "60652",
                Country = "United States"
            },
        }
    };

    _context.Persons.Add(record);

    _context.SaveChanges();

    _personId = record.Id;
}
```

Now that we have a test record set up and have its inserted Id, let us implement the TearDown method before we get to testing the update logic. The TearDown method is quite simple and just retrieves the inserted person record and deletes it as seen in Listing 9-2.

Listing 9-2. TearDown Method in UpdateTests.cs

```
[TearDown]
public void TearDown()
{
    var person = _context.Persons.Single(x => x.Id == _personId);
    _context.Persons.Remove(person);
    _context.SaveChanges();
}
```

The final step is to implement our test method, which will retrieve the existing record by its Id and then update the person and its associated address. Then we call SaveChanges to perform the update. After that, we retrieve the person and verify it was updated fully. See Listing 9-3 for the test method implementation.

Listing 9-3. UpdateTests.cs Test Method

```
[Test]
 public void UpdatePersonWithAddresses()
 {
     var person = _context.Persons.Single(x => x.Id == _personId);
     string firstName = "Matt";
     string lastName = "Smith";
     string email = "doctor@who.com";
     person.FirstName = firstName;
     person.LastName = lastName;
     person.EmailAddress = email;
     var address = person.Addresses.First();
     string addressLine1 = "123 Update St";
     string addressLine2 = "APT B1";
     string city = "Okemos";
     string state = "MI";
     string country = "USA";
     string zipCode = "48864";
     address.AddressLine1 = addressLine1;
     address.AddressLine2 = addressLine2;
     address.City = city;
     address.State = state;
     address.Country = country;
     address.ZipCode = zipCode;
     _context.SaveChanges();
     var updatedPerson = _context.Persons.Single(x => x.Id == _personId);
     Assert.AreEqual(1, updatedPerson.Addresses.Count);
     Assert.AreEqual(firstName, updatedPerson.FirstName);
     Assert.AreEqual(lastName, updatedPerson.LastName);
     Assert.AreEqual(email, updatedPerson.EmailAddress);
     var updatedAddress = updatedPerson.Addresses.First();
     Assert.AreEqual(addressLine1, updatedAddress.AddressLine1);
     Assert.AreEqual(addressLine2, updatedAddress.AddressLine2);
     Assert.AreEqual(city, updatedAddress.City);
```

```
        Assert.AreEqual(state, updatedAddress.State);
        Assert.AreEqual(zipCode, updatedAddress.ZipCode);
        Assert.AreEqual(country, updatedAddress.Country);
 }
```

Your final test file should now look like Listing 9-4.

Listing 9-4. Completed UpdateTests Unit Test Class

```
using System;
using System.Collections.Generic;
using System.Linq;
using EFCore5WebApp.Core.Entities;

using Microsoft.EntityFrameworkCore;
using NUnit.Framework;

namespace EFCOre5WebApp.DAL.Tests
{
    [TestFixture]
    public class UpdateTests
    {
        private AppDbContext _context;
        private int _personId;

        [SetUp]
        public void SetUp()
        {
            _context = new AppDbContext(new DbContextOptionsBuilder
            <AppDbContext>()
          .UseSqlServer("Server=(localdb)\\mssqllocaldb;Database=
          EfCore5WebApp;Trusted_Connection=True;MultipleActiveResult
          Sets=true")
                .Options);

            var record = new Person()
            {
                FirstName = "Clarke",
                LastName = "Kent",
```

```
            CreatedOn = DateTime.Now,
            EmailAddress = "clark@daileybugel.com",
            Addresses = new List<Address>
            {
                new Address
                {
                    AddressLine1 = "1234 Fake Street",
                    AddressLine2 = "Suite 1",
                    City = "Chicago",
                    State = "IL",
                    ZipCode = "60652",
                    Country = "United States"
                },
            }
        };
        _context.Persons.Add(record);
        _context.SaveChanges();
        _personId = record.Id;
    }

    [Test]
    public void UpdatePersonWithAddresses()
    {
        var person = _context.Persons.Single(x => x.Id == _personId);
        string firstName = "Matt";
        string lastName = "Smith";
        string email = "doctor@who.com";
        person.FirstName = firstName;
        person.LastName = lastName;
        person.EmailAddress = email;
        var address = person.Addresses.First();
        string addressLine1 = "123 Update St";
        string addressLine2 = "APT B1";
        string city = "Okemos";
```

```
            string state = "MI";
            string country = "USA";
            string zipCode = "48864";
            address.AddressLine1 = addressLine1;
            address.AddressLine2 = addressLine2;
            address.City = city;
            address.State = state;
            address.Country = country;
            address.ZipCode = zipCode;
            _context.SaveChanges();

            var updatedPerson = _context.Persons.Single(x => x.Id == _
            personId);
            Assert.AreEqual(1, updatedPerson.Addresses.Count);
            Assert.AreEqual(firstName, updatedPerson.FirstName);
            Assert.AreEqual(lastName, updatedPerson.LastName);
            Assert.AreEqual(email, updatedPerson.EmailAddress);
            var updatedAddress = updatedPerson.Addresses.First();
            Assert.AreEqual(addressLine1, updatedAddress.AddressLine1);
            Assert.AreEqual(addressLine2, updatedAddress.AddressLine2);
            Assert.AreEqual(city, updatedAddress.City);
            Assert.AreEqual(state, updatedAddress.State);
            Assert.AreEqual(zipCode, updatedAddress.ZipCode);
            Assert.AreEqual(country, updatedAddress.Country);
        }

        [TearDown]
        public void TearDown()
        {
            var person = _context.Persons.Single(x => x.Id == _personId);
            _context.Persons.Remove(person);
            _context.SaveChanges();
        }
    }
}
```

Summary

In this chapter, I have covered how to update entity records using Entity Framework Core 5 and test the logic. The basic steps are to first retrieve the record or records that will be updated. Next, change any property values. Lastly, call SaveChanges to persist the update. In the next chapter, I will cover strategies for deleting data from your database through EF Core 5.

Summary

CHAPTER 10

Deleting Data

In this chapter, I will cover how to delete data using Entity Framework Core 5. There are generally two ways to delete a record. These two methods are often referred to as soft delete and hard delete. A soft delete is flagging a record as deleted and can be achieved by doing a database update and setting a flag to mark a record as deleted. A hard delete is removing the record from the database, and it can no longer be retrieved afterward. In this chapter, I will be covering how to implement a hard delete.

Deleting the Root Entity

There are two steps to removing an item. The first is retrieving that item, and the second is removing that record by using the Remove method on DbSet<T> like this:

```
var existing = _context.Persons.Single(x => x.FirstName == "Clarke" &&
x.LastName == "Kent");
_context.Persons.Remove(existing);
_context.SaveChanges();
```

As you can see, removing a root entity is simple.

Deleting a Child Entity

By default, Entity Framework Core 5 will delete child entities when the root entity is deleted. In our database, if we delete a person record, its associated address records will also be deleted. You can also configure how you want to handle deleting child entities in OnModelCreating in our custom AppDbContext class. The options you have are cascade, client set null, restrict, and set null. These options are specified through the DeleteBehavior enum. I will now cover how each of these options works one by one.

E. Vogel, *Beginning Entity Framework Core 5*, https://doi.org/10.1007/978-1-4842-6882-7_10

Cascade Delete

Cascade delete is the default behavior for removing child entities. Cascade means that all related child entities will be deleted when the parent entity is deleted. In our case, when a person is deleted, its address records will also be deleted. In order to explicitly define this behavior, we need to finish the one-to-many mapping between Address and Person. We will do this by adding a Person type property on the Address entity named Person as seen in Listing 10-1.

Listing 10-1. Address Class Updated with Person Navigation Property

```
namespace EFCore5WebApp.Core.Entities
{
    public class Address
    {
        public int Id { get; set; }
        public string AddressLine1 { get; set; }
        public string AddressLine2 { get; set; }
        public string City { get; set; }
        public string State { get; set; }
        public string Country { get; set; }
        public string ZipCode { get; set; }
        public int PersonId { get; set; }
        public Person Person { get; set; }
    }
}
```

You can also explicitly define this behavior in the OnModelCreating event like Listing 10-2.

Listing 10-2. Define Cascade Delete for Person Address Records

```
modelBuilder.Entity<Person>(entity =>
{
    entity.HasMany(x => x.Addresses)
   .WithOne(x => x.Person)
        .OnDelete(DeleteBehavior.Cascade);
});
```

You can see in our code that we defined that a person has many addresses via the Addresses property and that an address has a single person mapped via the Person property on the Address entity. Lastly, we defined the delete behavior as cascade.

Client Set Null Delete Behavior

The client set null delete behavior will set any foreign key properties to null on the child entities instead of removing the child entities. This will only set the foreign key properties to null in memory. You have to explicitly call SaveChanges for this to be persisted to the database. In order to use this behavior in our code, we would need to set the PersonId property to be null in the Address entity. This update would look like Listing 10-3.

Listing 10-3. Address with Nullable PersonId

```
namespace EFCore5WebApp.Core.Entities
{
    public class Address
    {
        public int Id { get; set; }
        public string AddressLine1 { get; set; }
        public string AddressLine2 { get; set; }
        public string City { get; set; }
        public string State { get; set; }
        public string Country { get; set; }
        public string ZipCode { get; set; }
        public int? PersonId { get; set; }
        public Person Person { get; set; }
    }
}
```

The next step would be to update the OnModelCreating method in AppDbContext to set the delete behavior to be ClientSetNull as seen in Listing 10-4.

Listing 10-4. Client Set Null Delete Behavior on Person's Addresses

```
modelBuilder.Entity<Person>(entity =>
{
    entity.HasMany(x => x.Addresses)
   .WithOne(x => x.Person)
   .HasForeignKey(x => x.PersonId)
        .OnDelete(DeleteBehavior.Cascade);
});
```

As you can see in the code example, we also explicitly state the foreign key property to PersonId to help Entity Framework Core know what property value to null out.

Restrict Delete Behavior

The restrict delete behavior specifies not to perform a cascade delete. This forces you to handle deleting the child entities yourself in your code. To specify the restrict delete behavior, we would update the OnModelCreating method in our AppDbContext to set the Addresses delete behavior to Restrict on the Person entity as seen in Listing 10-5.

Listing 10-5. Restrict Delete Behavior on Person's Addresses

```
modelBuilder.Entity<Person>(entity =>
 {
     entity.HasMany(x => x.Addresses)
    .WithOne(x => x.Person)
    .HasForeignKey(x => x.PersonId)
         .OnDelete(DeleteBehavior.Restrict);
 });
```

You can see that the code is the same as client set null except we set the delete behavior enum value to DeleteBehavior.Restrict.

Set Null Delete Behavior

The set null delete behavior is the same as client set null except the foreign key properties are automatically set to null without your intervention when the parent entity is deleted. Look at Listing 10-6 to see the needed code in the OnModelCreating method for our AppDbContext.

Listing 10-6. Set Null Delete for Person's Addresses

```
modelBuilder.Entity<Person>(entity =>
{
    entity.HasMany(x => x.Addresses)
   .WithOne(x => x.Person)
   .HasForeignKey(x => x.PersonId)
        .OnDelete(DeleteBehavior.SetNull);
});
```

As you can see, the code is the exact same as ClientSetNull except we pass in the DeleteBehavior.SetNull value into the OnDelete() chained method.

Integration Test

Now that we have seen how to delete an entity record using Entity Framework Core 5, let us see this in action by creating an integration test. Open the DAL.Tests project and create a new class named DeleteTests. See Listing 10-7 for the unit test class.

Listing 10-7. DeleteTests Class File

```
using System;
using System.Collections.Generic;
using System.Linq;
using EFCore5WebApp.Core.Entities;
using Microsoft.EntityFrameworkCore;
using NUnit.Framework;
```

```
namespace EFCore5WebApp.DAL.Tests
{
    [TestFixture]
    public class DeleteTests
    {
        private AppDbContext _context;

        [SetUp]
        public void SetUp()
        {
            _context = new AppDbContext(new DbContextOptionsBuilder
            <AppDbContext>()
    .UseSqlServer("Server=(localdb)\\mssqllocaldb;Database=
    EfCore5WebApp;Trusted_Connection=True;MultipleActiveResult
    Sets=true")
                .Options);

            // add person record
            var record = new Person()
            {
                FirstName = "Clarke",
                LastName = "Kent",
                CreatedOn = DateTime.Now,
                EmailAddress = "clark@daileybugel.com",
                Addresses = new List<Address>
                {
                    new Address
                    {
                        AddressLine1 = "1234 Fake Street",
                        AddressLine2 = "Suite 1",
                        City = "Chicago",
                        State = "IL",
                        ZipCode = "60652",
                        Country = "United States"
                    },
```

```
                new Address
                {
                    AddressLine1 = "555 Waverly Street",
                    AddressLine2 = "APT B2",
                    City = "Mt. Pleasant",
                    State = "MI",
                    ZipCode = "48858",
                    Country = "USA"
                }
            }
        };
        _context.Persons.Add(record);

        _context.SaveChanges();
    }

    [Test]
    public void DeletePerson()
    {
        var existing = _context.Persons.Single(x => x.FirstName ==
        "Clarke" && x.LastName == "Kent");
        var personId = existing.Id;
        _context.Persons.Remove(existing);
        _context.SaveChanges();
        var found = _context.Persons.SingleOrDefault(x => x.FirstName
        == "Clarke" && x.LastName == "Kent");
        Assert.IsNull(found);
        var addresses = _context.Addresses.Where(x => x.PersonId ==
        personId);
        Assert.AreEqual(0, addresses.Count());
    }
  }
}
```

Like the other unit tests, we first get a connection to our SQL Server in the SetUp method. Next, I add a person record with two addresses. In the DeletePerson method, we test the delete functionality by retrieving the person record. Then we remove the record and commit the change. After the person record is removed, we make sure it can no longer be retrieved and that its addresses have also been removed.

Summary

In this chapter, I have covered how to delete a root entity and its child entities. By default, Entity Framework Core 5 will delete child entities when the root entity is removed. I also covered how you can change this default behavior if desired. After that, I covered how to test this functionality through an integration test. In the next chapter, I will cover navigation properties in depth.

CHAPTER 11

Navigation Properties

In this chapter, I will cover how to map both a one-to-many and a many-to-many entity relationship using Entity Framework Core 5 through using navigation properties. We have already created half of the code to create these relationships earlier in the book when we mapped one-to-many addresses to a person record. I will now show how to complete the one-to-many mapping between Person and Address entities. I will also cover how to add a many-to-many parent/child relationship through navigation properties.

Mapping a Parent Entity in a One-to-Many Relationship

In our example in Chapter 10 to map many Address entities to one person record, we created a collection property to store our addresses in the Person class as follows:

```
public List<Address> Addresses { get; set; } - new List<Address>();
```

The entire code for the Person class for reference is in Listing 11-1.

Listing 11-1. Person Class

```
using System;
using System.Collections.Generic;
using System.ComponentModel.DataAnnotations;
using System.ComponentModel.DataAnnotations.Schema;

namespace EFCore5WebApp.Core.Entities
{
    [Table("Persons", Schema ="dbo")]
    public class Person
```


E. Vogel, *Beginning Entity Framework Core 5*, https://doi.org/10.1007/978-1-4842-6882-7_11

```
    {
        public int Id { get; set; }
        [Required]
        [MaxLength(255)]
        public string FirstName { get; set; }
        [Required]
        [MaxLength(255)]
        public string LastName { get; set; }
        [Required]
        public string EmailAddress { get; set; }
        public List<Address> Addresses { get; set; } = new List<Address>();
        [NotMapped]
        public string FullName => $"{FirstName} {LastName}";

        public DateTime CreatedOn { get; set; }
    }
}
```

The Addresses navigation property allows us to retrieve one-to-many address records from a retrieved person record.

Mapping a Related Entity to Parent

To complete the one-to-many relationship between Person and Address entities, we map a single Person type property named Person to the Address entity class as seen in Listing 11-2.

Listing 11-2. Updated Address Class

```
namespace EFCore5WebApp.Core.Entities
{
    public class Address
    {
        public int Id { get; set; }
        public string AddressLine1 { get; set; }
        public string AddressLine2 { get; set; }
        public string City { get; set; }
```

```
        public string State { get; set; }
        public string Country { get; set; }
        public string ZipCode { get; set; }
        public int PersonId { get; set; }
        public Person Person { get; set; }
    }
}
```

The reason for this mapping in Listing 11-2 is so that we can retrieve any address in the database and follow the PersonId value to determine whom the address belongs to. Each address is owned by one person.

One-to-Many Integration Test

Now that we have completed both sides of the one-to-many relationship between person and address records, let us see it in action through some unit tests. Create a new NUnit unit test class file named NavigationPropertyTests under the DAL.Tests project. See Listing 11-3 for the completed navigation property unit tests.

Listing 11-3. Navigation Property Unit Tests

```
using EFCore5WebApp.Core.Entities;
using EFCOre5WebApp.DAL;
using Microsoft.EntityFrameworkCore;
using NUnit.Framework;
using System.Collections.Generic;
using System.Linq;

namespace EFCore5WebApp.DAL.Tests
{
    [TestFixture]
    public class NavigationPropertyTests
    {
        private AppDbContext _context;
        private Person _person;
```

```
        [SetUp]
        public void SetUp()
        {
            _context = new AppDbContext(new DbContextOptionsBuilder
            <AppDbContext>()
    .UseSqlServer("Server=(localdb)\\mssqllocaldb;Database=
    EfCore5WebApp;Trusted_Connection=True;MultipleActiveResult
    Sets=true")
                .Options);

            _person = new Person()
            {
                FirstName = "Clarke",
                LastName = "Kent",
                EmailAddress = "clark@daileybugel.com",
                Addresses = new List<Address>
                {
                    new Address
                    {
                        AddressLine1 = "1234 Fake Street",
                        AddressLine2 = "Suite 1",
                        City = "Chicago",
                        State = "IL",
                        ZipCode = "60652",
                        Country = "United States"
                    },
                    new Address
                    {
                        AddressLine1 = "555 Waverly Street",
                        AddressLine2 = "APT B2",
                        City = "Mt. Pleasant",
                        State = "MI",
                        ZipCode = "48858",
                        Country = "USA"
                    }
                }
            };
```

```
            _context.Persons.Add(_person);

            _context.SaveChanges();
        }

        [Test]
        public void GetAddressesFromPerson()
        {
            Assert.AreEqual(2, _person.Addresses.Count);
        }

        [Test]
        public void GetPersonFromAddress()
        {
            var address = _person.Addresses.First();
            Assert.IsNotNull(address.Person);
        }

        [TearDown]
        public void TearDown()
        {
            _context.Persons.Remove(_person);
            _context.SaveChanges();
        }
    }
}
```

Just like the other unit tests, we first create AppDbContext and initialize it in our SetUp method to connect to our SQL Server database. In the GetAddressesFromPerson unit test, we first retrieve a person record and then make sure its address was included. In the GetPersonFromAddress unit test, we retrieve an address record and then make sure it has a set person record. These unit tests ensure that both ends of the one-to-many entity mapping are working correctly.

Many-to-Many Relationships

Our many-to-many relationship is parents to children. A child can have many parents, and a parent can have many children. Prior to Entity Framework Core 5, we would need to explicitly create a mapping between the two using the OnModelCreating method in our DbContext class. In Entity Framework Core 5, we can now simply add both sides of the relationship through collections, and Entity Framework Core 5 will create the cross-reference table for us when we create our migration. In prior versions of Entity Framework Core, we would need to create our own cross-reference entity that would contain foreign keys to both sides of the many-to-many relationship. Let's now go through the process step by step.

Map a Relationship Through Navigation Properties

We will now update our Person class to have a collection of Person objects for both the parents and the children of the person as seen in Listing 11-4.

Listing 11-4. Person Class with Parents and Children

```
using System;
using System.Collections.Generic;
using System.ComponentModel.DataAnnotations;
using System.ComponentModel.DataAnnotations.Schema;

namespace EFCore5WebApp.Core.Entities
{
    [Table("Persons")]
    public class Person
    {
        public int Id { get; set; }
        [Required]
        [MaxLength(255)]
        public string FirstName { get; set; }
        [Required]
        [MaxLength(255)]
        public string LastName { get; set; }
```

```
        [Required]
        public string EmailAddress { get; set; }
        public List<Address> Addresses { get; set; } = new List<Address>();
        public DateTime CreatedOn { get; set; }
        public List<Person> Parents { get; set; } = new List<Person>();
        public List<Person> Children { get; set; } = new List<Person>();
    }
}
```

The final two properties in Listing 11-4 are the ones to focus on. Both are List<Person> entities. The list named Parents contains a list of the parents for a given person. The list named Children contains a list of that person's children. Using these properties, you can navigate upward and downward in the hierarchy.

Create and Run Migration

Now that we have the many-to-many relationship defined through our Parents and Children navigation properties on the Person model, let's create the migration for that relationship. In the NuGet Package Manager Console, run the "Add-Migration" command to add a migration called "PersonParentChildren" as follows:

```
Add-Migration PersonParentChildren
```

You should now see a new migration created in the "Migrations" folder in your "DAL" project, and that new migration will be named PersonParentChildren. The migration should look like that in Listing 11-5.

Listing 11-5. PersonParentChildren Migration Class

```
using System;
using Microsoft.EntityFrameworkCore.Migrations;

namespace EFCore5WebApp.DAL.Migrations
{
    public partial class PersonParentChildren : Migration
    {
        protected override void Up(MigrationBuilder migrationBuilder)
```

```
        {
            migrationBuilder.AddColumn<DateTime>(
                name: "CreatedOn",
                table: "Persons",
                type: "datetime2",
                nullable: false,
                defaultValue: new DateTime(1, 1, 1, 0, 0, 0, 0,
                DateTimeKind.Unspecified));

            migrationBuilder.AlterColumn<int>(
                name: "PersonId",
                table: "Addresses",
                type: "int",
                nullable: true,
                oldClrType: typeof(int),
                oldType: "int");

            migrationBuilder.CreateTable(
                name: "PersonPerson",
                columns: table => new
                {
                    ChildrenId = table.Column<int>(type: "int",
                    nullable: false),
                    ParentsId = table.Column<int>(type: "int",
                    nullable: false)
                },
                constraints: table =>
                {
                    table.PrimaryKey("PK_PersonPerson", x => new {
                    x.ChildrenId, x.ParentsId });
                    table.ForeignKey(
                        name: "FK_PersonPerson_Persons_ChildrenId",
                        column: x => x.ChildrenId,
                        principalTable: "Persons",
                        principalColumn: "Id",
                        onDelete: ReferentialAction.Cascade);
```

```
                    table.ForeignKey(
                        name: "FK_PersonPerson_Persons_ParentsId",
                        column: x => x.ParentsId,
                        principalTable: "Persons",
                        principalColumn: "Id",
                        onDelete: ReferentialAction.Restrict);
                });

            migrationBuilder.CreateIndex(
                name: "IX_PersonPerson_ParentsId",
                table: "PersonPerson",
                column: "ParentsId");
        }

        protected override void Down(MigrationBuilder migrationBuilder)
        {
            migrationBuilder.DropTable(
                name: "PersonPerson");

            migrationBuilder.DropColumn(
                name: "CreatedOn",
                table: "Persons");

            migrationBuilder.AlterColumn<int>(
                name: "PersonId",
                table: "Addresses",
                type: "int",
                nullable: false,
                defaultValue: 0,
                oldClrType: typeof(int),
                oldType: "int",
                oldNullable: true);
        }
    }
}
```

You can see that EF Core 5 decided to add a PersonPerson cross-reference table to store the many-to-many mapping between parents and children. The PersonPerson table will have columns named "ChildrenId" and "ParentsId" that link the parents to their children and vice versa.

Now let's run the migration on our database by running the "Update-Database" command from the NuGet Package Manager Console. You can now see that the "PersonPerson" table was successfully created in our database as seen in Figure 11-1.

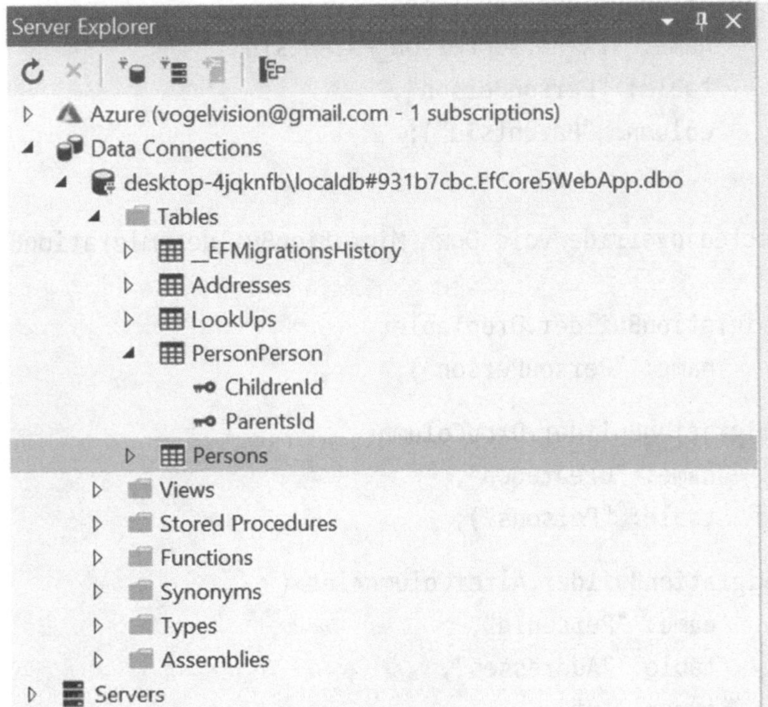

Figure 11-1. *PersonPerson Table*

Many-to-Many Integration Test

Now let's put our parent-children relationship to the test through an NUnit integration test. Let's create a new NUnit test class named "ManyToManyTests". The integration tests are a little complicated, so let's break them down piece by piece. First, we declare our AppDbContext and a collection of Person objects that will hold our entire family:

```
private AppDbContext _context;
private List<Person> _family;
```

After that, we define our SetUp method as seen in Listing 11-6.

Listing 11-6. ManyToManyTests SetUp Method

```
[SetUp]
 public void SetUp()
 {
     _context = new AppDbContext(new DbContextOptionsBuilder<AppDbContext>()
  .UseSqlServer("Server=(localdb)\\mssqllocaldb;Database=EfCore5
  WebApp;Trusted_Connection=True;MultipleActiveResultSets=true")
  .Options);

     _family = new List<Person>();

     var parent1 = new Person()
     {
         FirstName = "Clarke",
         LastName = "Kent",
         EmailAddress = "clark@daileybugel.com",
         Addresses = new List<Address>
         {
             new Address
             {
                 AddressLine1 = "1234 Fake Street",
                 AddressLine2 = "Suite 1",
                 City = "Chicago",
                 State = "IL",
                 ZipCode = "60652",
                 Country = "United States"
             },
         }
     };

     var parent2 = new Person()
     {
         FirstName = "Lois",
         LastName = "Lane",
         EmailAddress = "Lois@daileybugel.com",
```

```
            Addresses = new List<Address>
            {
                new Address
                {
                    AddressLine1 = "1234 Fake Street",
                    AddressLine2 = "Suite 1",
                    City = "Chicago",
                    State = "IL",
                    ZipCode = "60652",
                    Country = "United States"
                },
            }
        };

        var child1 = new Person()
        {
            FirstName = "David",
            LastName = "Kent",
            EmailAddress = "Lois@daileybugel.com",
            Addresses = new List<Address>
            {
                new Address
                {
                    AddressLine1 = "1234 Fake Street",
                    AddressLine2 = "Suite 1",
                    City = "Chicago",
                    State = "IL",
                    ZipCode = "60652",
                    Country = "United States"
                },
            }
        };

        var child2 = new Person()
        {
            FirstName = "Anna",
            LastName = "Kent",
```

```
            EmailAddress = "Lois@daileybugel.com",
            Addresses = new List<Address>
            {
                new Address
                {
                    AddressLine1 = "1234 Fake Street",
                    AddressLine2 = "Suite 1",
                    City = "Chicago",
                    State = "IL",
                    ZipCode = "60652",
                    Country = "United States"
                },
            }
        };

        _context.Persons.Add(parent1);
        _context.Persons.Add(parent2);
        _context.Persons.Add(child1);
        _context.Persons.Add(child2);

        parent1.Children.Add(child1);
        parent1.Children.Add(child2);

        child1.Parents.Add(parent1);
        child1.Parents.Add(parent2);

        child2.Parents.Add(parent1);
        child2.Parents.Add(parent2);

        _family.Add(parent1);
        _family.Add(parent2);
        _family.Add(child1);
        _family.Add(child2);

        _context.SaveChanges();
    }
```

Our SetUp method is quite extensive, so let's go through it piece by piece. First, we initialize our _context class just like in our other NUnit test classes:

```
_context = new AppDbContext(new DbContextOptionsBuilder<AppDbContext>()
.UseSqlServer("Server=(localdb)\\mssqllocaldb;Database=EfCore5WebApp;
Trusted_Connection=True;MultipleActiveResultSets=true")
     .Options);
```

After that, we initialize our _family to be an empty collection:

```
_family = new List<Person>();
```

Now we are going to add both parents, the father as "Clarke Kent" and the mother as "Lois Lane":

```
var parent1 = new Person()
{
    FirstName = "Clarke",
    LastName = "Kent",
    EmailAddress = "clark@daileybugel.com",
    Addresses = new List<Address>
    {
        new Address
        {
            AddressLine1 = "1234 Fake Street",
            AddressLine2 = "Suite 1",
            City = "Chicago",
            State = "IL",
            ZipCode = "60652",
            Country = "United States"
        },
    }
};

var parent2 = new Person()
{
    FirstName = "Lois",
    LastName = "Lane",
    EmailAddress = "Lois@daileybugel.com",
```

```
    Addresses = new List<Address>
    {
        new Address
        {
            AddressLine1 = "1234 Fake Street",
            AddressLine2 = "Suite 1",
            City = "Chicago",
            State = "IL",
            ZipCode = "60652",
            Country = "United States"
        },
    }
};
```

Next, we add their two children, a son named "David" and a daughter named "Anna":

```
var child1 = new Person()
{
    FirstName = "David",
    LastName = "Kent",
    EmailAddress = "Lois@daileybugel.com",
    Addresses = new List<Address>
    {
        new Address
        {
            AddressLine1 = "1234 Fake Street",
            AddressLine2 = "Suite 1",
            City = "Chicago",
            State = "IL",
            ZipCode = "60652",
            Country = "United States"
        },
    }
};
```

```
var child2 = new Person()
{
    FirstName = "Anna",
    LastName = "Kent",
    EmailAddress = "Lois@daileybugel.com",
    Addresses = new List<Address>
    {
        new Address
        {
            AddressLine1 = "1234 Fake Street",
            AddressLine2 = "Suite 1",
            City = "Chicago",
            State = "IL",
            ZipCode = "60652",
            Country = "United States"
        },
    }
};
```

Next, we add all of the Person objects to our DbContext:

```
_context.Persons.Add(parent1);
_context.Persons.Add(parent2);
_context.Persons.Add(child1);
_context.Persons.Add(child2);
```

After that, we add both children to the first parent:

```
parent1.Children.Add(child1);
parent1.Children.Add(child2);
```

Next, we add both children to the second parent:

```
parent2.Children.Add(child1);
parent2.Children.Add(child2);
```

Then we add both parents to the first child:

```
child1.Parents.Add(parent1);
child1.Parents.Add(parent2);
```

Next, we add both parents to the second child:

```
child2.Parents.Add(parent1);
child2.Parents.Add(parent2);
```

Then we add all of the Person objects in our family to the _family collection:

```
_family.Add(parent1);
 _family.Add(parent2);
 _family.Add(child1);
 _family.Add(child2);
```

Lastly, we save our family to the database:

```
_context.SaveChanges();
```

Your completed SetUp method should now look like Listing 11-7.

Listing 11-7. Completed ManyToManyTests SetUp Method

```
[TestFixture]
 public class ManyToManyTests
 {
     private AppDbContext _context;
     private List<Person> _family;

     [SetUp]
     public void SetUp()
     {
         _context = new AppDbContext(new DbContextOptionsBuilder
         <AppDbContext>()
 .UseSqlServer("Server=(localdb)\\mssqllocaldb;Database=EfCore5WebApp;
 Trusted_Connection=True;MultipleActiveResultSets=true")
             .Options);

         _family = new List<Person>();

         var parent1 = new Person()
         {
             FirstName = "Clarke",
             LastName = "Kent",
```

```
            EmailAddress = "clark@daileybugel.com",
            Addresses = new List<Address>
            {
                new Address
                {
                    AddressLine1 = "1234 Fake Street",
                    AddressLine2 = "Suite 1",
                    City = "Chicago",
                    State = "IL",
                    ZipCode = "60652",
                    Country = "United States"
                },
            }
        };

        var parent2 = new Person()
        {
            FirstName = "Lois",
            LastName = "Lane",
            EmailAddress = "Lois@daileybugel.com",
            Addresses = new List<Address>
            {
                new Address
                {
                    AddressLine1 = "1234 Fake Street",
                    AddressLine2 = "Suite 1",
                    City = "Chicago",
                    State = "IL",
                    ZipCode = "60652",
                    Country = "United States"
                },
            }
        };
```

```
var child1 = new Person()
{
    FirstName = "David",
    LastName = "Kent",
    EmailAddress = "Lois@daileybugel.com",
    Addresses = new List<Address>
    {
        new Address
        {
            AddressLine1 = "1234 Fake Street",
            AddressLine2 = "Suite 1",
            City = "Chicago",
            State = "IL",
            ZipCode = "60652",
            Country = "United States"
        },
    }
};

var child2 = new Person()
{
    FirstName = "Anna",
    LastName = "Kent",
    EmailAddress = "Lois@daileybugel.com",
    Addresses = new List<Address>
    {
        new Address
        {
            AddressLine1 = "1234 Fake Street",
            AddressLine2 = "Suite 1",
            City = "Chicago",
            State = "IL",
            ZipCode = "60652",
            Country = "United States"
        },
    }
};
```

```
        _context.Persons.Add(parent1);
        _context.Persons.Add(parent2);
        _context.Persons.Add(child1);
        _context.Persons.Add(child2);

        parent1.Children.Add(child1);
        parent1.Children.Add(child2);

        parent2.Children.Add(child1);
        parent2.Children.Add(child2);

        child1.Parents.Add(parent1);
        child1.Parents.Add(parent2);

        child2.Parents.Add(parent1);
        child2.Parents.Add(parent2);

        _family.Add(parent1);
        _family.Add(parent2);
        _family.Add(child1);
        _family.Add(child2);

        _context.SaveChanges();
    }
```

Now that our family is saved to the database in our SetUp method, we will test that we can get both parents from their children in our GetParentsFromChildren test method:

```
[Test]
public void GetParentsFromChildren()
{
    var daughter = _family.Single(x => x.FirstName == "Anna");
    var son = _family.Single(x => x.FirstName == "David");
    Assert.AreEqual(2, daughter.Parents.Count);
    Assert.AreEqual(2, son.Parents.Count);
}
```

Now let's test that we can get both children from both of our parents in our GetChildrenFromParents test method:

```
[Test]
public void GetChildrenFromParents()
{
    var mother = _family.Single(x => x.FirstName == "Lois");
    var father = _family.Single(x => x.FirstName == "Clarke");
    Assert.AreEqual(2, mother.Children.Count);
    Assert.AreEqual(2, father.Children.Count);
}
```

Lastly, let's clean up our created Person objects in our TearDown method:

```
[TearDown]
public void TearDown()
{
    _context.Persons.RemoveRange(_family);
    _context.SaveChanges();
}
```

We are using the RemoveRange() method to remove the entire collection of Person objects at once, and then we save that change through SaveChanges().

Your complete ManyToManyTests NUnit class should now look like Listing 11-8.

Listing 11-8. ManyToManyTests NUnit Class

```
using EFCore5WebApp.Core.Entities;
using EFCOre5WebApp.DAL;
using Microsoft.EntityFrameworkCore;
using NUnit.Framework;
using System.Collections.Generic;
using System.Linq;

namespace EFCore5WebApp.DAL.Tests
{
    [TestFixture]
    public class ManyToManyTests
```

```
{
    private AppDbContext _context;
    private List<Person> _family;

    [SetUp]
    public void SetUp()
    {
        _context = new AppDbContext(new DbContextOptionsBuilder
        <AppDbContext>()
.UseSqlServer("Server=(localdb)\\mssqllocaldb;Database=
EfCore5WebApp;Trusted_Connection=True;MultipleActiveResult
Sets=true")
            .Options);

        _family = new List<Person>();

        var parent1 = new Person()
        {
            FirstName = "Clarke",
            LastName = "Kent",
            EmailAddress = "clark@daileybugel.com",
            Addresses = new List<Address>
            {
                new Address
                {
                    AddressLine1 = "1234 Fake Street",
                    AddressLine2 = "Suite 1",
                    City = "Chicago",
                    State = "IL",
                    ZipCode = "60652",
                    Country = "United States"
                },
            }
        };
```

```
var parent2 = new Person()
{
    FirstName = "Lois",
    LastName = "Lane",
    EmailAddress = "Lois@daileybugel.com",
    Addresses = new List<Address>
    {
        new Address
        {
            AddressLine1 = "1234 Fake Street",
            AddressLine2 = "Suite 1",
            City = "Chicago",
            State = "IL",
            ZipCode = "60652",
            Country = "United States"
        },
    }
};

var child1 = new Person()
{
    FirstName = "David",
    LastName = "Kent",
    EmailAddress = "Lois@daileybugel.com",
    Addresses = new List<Address>
    {
        new Address
        {
            AddressLine1 = "1234 Fake Street",
            AddressLine2 = "Suite 1",
            City = "Chicago",
            State = "IL",
            ZipCode = "60652",
            Country = "United States"
        },
    }
};
```

```
var child2 = new Person()
{
    FirstName = "Anna",
    LastName = "Kent",
    EmailAddress = "Lois@daileybugel.com",
    Addresses = new List<Address>
    {
        new Address
        {
            AddressLine1 = "1234 Fake Street",
            AddressLine2 = "Suite 1",
            City = "Chicago",
            State = "IL",
            ZipCode = "60652",
            Country = "United States"
        },
    }
};

_context.Persons.Add(parent1);
_context.Persons.Add(parent2);
_context.Persons.Add(child1);
_context.Persons.Add(child2);

parent1.Children.Add(child1);
parent1.Children.Add(child2);

parent2.Children.Add(child1);
parent2.Children.Add(child2);

child1.Parents.Add(parent1);
child1.Parents.Add(parent2);

child2.Parents.Add(parent1);
child2.Parents.Add(parent2);
```

```
            _family.Add(parent1);
            _family.Add(parent2);
            _family.Add(child1);
            _family.Add(child2);
            _context.SaveChanges();
        }

        [Test]
        public void GetParentsFromChildren()
        {
            var daughter = _family.Single(x => x.FirstName == "Anna");
            var son = _family.Single(x => x.FirstName == "David");
            Assert.AreEqual(2, daughter.Parents.Count);
            Assert.AreEqual(2, son.Parents.Count);
        }

        [Test]
        public void GetChildrenFromParents()
        {
            var mother = _family.Single(x => x.FirstName == "Lois");
            var father = _family.Single(x => x.FirstName == "Clarke");
            Assert.AreEqual(2, mother.Children.Count);
            Assert.AreEqual(2, father.Children.Count);
        }

        [TearDown]
        public void TearDown()
        {
            _context.Persons.RemoveRange(_family);
            _context.SaveChanges();
        }
    }
}
```

Summary

As you can see, Entity Framework Core 5 makes mapping a one-to-many relationship easy by using navigation properties. In this chapter, we first covered how to map many address records to the root Person entity. Next, we looked at how to map the other end of the relationship by mapping a single Person entity record to an address record. Next, we tested both sides of the relationship mapping through NUnit unit tests. We then repeated this process for a many-to-many relationship between parents and children, culminating in some integration tests. In the next chapter, I will show how to perform aggregation operations over your data using Entity Framework Core 5.

PART III

Advanced Features

CHAPTER 12

Aggregations

Entity Framework Core 5 includes several ways to aggregate your data. In this chapter, I will be covering count, min, max, average, sum, and group by. The group by clause is often used in conjunction with the aggregation operations. I will cover the simple operators first and then show how to use them with group by.

Unit Test Setup

We will be using unit tests to explore the various aggregation operators. Create a new NUnit class named AggregationTest in the DAL.Tests project. Initialize AppDbContext like in our other unit tests. Your code should now look like that in Listing 12-1.

Listing 12-1. Initial Aggregation Test Class

```
using System;
using System.Collections.Generic;
using System.Linq;
using EFCore5WebApp.Core.Entities;
using Microsoft.EntityFrameworkCore;
using NUnit.Framework;

namespace EFCOre5WebApp.DAL.Tests
{
    [TestFixture]
    public class AggregationTests
    {
        private AppDbContext _context;
```


E. Vogel, *Beginning Entity Framework Core 5*, https://doi.org/10.1007/978-1-4842-6882-7_12

```
        [SetUp]
        public void SetUp()
        {
            _context = new AppDbContext(new DbContextOptionsBuilder
            <AppDbContext>()
    .UseSqlServer("Server=(localdb)\\mssqllocaldb;Database=
    EfCore5WebApp;Trusted_Connection=True;MultipleActiveResult
    Sets=true")
                .Options);
        }
    }
}
```

Count

The simplest aggregation operation is count. Count simply returns the number of records in the collection. Let us first test the Count operator without a filter with a unit test as seen in Listing 12-2.

Listing 12-2. Person Count with No Filter Test

```
[Test]
 public void CountPersons()
 {
     int personCount = _context.Persons.Count();
     Assert.AreEqual(2, personCount);
 }
```

The number of person records may change if you have modified the records in the database. Next, let us test the Count operator with a filter by getting the number of person records with a first name of John and last name of Smith. We should expect a count of one. See Listing 12-3 for the unit test for this scenario.

Listing 12-3. Count with Filter Unit Test

```
[Test]
public void CountPersonsWithFilter()
{
    int personCount = _context.Persons.Count(x => x.FirstName == "John" &&
    x.LastName == "Smith");
    Assert.AreEqual(1, personCount);
}
```

The difference between Listing 12-2 and Listing 12-3 is the addition of the following predicate as an argument to Count:

```
x => x.FirstName == "John" && x.LastName == "Smith"
```

The predicate is given as a lambda expression. A predicate is a Boolean expression that must evaluate to true for the records to be filtered; in this case, when the predicate is true, the records will be included in the count. Hence, only the records for "John Smith" are counted, and there is only one such record.

Adding Age to Person

To demonstrate our aggregation operators on more real-world data, we'll add an Age property to the Person entity. Let us add Age to the Person entity by updating the Person class to match Listing 12-4.

Listing 12-4. Updated Person with Age

```
using System;
using System.Collections.Generic;
using System.ComponentModel.DataAnnotations;
using System.ComponentModel.DataAnnotations.Schema;

namespace EFCore5WebApp.Core.Entities
{
    [Table("Persons", Schema ="dbo")]
    public class Person
```

```
    {
        public int Id { get; set; }
        [Required]
        [MaxLength(255)]
        public string FirstName { get; set; }
        [Required]
        [MaxLength(255)]
        public string LastName { get; set; }
        [Required]
        public string EmailAddress { get; set; }
        public List<Address> Addresses { get; set; } = new List<Address>();
        [NotMapped]
        public string FullName => $"{FirstName} {LastName}";

        public DateTime CreatedOn { get; set; }
        public int Age { get; set; }
    }
}
```

Next, let us update the seeded person data in the AppDbContext class to set the Age property for our records. Open up the AppDbContext class and set the Age values in HasData for the Person entity to be

```
modelBuilder.Entity<Person>().HasData(new List<Person>()
{
    new Person(){ Id = 1, FirstName = "John", LastName = "Smith",
    EmailAddress = "john@smith.com", Age = 20 },
    new Person(){ Id = 2, FirstName = "Susan", LastName = "Jones",
    EmailAddress = "john@smith.com", Age = 30 }
});
```

The final step is to create and run a migration to update our database schema and seeded data. Create a migration from the NuGet Package Manager Console by running "Add-Migration AddedAgeToPerson". After that, run "Update-Database" from the NuGet Package Manager Console to run the migration.

Min

The Min operator returns the minimum property value in a collection. The Min operator is often used on numeric data. In our example, we will be getting the min Person Age value through a unit test as seen in Listing 12-5.

Listing 12-5. Min Value Unit Test

```
[Test]
public void MinPersonAge()
{
    var minPersonAge = _context.Persons.Min(x => x.Age);
    Assert.AreEqual(20, minPersonAge);
}
```

The argument to Min is a selector of the property we want the minimum value of. In this case, that property is the Age property.

Max

The Max method returns the maximum property value out of a collection. We will test out this method by getting the maximum Person Age value and making sure it is greater than the minimum Person Age value as seen in Listing 12-6.

Listing 12-6. Max Value Unit Test

```
[Test]
public void MaxPersonAge()
{
    var maxPersonAge = _context.Persons.Max(x => x.Age);
    Assert.Greater(maxPersonId, 20);
}
```

Average

The Average method returns the mean property value out of a collection. We do not have much numeric data in our database, so let us add an Age property to our Person entity. Then we will show how to compute the mean of the ages.

Average Unit Test

Now that we have an Age property on Person with some data, we can calculate the average and make sure it matches the expected value of 25 as our sample person records are age 20 and age 30. Execute the code in Listing 12-7 to compute the average age.

Listing 12-7. Average Person Age Unit Test

```
[Test]
 public void AveragePersonAge()
 {
     var average = _context.Persons.Average(x => x.Age);
     Assert.AreEqual(25, average);
 }
```

Sum

We can also calculate the sum of property values in a collection through the Sum method. For a simple test, we will execute the code in Listing 12-8 to calculate the sum of the Age values in the Person entity. The expected value is 50.

Listing 12-8. Sum Age Unit Test

```
[Test]
public void SumPersonAge()
{
    var sumAge = _context.Persons.Sum(x => x.Age);
    Assert.AreEqual(50, sumAge);
}
```

Group By

The group by clause is used to group records together. In our database, we could group address records by City, State, Country, or ZipCode, or we could use the Addresses property on the Person class to group person records by those same fields.

Direct Group By

Let us look at a simple example first by grouping address records directly. We are going to use our existing data first and group address records by State, so we should get two records for IL and one record for CA. To demonstrate this functionality, we will create a GroupAddressesByState unit test method as seen in Listing 12-9.

Listing 12-9. Address Group by State

```
[Test]
 public void GroupAddressesByState()
 {
     var expectedILAddressesCount = _context.Addresses.Where(x => x.State
     == "IL").Count();
     var expectedCAAddressesCount = _context.Addresses.Where(x => x.State
     == "CA").Count();

     var groupedAddresses = (from a in _context.Addresses.ToList()
                             group a by a.State into g
                             select new { State = g.Key, Addresses =
                             g.Select(x => x) }).ToList();

     Assert.AreEqual(expectedILAddressesCount, groupedAddresses.Single(x =>
     x.State == "IL").Addresses.Count());
     Assert.AreEqual(expectedCAAddressesCount, groupedAddresses.Single(x =>
     x.State == "CA").Addresses.Count());
 }
```

In the GroupAddressesByState test, we are first getting the number of addresses for Illinois and then California. After that, we group the addresses in AppDbContext by the State property, and we select a new collection of objects that have a property named

State and a property called Addresses that contains the addresses in that State. There is currently a limitation with Entity Framework Core 5 where you can't directly select all of the entities in a group by without first loading the entire collection into memory. Lastly, we assert that the grouped addresses for Illinois and then California are the same as the expected counts we initialized at the start of the test.

Group By with Count

Let us test group by with a count by modifying our previous query to just get the count of addresses per state instead of the full address record collection as seen in Listing 12-10.

Listing 12-10. Address Count by State

```
[Test]
public void GroupAddressesByStateCount()
{
    var expectedILAddressesCount = _context.Addresses.Where(x => x.State ==
    "IL").Count();
    var expectedCAAddressesCount = _context.Addresses.Where(x => x.State ==
    "CA").Count();

    var groupedAddresses = (from a in _context.Addresses
                            group a by a.State into g
                            select new { State = g.Key, Count = g.Count()
                            }).ToList();

    Assert.AreEqual(expectedILAddressesCount, groupedAddresses.Single(x =>
    x.State == "IL").Count);
    Assert.AreEqual(expectedCAAddressesCount, groupedAddresses.Single(x =>
    x.State == "CA").Count);
}
```

As you can see, it is quite easy to combine a group by with an aggregate method.

Group By with Min

Now let us test out using the Min method with a group by. In this example, we will get the minimum age per state. See Listing 12-11 for the unit test.

Listing 12-11. Min Person Age by State

```
[Test]
public void MinAgePerState()
{
    var expectedIlMinAge = 30;
    var expectedCaMinAge = 20;

    var groupedAddresses = from a in _context.Addresses
                           select new { State = a.State, Age = a.Person.Age
                           } into stateAge
                           group stateAge by stateAge.State into g
                           select new { State = g.Key, MinAge = g.Min(a =>
                           a.Age) };

    Assert.AreEqual(expectedIlMinAge, groupedAddresses.Single(x => x.State
    == "IL").MinAge);
    Assert.AreEqual(expectedCaMinAge, groupedAddresses.Single(x => x.State
    == "CA").MinAge);
}
```

Group By with Max

Now let us do the same test but get the maximum age by state as seen in Listing 12-12.

Listing 12-12. Max Person Age by State

```
[Test]
 public void MaxAgePerState()
 {
    var expectedIlMaxAge = 30;
    var expectedCaMaxAge = 20;

    var groupedAddresses = from a in _context.Addresses
                           select new { State = a.State, Age = a.Person.
                           Age } into stateAge
                           group stateAge by stateAge.State into g
                           select new { State = g.Key, MaxAge = g.Max(a =>
                           a.Age) };
```

```
    Assert.AreEqual(expectedIlMaxAge, groupedAddresses.Single(x => x.State
    == "IL").MaxAge);
    Assert.AreEqual(expectedCaMaxAge, groupedAddresses.Single(x => x.State
    == "CA").MaxAge);
}
```

Group By with Average

We can repeat the test, but switch Max with Average as seen in Listing 12-13.

Listing 12-13. Average Age by State

```
[Test]
public void AverageAgePerState()
{
    var expectedIlAge = 30;
    var expectedCaAge = 20;

    var groupedAddresses = from a in _context.Addresses
                           select new { State = a.State, Age = a.Person.
                           Age } into stateAge
                           group stateAge by stateAge.State into g
                           select new { State = g.Key, AverageAge =
                           g.Average(a => a.Age) };

    Assert.AreEqual(expectedIlAge, groupedAddresses.Single(x => x.State ==
    "IL").AverageAge);
    Assert.AreEqual(expectedCaAge, groupedAddresses.Single(x => x.State ==
    "CA").AverageAge);
}
```

Group By with Sum

Lastly, we can also get the sum age per state as seen in Listing 12-14.

Listing 12-14. Sum Age by State

```
[Test]
 public void SumAgePerState()
 {
     var expectedIlAge = 60;
     var expectedCaAge = 20;

     var groupedAddresses = from a in _context.Addresses
                            select new { State = a.State, Age = a.Person.
                            Age } into stateAge
                            group stateAge by stateAge.State into g
                            select new { State = g.Key, SumAge = g.Sum(a =>
                            a.Age) };

     Assert.AreEqual(expectedIlAge, groupedAddresses.Single(x => x.State ==
     "IL").SumAge);
     Assert.AreEqual(expectedCaAge, groupedAddresses.Single(x => x.State ==
     "CA").SumAge);
 }
```

Summary

In this chapter, we have covered a lot of ground. We have covered the count, min, max, average, and sum aggregation methods by unit testing them. Then we went over how to group data. Lastly, we covered how to perform aggregate operations over grouped data through unit tests. In the next chapter, I will cover how to create and call a stored procedure using Entity Framework Core 5.

CHAPTER 13

Stored Procedures

In this chapter, I will cover how to call stored procedures using Entity Framework Core 5. I will show how to call both a stored procedure that returns results and one that inserts a record. I will also show how you can pass parameters to stored procedures. Some examples of where it makes sense to use a stored procedure instead of directly using Entity Framework Core are when you have to do complex queries for reporting or when performing bulk data operations.

Add Stored Procedures to a Database

We first need to add our stored procedures to the database. To make this simple, I will be creating a database migration that adds the stored procedures to the database when it is executed.

To get started, we will add an empty migration using the NuGet Package Manager Console by running "Add-Migration AddStoredProcedures". You should now have an empty class file that ends in "_AddStoredProcedures" added to your DAL project that looks like Listing 13-1.

Listing 13-1. Empty Migration

```
using Microsoft.EntityFrameworkCore.Migrations;

namespace EFCOre5WebApp.DAL.Migrations
{
    public partial class AddStoredProcedures : Migration
    {
        protected override void Up(MigrationBuilder migrationBuilder)
        {

        }
```


E. Vogel, *Beginning Entity Framework Core 5*, https://doi.org/10.1007/978-1-4842-6882-7_13

```
        protected override void Down(MigrationBuilder migrationBuilder)
        {

        }
    }
}
```

In the "Up" method, we will add our stored procedures; and in the "Down" method, we will remove the stored procedures. We will be adding two stored procedures. The first stored procedure named "GetPersonsByState" will return all person records that have an address in a given state. The second stored procedure named "AddLookUpItem" simply inserts a new LookUp record.

First, let us implement the "Up" method to match Listing 13-2.

Listing 13-2. Updated Migration Up Method

```
protected override void Up(MigrationBuilder migrationBuilder)
{
    var proc1 = @"
    IF OBJECT_ID('GetPersonsByState', 'P') IS NOT NULL
    DROP PROC UpdateProfilesCountry
    GO

    CREATE PROCEDURE [dbo].[GetPersonsByState]
        @State varchar(255)
    AS
    BEGIN
        SELECT p.*
        FROM Persons p
        INNER JOIN Addresses a on p.Id = a.PersonId
        WHERE a.State =  @State
    END";

    var proc2 = @"
    IF OBJECT_ID('AddLookUpItem', 'P') IS NOT NULL
    DROP PROC AddLookUpItem
    GO
```

```
    CREATE PROCEDURE [dbo].[AddLookUpItem]
        @Code varchar(255),
        @Description varchar(255),
        @LookUpTypeId int
    AS
    BEGIN
        INSERT INTO LookUps (Code, Description, LookUpType) VALUES (@Code,
        @Description, @LookUpTypeId)
    END";

    migrationBuilder.Sql(proc1);
    migrationBuilder.Sql(proc2);
}
```

The "Down" method simply drops both added stored procedures as seen in Listing 13-3.

Listing 13-3. Updated Migration Down Method

```
protected override void Down(MigrationBuilder migrationBuilder)
{
    migrationBuilder.Sql(@"DROP PROC GetPersonsByState");
    migrationBuilder.Sql(@"DROP PROC AddLookUpItem");
}
```

Your completed "AddStoredProcedures" class should now look like Listing 13-4 that follows.

Listing 13-4. Completed AddStoredProcedures Migration Class

```
using Microsoft.EntityFrameworkCore.Migrations;

namespace EFCore5WebApp.DAL.Migrations
{
    public partial class AddStoredProcedures : Migration
    {
        protected override void Up(MigrationBuilder migrationBuilder)
```

```
{
    var proc1 = @"
    IF OBJECT_ID('GetPersonsByState', 'P') IS NOT NULL
    DROP PROC UpdateProfilesCountry
    GO

    CREATE PROCEDURE [dbo].[GetPersonsByState]
        @State varchar(255)
    AS
    BEGIN
        SELECT p.*
        FROM Persons p
        INNER JOIN Addresses a on p.Id = a.PersonId
        WHERE a.State =  @State
    END";

    var proc2 = @"
    IF OBJECT_ID('AddLookUpItem', 'P') IS NOT NULL
    DROP PROC AddLookUpItem
    GO

    CREATE PROCEDURE [dbo].[AddLookUpItem]
        @Code varchar(255),
        @Description varchar(255),
        @LookUpTypeId int
    AS
    BEGIN
        INSERT INTO LookUps (Code, Description, LookUpType) VALUES
        (@Code, @Description, @LookUpTypeId)
    END";

    migrationBuilder.Sql(proc1);
    migrationBuilder.Sql(proc2);
}
```

```
        protected override void Down(MigrationBuilder migrationBuilder)
        {
            migrationBuilder.Sql(@"DROP PROC GetPersonsByState");
            migrationBuilder.Sql(@"DROP PROC AddLookUpItem");
        }
    }
}
```

Now run "Update-Database" in the NuGet Package Manager Console to run the "AddStoredProcedures" migration on your SQL Server database.

Set Up Unit Tests

We will be testing our newly added stored procedures through some unit tests. Create a new NUnit test class named "StoredProceduresTests" in the "DAL.Tests" project. Your initial class file should look like Listing 13-5.

Listing 13-5. Initial Stored Procedures Unit Test Class

```
using EFCore5WebApp.Core.Entities;
using Microsoft.EntityFrameworkCore;
using NUnit.Framework;
using System;
using System.Collections.Generic;
using System.Linq;

namespace EFCOre5WebApp.DAL.Tests
{
    [TestFixture]
    public class StoredProceduresTests
    {
        private AppDbContext _context;

        [SetUp]
        public void SetUp()
        {
            _context = new AppDbContext(new DbContextOptionsBuilder
            <AppDbContext>()
```

```
                .UseSqlServer("Server=(localdb)\\mssqllocaldb;Database=
                EfCore5WebApp;Trusted_Connection=True;MultipleActiveResult
                Sets=true")
                .Options);
        }
    }
}
```

Test the GetPersonsByState Stored Procedure

Now it is time to test out our "GetPersonsByState" stored procedure through a unit test. To call the stored procedure, we will use the DbSet<T>.FromSqlInterpolated() method that takes in the stored procedure name with its parameters given in each variable in the string. Now that we know that, let us test it out in a unit test method named "GetPersonsByStateInterpolated" as seen in Listing 13-6.

Listing 13-6. GetPersonsByStateInterpolated Unit Test

```
[Test]
public void GetPersonsByStateInterpolated()
{
    string state = "IL";
    var persons = _context.Persons.FromSqlInterpolated($"GetPersonsByState
    {state}").ToList();
    Assert.AreEqual(2, persons.Count);
}
```

The FromSqlInterpreted() method can also be used to run any SQL query or command. Similarly, we can also use the DbSet<T>.FromSqlRaw() method to run our stored procedure. The FromSqlRaw method takes in the name of the stored procedure along with the variable names as the first argument; the second parameter is a collection of parameter values to pass into the stored procedures. Let us test out FromSqlRaw in a new unit test called GetPersonsByStateRaw as seen in Listing 13-7.

Listing 13-7. GetPersonsByStateRaw Unit Test

```
[Test]
public void GetPersonsByStateRaw()
{
    string state = "IL";
    var persons = _context.Persons.FromSqlRaw($"GetPersonsByState @p0",
    new[] { state }).ToList();
    Assert.AreEqual(2, persons.Count);
}
```

The FromSqlRaw() method can also be used to call any SQL query or command.

Test the AddLookUpItem Stored Procedure

Next, we will test out the "AddLookUpItem" stored procedure. To run non-query command SQL, we will use either the ExecuteSqlInterpolated or the ExecuteSqlRaw method, both of which are exposed through the Database property on DbContext. Let us first test out the ExecuteSqlInterpolated method to call our "AddLookUpItem" stored procedure through the unit test defined in Listing 13-8.

Listing 13-8. AddLookUpItemInterpolated Unit Test

```
[Test]
public void AddLookUpItemInterpolated()
{
    string code = "CAN";
    string description = "Canada";
    LookUpType lookUpType = LookUpType.Country;
    _context.Database.ExecuteSqlInterpolated($"AddLookUpItem {code},
    {description}, {lookUpType}");

    var addedItem = _context.LookUps.Single(x => x.Code == "CAN");
    Assert.IsNotNull(addedItem);

    _context.LookUps.Remove(addedItem);
    _context.SaveChanges();
}
```

Next, let us test calling "AddLookUpItem" via the ExecuteSqlRaw method as seen in Listing 13-9.

Listing 13-9. AddLookUpItemRaw Unit Test

```
[Test]
public void AddLookUpItemRaw()
{
    string code = "MEX";
    string description = "Mexico";
    LookUpType lookUpType = LookUpType.Country;
    _context.Database.ExecuteSqlRaw("AddLookUpItem @p0,@p1,@p2",
    new object[] { code, description, lookUpType });

    var addedItem = _context.LookUps.Single(x => x.Code == "MEX");
    Assert.IsNotNull(addedItem);

    _context.LookUps.Remove(addedItem);
    _context.SaveChanges();
}
```

Summary

In this chapter, I covered how to call query and non-query parameterized stored procedures through Entity Framework Core 5. We went over how there are both a Raw and an Interpolated approach for both use cases. The Interpolated string is the newest way to call stored procedures using Entity Framework Core 5. I think the Interpolated approach is a little more concise and cleaner, so we will be using this method in future code in the book. Both approaches are valid, so feel free to use either approach in your own projects.

CHAPTER 14

Migrations

In this chapter, I will cover how migrations work in Entity Framework Core 5. A migration allows you to version database changes in your application. I will cover how you can add and run migrations. I will also cover how you can update to a given database version or revert to a previous migration.

What Is a Migration?

In prior chapters, I have covered how to add a new migration and how to update your database to the latest migration. A migration is code that alters your database and contains two methods: Up() and Down(). The Up() method will make the necessary changes to your database to update it. The Down() method reverses the changes that were made in the Up() method. This allows you to either update to that version of the database or to revert to a previous version.

How to Add a Migration?

There are two ways to fill in the code for a migration, either automatic or manual. An automatic migration can be created by making a change to your database model and then running “Add-Database X” where X is the name you assign to that migration. Entity Framework Core 5 will automatically create the necessary code for the Up() and Down() methods to make the necessary schema and data changes.

In the previous chapter, we covered how to create a manual migration. To create a manual migration, you run the same command “Add-Migration X” from the Package Manager Console; but because there are no model changes, the Up() and Down() methods will be empty. You can then use the migration API to make the necessary changes in the Up() and Down() methods.

E. Vogel, *Beginning Entity Framework Core 5*, https://doi.org/10.1007/978-1-4842-6882-7_14

The Migration API

You can add custom changes to an automatically or manually created migration by using the Migration Builder API. The simplest way to make changes is to the MigrationBuilder.Sql() method to run arbitrary SQL. There are also methods on the MigrationBuilder class for making common schema and data changes. When you make a change to the entity model and add a new migration, Entity Framework Core 5 will generate code that calls these common schema commands. In the off case where you need to define these changes yourself, you can add these commands to the generated code or to an empty migration. Next, I will cover some of these common Migration Builder API methods.

Common Schema Commands

Two of the more common schema commands are to add a column to a table and to change a column in a table. These are two different commands, and they are described in the following subsections.

Add a Column to a Table

The AddColumn() method allows you to add a new column to your target database in a database-agnostic way. This command is used if you add a new mapped property to an entity class. See Listing 14-1 for the method signature.

Listing 14-1. AddColumn Migration Builder Method Declaration

```
public virtual OperationBuilder<AddColumnOperation>
AddColumn<T>([NotNullAttribute] string name, [NotNullAttribute] string
table, [CanBeNullAttribute] string type = null, bool? unicode = null,
int? maxLength = null, bool rowVersion = false, [CanBeNullAttribute]
string schema = null, bool nullable = false, [CanBeNullAttribute] object
defaultValue = null, [CanBeNullAttribute] string defaultValueSql = null,
[CanBeNullAttribute] string computedColumnSql = null, bool? fixedLength
= null, [CanBeNullAttribute] string comment = null, [CanBeNullAttribute]
string collation = null, int? precision = null, int? scale = null, bool?
stored = null);
```

Change a Column in a Table

The AlterColumn() method is used if you want to change an attribute on a column such as its data type. You can also customize other properties on a column such as precision and scale on a numeric data type or change the nullability of a column. See Listing 14-2 for the AlterColumn full method signature.

Listing 14-2. AlterColumn Migration Builder Declaration

```
public virtual AlterOperationBuilder<AlterColumnOperation> AlterColum
n<T>([NotNullAttribute] string name, [NotNullAttribute] string table,
[CanBeNullAttribute] string type = null, bool? unicode = null, int?
maxLength = null, bool rowVersion = false, [CanBeNullAttribute] string
schema = null, bool nullable = false, [CanBeNullAttribute] object
defaultValue = null, [CanBeNullAttribute] string defaultValueSql = null,
[CanBeNullAttribute] string computedColumnSql = null, [CanBeNullAttribute]
Type oldClrType = null, [CanBeNullAttribute] string oldType = null, bool?
oldUnicode = null, int? oldMaxLength = null, bool oldRowVersion = false,
bool oldNullable = false, [CanBeNullAttribute] object oldDefaultValue
= null, [CanBeNullAttribute] string oldDefaultValueSql = null,
[CanBeNullAttribute] string oldComputedColumnSql = null, bool? fixedLength
= null, bool? oldFixedLength = null, [CanBeNullAttribute] string comment =
null, [CanBeNullAttribute] string oldComment = null, [CanBeNullAttribute]
string collation = null, [CanBeNullAttribute] string oldCollation = null,
int? precision = null, int? oldPrecision = null, int? scale = null, int?
oldScale = null, bool? stored = null, bool? oldStored = null);
```

Common Data Commands

There are also Migration Builder API commands for inserting, updating, and deleting data in a migration. These methods are described in the following sections.

Inserting Data

You can use one of the InsertData() methods if you simply want to insert data into a table. To insert a single value, you can use one of the following methods in Listing 14-3.

Listing 14-3. Insert a Single Value in a Migration

```
public virtual OperationBuilder<InsertDataOperation>
InsertData([NotNullAttribute] string table, [NotNullAttribute] string
column, [CanBeNullAttribute] object value, [CanBeNullAttribute] string
schema = null);
public virtual OperationBuilder<InsertDataOperation>
InsertData([NotNullAttribute] string table, [NotNullAttribute] string
column, [NotNullAttribute] object[] values, [CanBeNullAttribute] string
schema = null);
```

You can also insert values for multiple columns using the method defined in Listing 14-4.

Listing 14-4. Insert Data for Multiple Columns in a Migration

```
public virtual OperationBuilder<InsertDataOperation>
InsertData([NotNullAttribute] string table, [NotNullAttribute] string[]
columns, [NotNullAttribute] object[] values, [CanBeNullAttribute] string
schema = null);
```

Deleting Data

The Migration Builder API contains methods for either deleting a single row or multiple rows of data.

Delete a Single Row

To delete a single row of data by its key Id value, use the DeleteData method defined in Listing 14-5.

Listing 14-5. Delete a Single Row of Data in a Migration

```
public virtual OperationBuilder<DeleteDataOperation>
DeleteData([NotNullAttribute] string table, [NotNullAttribute] string
keyColumn, [CanBeNullAttribute] object keyValue, [CanBeNullAttribute]
string schema = null);
```

Delete Multiple Rows of Data

There is also a DeleteData method where you can pass in multiple key Id values to remove as seen in Listing 14-6.

Listing 14-6. Delete Multiple Rows of Data in a Migration

```
public virtual OperationBuilder<DeleteDataOperation>
DeleteData([NotNullAttribute] string table, [NotNullAttribute] string[]
keyColumns, [NotNullAttribute] object[] keyValues, [CanBeNullAttribute]
string schema = null);
```

Update Data in a Migration

There are a variety of UpdateData() methods defined in the Migration Builder API. First, you can update a single row of data with a single value or update a single row with multiple column values. Second, you can update a single value for multiple key values or update multiple column values on multiple rows of data. See Listing 14-7 for the various update data methods.

Listing 14-7. Update Data in a Migration

```
public virtual OperationBuilder<UpdateDataOperation>
UpdateData([NotNullAttribute] string table, [NotNullAttribute] string[]
keyColumns, [NotNullAttribute] object[] keyValues, [NotNullAttribute]
string[] columns, [NotNullAttribute] object[] values, [CanBeNullAttribute]
string schema = null);
public virtual OperationBuilder<UpdateDataOperation>
UpdateData([NotNullAttribute] string table, [NotNullAttribute] string
keyColumn, [NotNullAttribute] object[] keyValues, [NotNullAttribute] string
column, [NotNullAttribute] object[] values, [CanBeNullAttribute] string
schema = null);
public virtual OperationBuilder<UpdateDataOperation>
UpdateData([NotNullAttribute] string table, [NotNullAttribute] string
keyColumn, [NotNullAttribute] object[] keyValues, [NotNullAttribute]
string[] columns, [NotNullAttribute] object[,] values, [CanBeNullAttribute]
string schema = null);
```

```
public virtual OperationBuilder<UpdateDataOperation>
UpdateData([NotNullAttribute] string table, [NotNullAttribute] string[]
keyColumns, [NotNullAttribute] object[,] keyValues, [NotNullAttribute]
string column, [NotNullAttribute] object[] values, [CanBeNullAttribute]
string schema = null);
public virtual OperationBuilder<UpdateDataOperation>
UpdateData([NotNullAttribute] string table, [NotNullAttribute] string[]
keyColumns, [NotNullAttribute] object[,] keyValues, [NotNullAttribute]
string[] columns, [NotNullAttribute] object[,] values, [CanBeNullAttribute]
string schema = null);
public virtual OperationBuilder<UpdateDataOperation>
UpdateData([NotNullAttribute] string table, [NotNullAttribute] string
keyColumn, [CanBeNullAttribute] object keyValue, [NotNullAttribute] string
column, [CanBeNullAttribute] object value, [CanBeNullAttribute] string
schema = null);
public virtual OperationBuilder<UpdateDataOperation>
UpdateData([NotNullAttribute] string table, [NotNullAttribute] string[]
keyColumns, [NotNullAttribute] object[] keyValues, [NotNullAttribute]
string column, [CanBeNullAttribute] object value, [CanBeNullAttribute]
string schema = null);
public virtual OperationBuilder<UpdateDataOperation>
UpdateData([NotNullAttribute] string table, [NotNullAttribute] string
keyColumn, [CanBeNullAttribute] object keyValue, [NotNullAttribute]
string[] columns, [NotNullAttribute] object[] values, [CanBeNullAttribute]
string schema = null);
```

How to Run Migrations

Migrations can easily be run via the NuGet Package Manager Console “Update-Database” command. I will show how to update to the most recent migration, how to migrate to a specific migration, and how to update your app to the most recent migration via code.

Update to the Most Recent Migration

Now that you have seen how to create an automatic or manual migration, let us see how to control which migration to run. The simplest way to run a migration is by running the "Update-Database" method from the Package Manager Console. This will update your database to the latest migration.

Migrate to a Specific Migration

To update to a specific migration, run "Update-Database -Migration X", where "X" is the name of the migration you want to migrate to. This will upgrade or downgrade your database to the given migration by name.

Run Migration from Code

Entity Framework Core 5 allows you to migrate your database programmatically if you want. This can be done by running the Migrate() method on the Database property of DbContext as seen in Listing 14-8.

Listing 14-8. Update the Database Through Code

```
using (var context = new AppDbContext())
{
    context.Database.Migrate();
}
```

Later in the book, we will add code to the StartUp class to upgrade the database on app startup.

Automatic Data Migrations

The aforementioned migration builder data commands are used automatically by Entity Framework Core 5 tooling's "Add-Migration" command when you change the data in the OnModelCreating() method in our DbContext. For example, when we added the Age property in Chapter 12 to the Person entity and seeded data with the following code in OnModelCreating()

```
modelBuilder.Entity<Person>().HasData(new List<Person>()
        {
            new Person(){ Id = 1, FirstName = "John", LastName = "Smith",
            EmailAddress = "john@smith.com", Age = 20 },
            new Person(){ Id = 2, FirstName = "Susan", LastName = "Jones",
            EmailAddress = "john@smith.com", Age = 30 }
        });
```

the created AddedAgeToPerson migration class used the UpdateData() method to add the Age column values as seen in Listing 14-9.

Listing 14-9. AddedAgeToPerson Migration

```
using Microsoft.EntityFrameworkCore.Migrations;

namespace EFCore5WebApp.DAL.Migrations
{
    public partial class AddedAgeToPerson : Migration
    {
        protected override void Up(MigrationBuilder migrationBuilder)
        {
            migrationBuilder.AddColumn<int>(
                name: "Age",
                table: "Persons",
                type: "int",
                nullable: false,
                defaultValue: 0);

            migrationBuilder.UpdateData(
                table: "Persons",
                keyColumn: "Id",
                keyValue: 1,
                column: "Age",
                value: 20);
```

```
            migrationBuilder.UpdateData(
                table: "Persons",
                keyColumn: "Id",
                keyValue: 2,
                column: "Age",
                value: 30);
        }

        protected override void Down(MigrationBuilder migrationBuilder)
        {
            migrationBuilder.DropColumn(
                name: "Age",
                table: "Persons");
        }
    }
}
```

Summary

In this chapter, I covered how automatic and manual migrations work in Entity Framework Core 5. I covered some of the most common schema and data migration methods that are defined through the Migration Builder API. Next, I covered how you can update your database to the current migration or a specific migration. Lastly, I covered how you can upgrade your database directly in your application. In the next several chapters, I will go over how to build and use an ASP.NET Core MVC web app that uses Entity Framework Core 5 to retrieve, update, create, and delete data.

PART IV

A Model Web Application

CHAPTER 15

Authentication on the Web

In this chapter, I will cover how to set up authentication on our ASP.NET Core MVC application. Our users will be stored in our SQL Server database, and Entity Framework Core 5 will be used to access it.

Install Identity NuGet Packages

The first thing we need to get out of the way is to install the needed NuGet packages for Entity Framework Core 5 Identity and AspNetCore.Identity.UI. Right-click the web project and click Manage NuGet Packages. Then install the Microsoft.AspNetCore.Identity.UI package as seen in Figure 15-1.

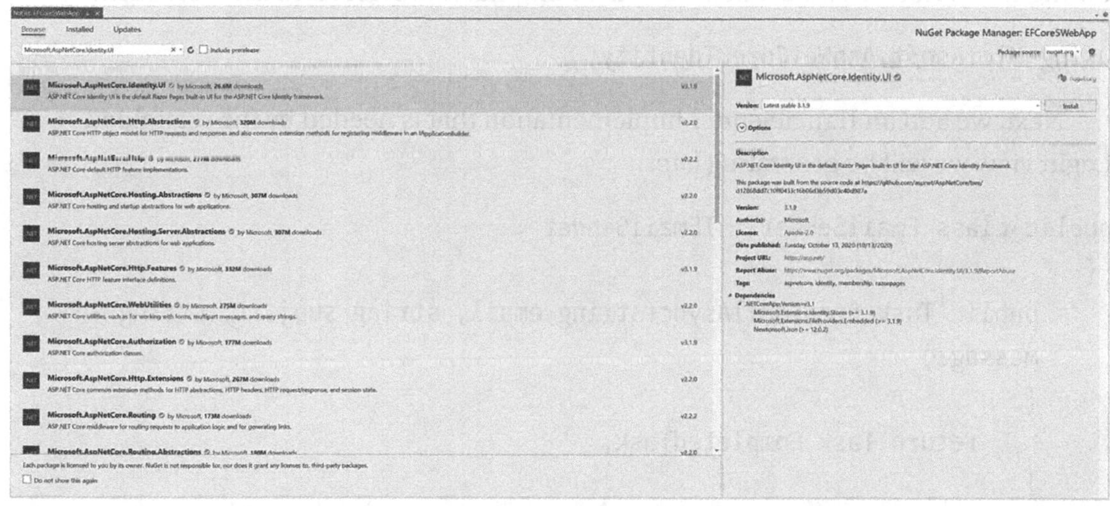

***Figure 15-1.** Install the ASP.NET Core Identity UI Package*

The next step is to install the Microsoft.AspNetCore.Identity.EntityFrameworkCore NuGet package as seen in Figure 15-2.

E. Vogel, *Beginning Entity Framework Core 5*, https://doi.org/10.1007/978-1-4842-6882-7_15

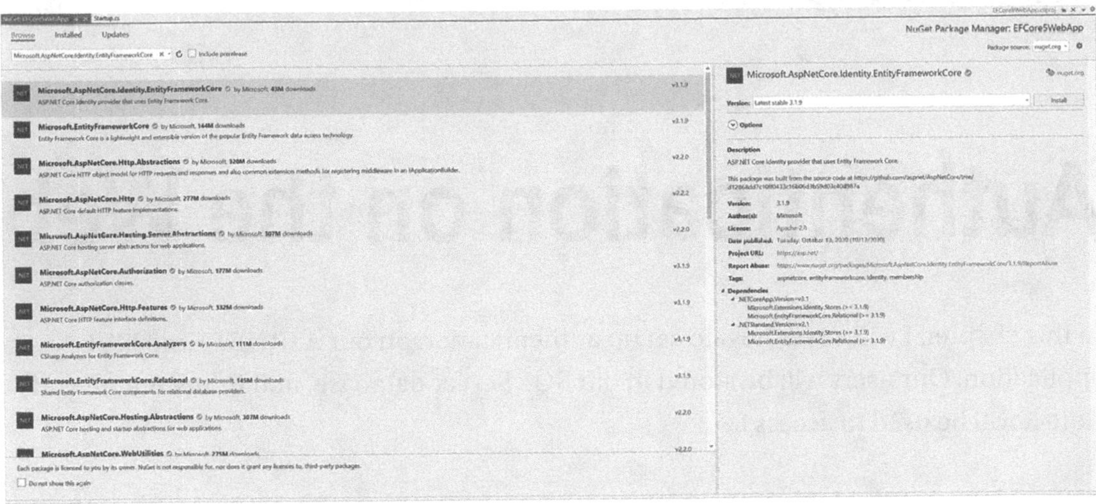

Figure 15-2. Install the Entity Framework Core 5 Identity Package

Initialize Identity on App Startup

The next step is to update the Startup class to wire up ASP.NET Core Identity management using EF Core 5. To get started, we are going to update the ConfigureServices method. First, we add a using statement for ASP.NET Core Identity:

```
using Microsoft.AspNetCore.Identity;
```

Next, we add an IEmailSender implementation that is needed by the scaffolded Login view we will be generating later:

```
public class EmailSender : IEmailSender
 {
     public Task SendEmailAsync(string email, string subject, string
     message)
     {
         return Task.CompletedTask;
     }
 }
```

Then we wire up ASP.NET Core Identity to use Entity Framework Core 5 in the ConfigureServices method:

```
services.AddIdentity<IdentityUser,IdentityRole>(options => options.SignIn.
RequireConfirmedAccount = true)
               .AddEntityFrameworkStores<AppDbContext>();
```

Next, we want to use the baked-in UI code for authentication, so we call

```
 services.AddRazorPages();
 services.AddControllersWithViews();
```

After that, we configure the ASP.NET Core Identity password, username, and lockout settings:

```
services.Configure<IdentityOptions>(options =>
{
    // Password settings.
    options.Password.RequireDigit = true;
    options.Password.RequireLowercase = true;
    options.Password.RequireNonAlphanumeric = true;
    options.Password.RequireUppercase = true;
    options.Password.RequiredLength = 6;
    options.Password.RequiredUniqueChars = 1;

    // Lockout settings.
    options.Lockout.DefaultLockoutTimeSpan = TimeSpan.FromMinutes(5);
    options.Lockout.MaxFailedAccessAttempts = 5;
    options.Lockout.AllowedForNewUsers = true;

    // User settings.
    options.User.AllowedUserNameCharacters =
    "abcdefghijklmnopqrstuvwxyzABCDEFGHIJKLMNOPQRSTUVWXYZ0123456789-._@+";
    options.User.RequireUniqueEmail = false;
});
```

Next, we configure the authentication cookie to use a five-minute sliding expiration and use the built-in login and access denied URLs:

```
services.ConfigureApplicationCookie(options =>
{
    // Cookie settings
    options.Cookie.HttpOnly = true;
    options.ExpireTimeSpan = TimeSpan.FromMinutes(5);

    options.LoginPath = "/Identity/Account/Login";
    options.AccessDeniedPath = "/Identity/Account/AccessDenied";
    options.SlidingExpiration = true;
});
```

Next, we wire up a test email sender:

```
services.AddSingleton<IEmailSender, EmailSender>();
```

Then we need to update the Configure method to enable authentication. Go to the Configure method and add this line after app.UseRouting():

```
app.UseAuthentication();
```

Your StartUp class should now look like Listing 15-1.

Listing 15-1. Updated StartUp Class with Identity Management Added

```
using EFCOre5WebApp.DAL;
using Microsoft.AspNetCore.Builder;
using Microsoft.AspNetCore.Hosting;
using Microsoft.AspNetCore.Identity;
using Microsoft.AspNetCore.Identity.UI.Services;
using Microsoft.EntityFrameworkCore;
using Microsoft.Extensions.Configuration;
using Microsoft.Extensions.DependencyInjection;
using Microsoft.Extensions.Hosting;
using System;
using System.Threading.Tasks;
```

```
namespace EFCore5WebApp
{
    public class EmailSender : IEmailSender
    {
        public Task SendEmailAsync(string email, string subject, string
        message)
        {
            return Task.CompletedTask;
        }
    }

    public class Startup
    {
        public Startup(IConfiguration configuration)
        {
            Configuration = configuration;
        }

        public IConfiguration Configuration { get; }

        // This method gets called by the runtime. Use this method to add
        services to the container.
        public void ConfigureServices(IServiceCollection services)
        {

            services.AddDbContext<AppDbContext>(options =>
            options.UseSqlServer(Configuration.GetConnectionString(
            "connection")));

            services.AddIdentity<IdentityUser, IdentityRole>()
            .AddEntityFrameworkStores<AppDbContext>();
            services.AddRazorPages();
            services.AddControllersWithViews();

            services.Configure<IdentityOptions>(options =>
            {
                // Password settings.
                options.Password.RequireDigit = true;
                options.Password.RequireLowercase = true;
```

```
            options.Password.RequireNonAlphanumeric = true;
            options.Password.RequireUppercase = true;
            options.Password.RequiredLength = 6;
            options.Password.RequiredUniqueChars = 1;

            // Lockout settings.
            options.Lockout.DefaultLockoutTimeSpan = TimeSpan.
            FromMinutes(5);
            options.Lockout.MaxFailedAccessAttempts = 5;
            options.Lockout.AllowedForNewUsers = true;

            // User settings.
            options.User.AllowedUserNameCharacters =
            "abcdefghijklmnopqrstuvwxyzABCDEFGHIJKLMNOPQRSTUVWXYZ0123
            456789-._@+";
            options.User.RequireUniqueEmail = false;
        });

        services.ConfigureApplicationCookie(options =>
        {
            // Cookie settings
            options.Cookie.HttpOnly = true;
            options.ExpireTimeSpan = TimeSpan.FromMinutes(5);

            options.LoginPath = "/Identity/Account/Login";
            options.AccessDeniedPath = "/Identity/Account/AccessDenied";
            options.SlidingExpiration = true;
        });

        services.AddSingleton<IEmailSender, EmailSender>();
    }

    // This method gets called by the runtime. Use this method to
    configure the HTTP request pipeline.
    public void Configure(IApplicationBuilder app, IWebHostEnvironment
    env)
    {
        if (env.IsDevelopment())
```

```
            {
                app.UseDeveloperExceptionPage();
            }
            else
            {
                app.UseExceptionHandler("/Home/Error");
                // The default HSTS value is 30 days. You may want to
                change this for production scenarios, see https://aka.ms/
                aspnetcore-hsts.
                app.UseHsts();
            }
            app.UseHttpsRedirection();
            app.UseStaticFiles();

            app.UseRouting();
            app.UseAuthentication();
            app.UseAuthorization();

            app.UseEndpoints(endpoints =>
            {
                endpoints.MapControllerRoute(
                    name: "default",
                    pattern: "{controller=Home}/{action=Index}/{id?}");
                endpoints.MapRazorPages();
            });
        }
    }
}
```

Next, we need to update our AppDbContext class to inherit from IdentityDbContext so that it can be scaffolded in the next section. We do this so to tell Entity Framework Core 5 to manage our users, roles, and claims in our SQL Server database. To do this, we first need to install the Microsoft.AspNetCore.Identity.EntityFrameworkCore NuGet package to our DAL project. To do this, click Manage NuGet Packages on the main solution node. Then go to Installed and select the Microsoft.AspNetCore.Identity.EntityFrameworkCore package and click the DAL project checkbox as seen in Figure 15-3.

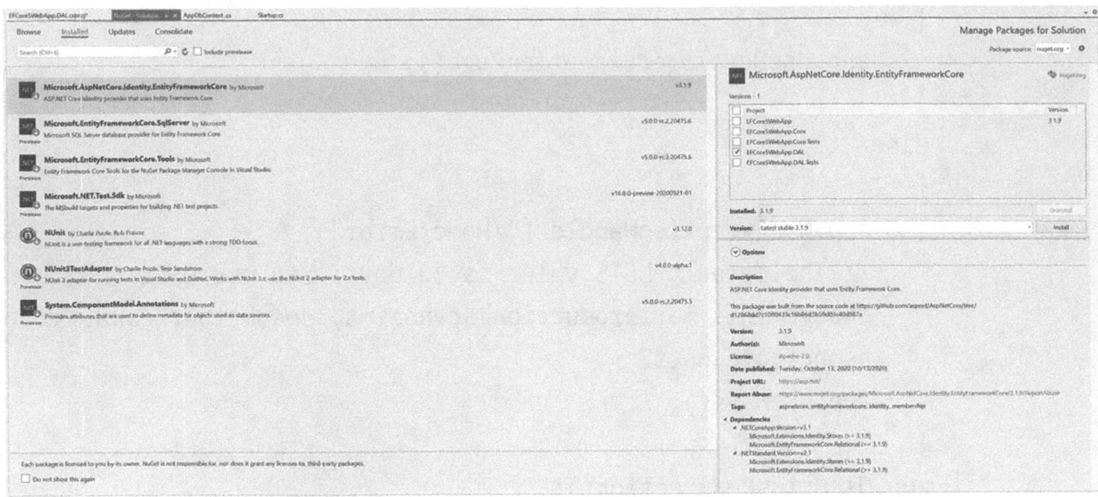

Figure 15-3. *Install the Identity EF Core 5 Package into the DAL Project*

Click the Install button to finish the installation. Now we can update our AppDbContext class to inherit from IdentityDbContext. To do this, add the following namespace first:

```
using Microsoft.AspNetCore.Identity.EntityFrameworkCore;
```

Then update the AppDbContext class declaration to match:

```
public class AppDbContext : IdentityDbContext
```

Scaffold UI

Now we are going to use Visual Studio to scaffold our Identity UI. We are doing this so we get pre-built authentication UI pages like login and user registration. To do this, right-click the web project and select "Add New Scaffolded Item". Then select Identity as seen in Figure 15-4.

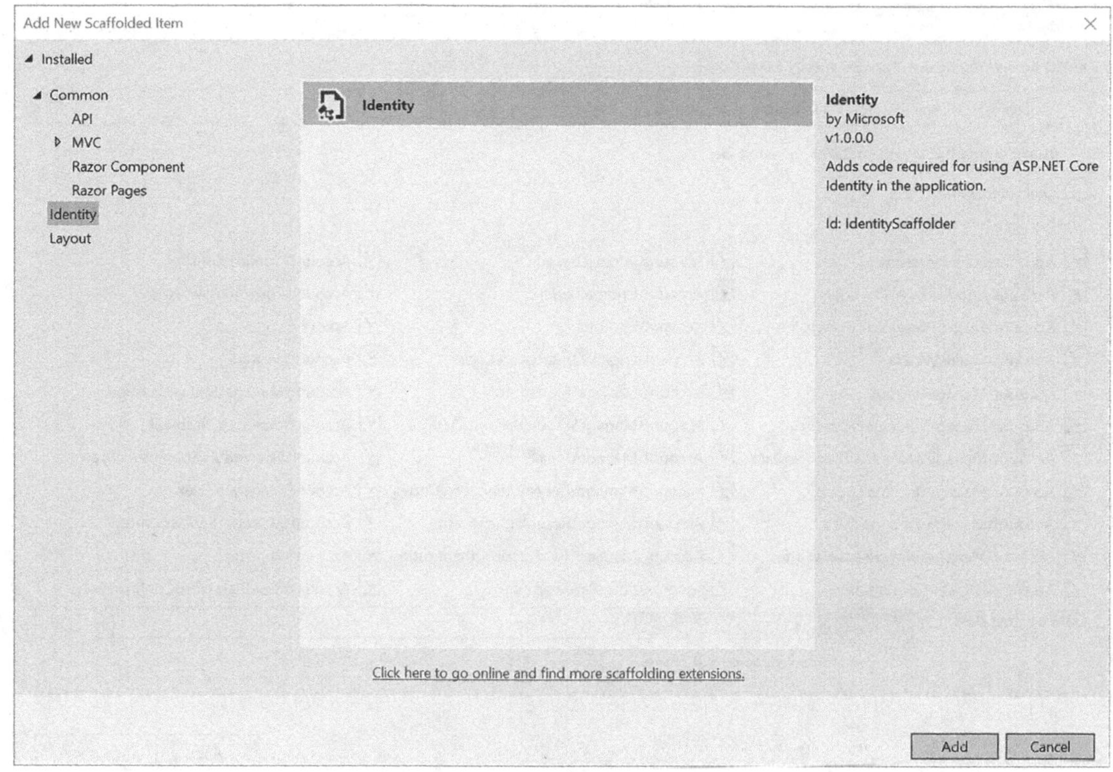

***Figure 15-4.** Add an Identity Scaffolded Item*

Then click the "Add" button. Next, select our AppDbContext class in the Data context class section and click the Override all files checkbox as seen in Figure 15-5.

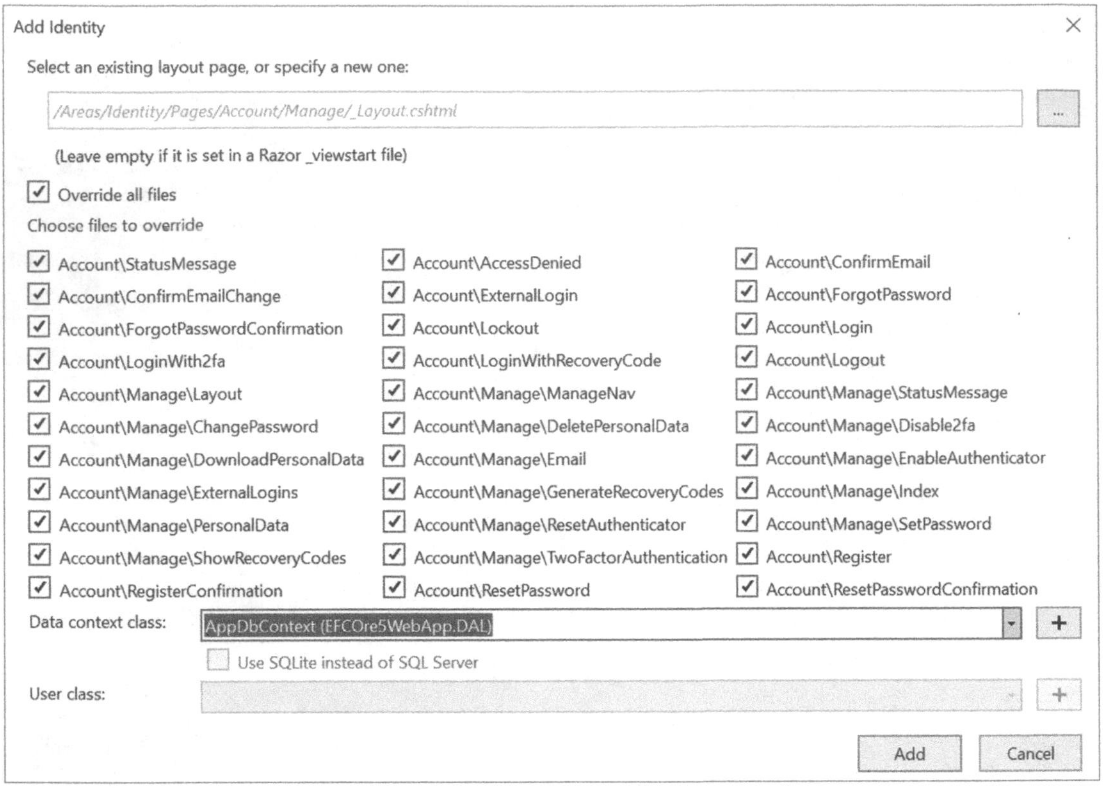

***Figure 15-5.** Select AppDbContext for Identity UI Scaffold*

Then click the Add button.

Update Database

Now we need to create and run a migration to add the Identity tables. First, create a new migration named “InitialIdentity” by running “Add-Migration InitialIdentity” in the Package Manager Console. Now run the migration by running “Update-Database” from the Package Manager Console. You can now see there are a bunch of added AspNet tables into our database as seen in Figure 15-6.

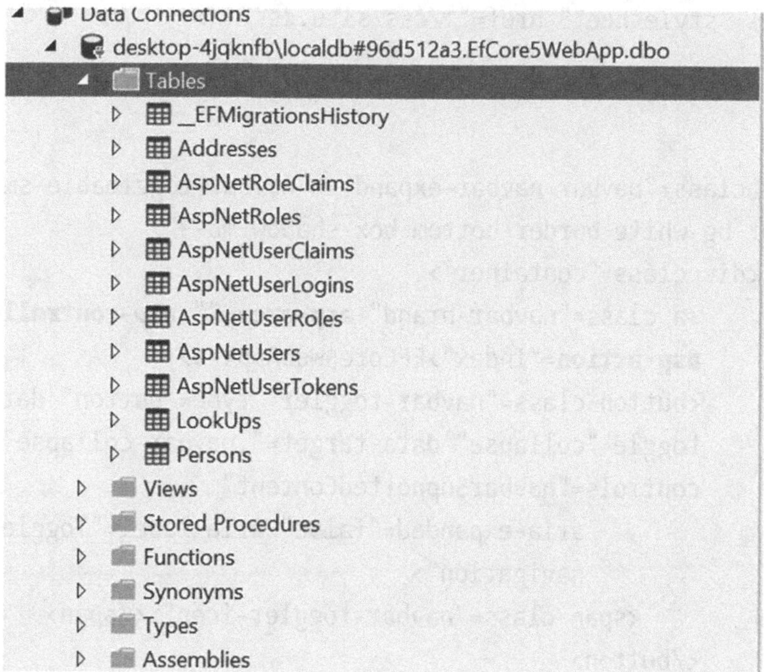

***Figure 15-6.** Added AspNet Identity Tables*

Updating UI

Now it is time to update the UI to call into the scaffolded register and login functionality. We are going to simply render the LoginPartial Razor in the top nav bar by adding the following markup to the Layout Razor view:

```
<partial name="_LoginPartial" />
```

Open Views/Shared/_Layout.cshtml and make it match Listing 15-2.

Listing 15-2. Updated _Layout Partial with Login Partial Render Added

```
<!DOCTYPE html>
<html lang="en">
<head>
    <meta charset="utf-8" />
    <meta name="viewport" content="width=device-width, initial-scale=1.0" />
    <title>@ViewData["Title"] - EFCore5WebApp</title>
    <link rel="stylesheet" href="~/lib/bootstrap/dist/css/bootstrap.min.css" />
```

```
    <link rel="stylesheet" href="~/css/site.css" />
</head>
<body>
    <header>
        <nav class="navbar navbar-expand-sm navbar-toggleable-sm navbar-
        light bg-white border-bottom box-shadow mb-3">
            <div class="container">
                <a class="navbar-brand" asp-area="" asp-controller="Home"
                asp-action="Index">EFCore5WebApp</a>
                <button class="navbar-toggler" type="button" data-
                toggle="collapse" data-target=".navbar-collapse" aria-
                controls="navbarSupportedContent"
                        aria-expanded="false" aria-label="Toggle
                        navigation">
                    <span class="navbar-toggler-icon"></span>
                </button>
                <div class="navbar-collapse collapse d-sm-inline-flex flex-
                sm-row-reverse">
                    <partial name="_LoginPartial" />
                    <ul class="navbar-nav flex-grow-1">
                        <li class="nav-item">
                            <a class="nav-link text-dark" asp-area="" asp-
                            controller="Home" asp-action="Index">Home</a>
                        </li>
                        <li class="nav-item">
                            <a class="nav-link text-dark" asp-
                            area="" asp-controller="Home" asp-
                            action="Privacy">Privacy</a>
                        </li>
                    </ul>
                </div>
            </div>
        </nav>
    </header>
    <div class="container">
```

```
        <main role="main" class="pb-3">
            @RenderBody()
        </main>
    </div>

    <footer class="border-top footer text-muted">
        <div class="container">
            &copy; 2020 - EFCore5WebApp - <a asp-area="" asp-
            controller="Home" asp-action="Privacy">Privacy</a>
        </div>
    </footer>
    <script src="~/lib/jquery/dist/jquery.min.js"></script>
    <script src="~/lib/bootstrap/dist/js/bootstrap.bundle.min.js"></script>
    <script src="~/js/site.js" asp-append-version="true"></script>
    @await RenderSectionAsync("Scripts", required: false)
</body>
</html>
```

You should now be able to see the Register and Login links on your web app as seen in Figure 15-7.

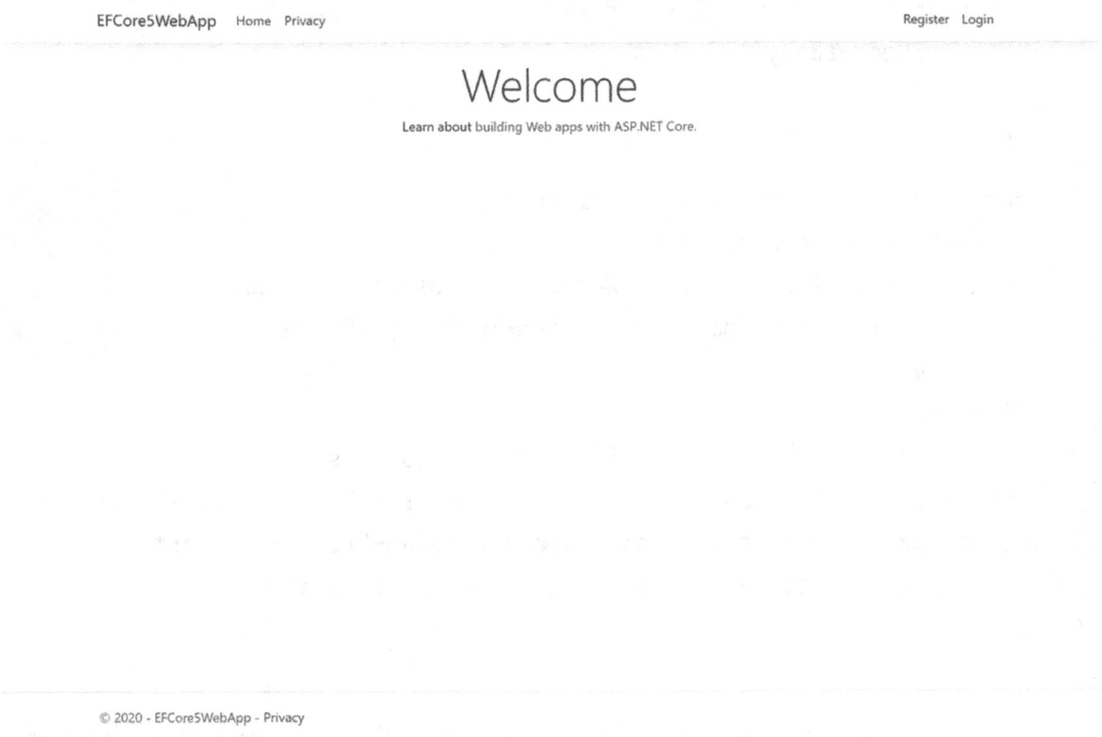

EFCore5WebApp Home Privacy Register Login

Welcome

Learn about building Web apps with ASP.NET Core.

© 2020 - EFCore5WebApp - Privacy

Figure 15-7. *App with Register and Login Functionality*

You can now access the Register page as seen in Figure 15-8.

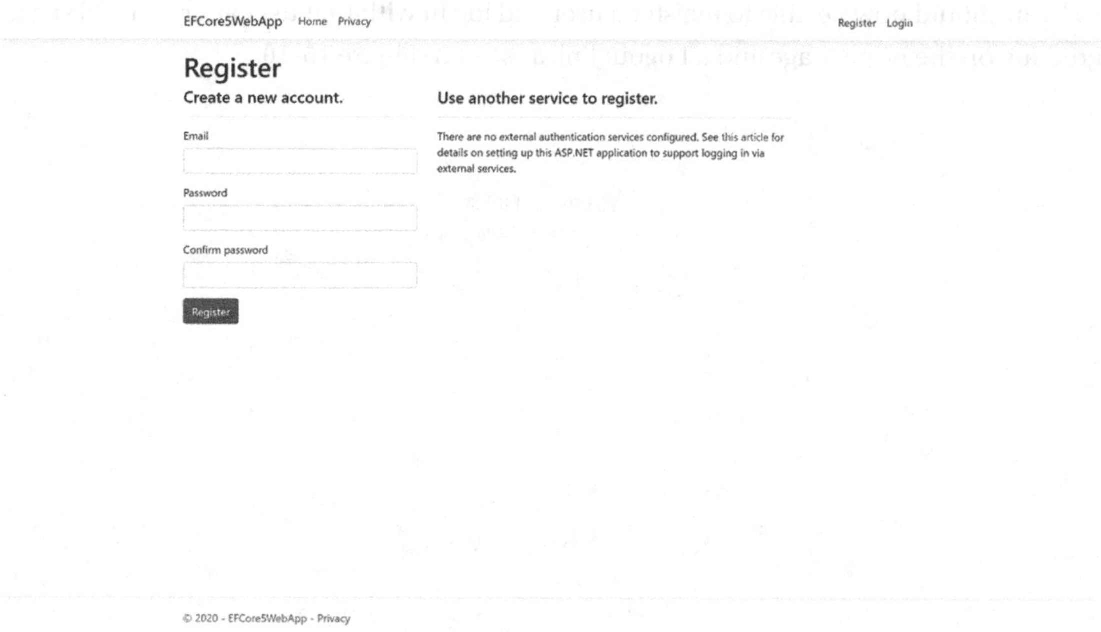

Figure 15-8. *Register User Page*

You should now also be able to access the Login page as seen in Figure 15-9.

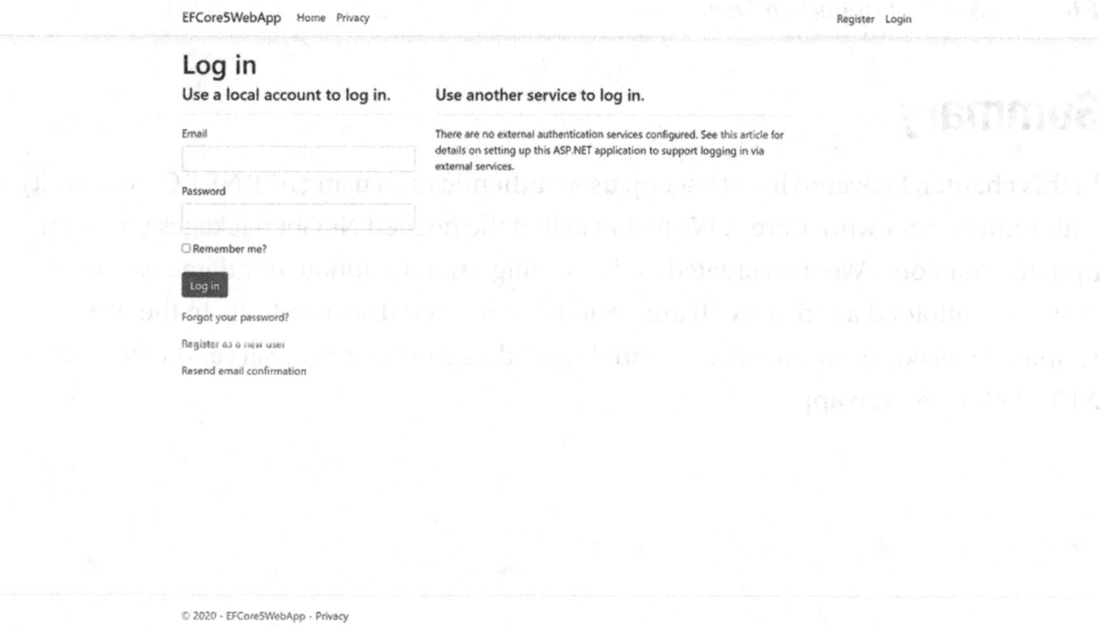

Figure 15-9. *Login Page*

You should now be able to register a user and log in with that user after you will see a greeting on the home page and a Logout link as seen in Figure 15-10.

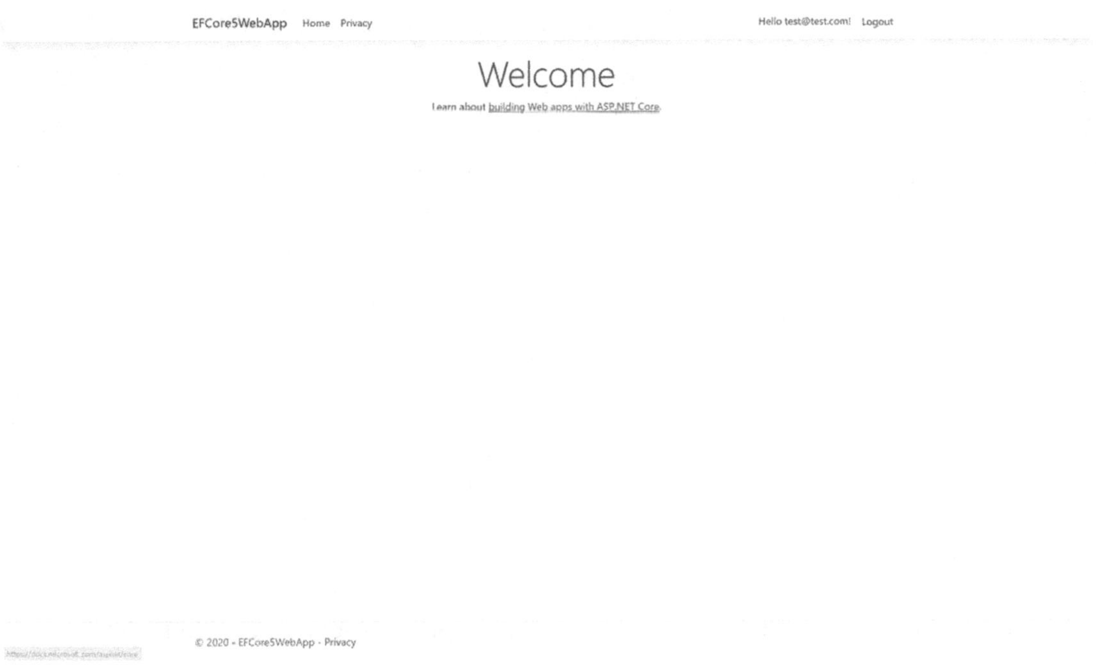

Figure 15-10. *Logged-In User*

Summary

In this chapter, I covered how to set up user authentication using ASP.NET Core Identity with Entity Framework Core 5. We first installed the needed NuGet packages and then updated our code. We then created and ran a migration to update our database. After that, we scaffolded an Identity UI and tested that it worked successfully. In the next chapter, I will cover how to retrieve and display data from our SQL Server on our ASP.NET MVC Core web app.

CHAPTER 16

Displaying Data on the Web

In this chapter, I will cover how to display a list of people with their addresses on our ASP.NET Core Razor Pages application using Entity Framework Core 5. I will show how to use Visual Studio scaffolding to create the initial Razor Pages and then how to customize it to display addresses on the details page. Lastly, we will add a menu link named "Contacts" that points to the generated Index page.

Scaffolding UI

We are going to use Visual Studio to scaffold Create, Read, Update, and Delete Razor Pages using Entity Framework. To keep everything tidy, create a new folder named "Pages" and then create a subdirectory named "Contacts" under the "Pages" folder in your web project. Next, right-click the "Contacts" folder and add a new scaffolded item. Then select Razor Pages and then the Razor Pages using Entity Framework (CRUD) option as seen in Figure 16-1.

E. Vogel, *Beginning Entity Framework Core 5*, https://doi.org/10.1007/978-1-4842-6882-7_16

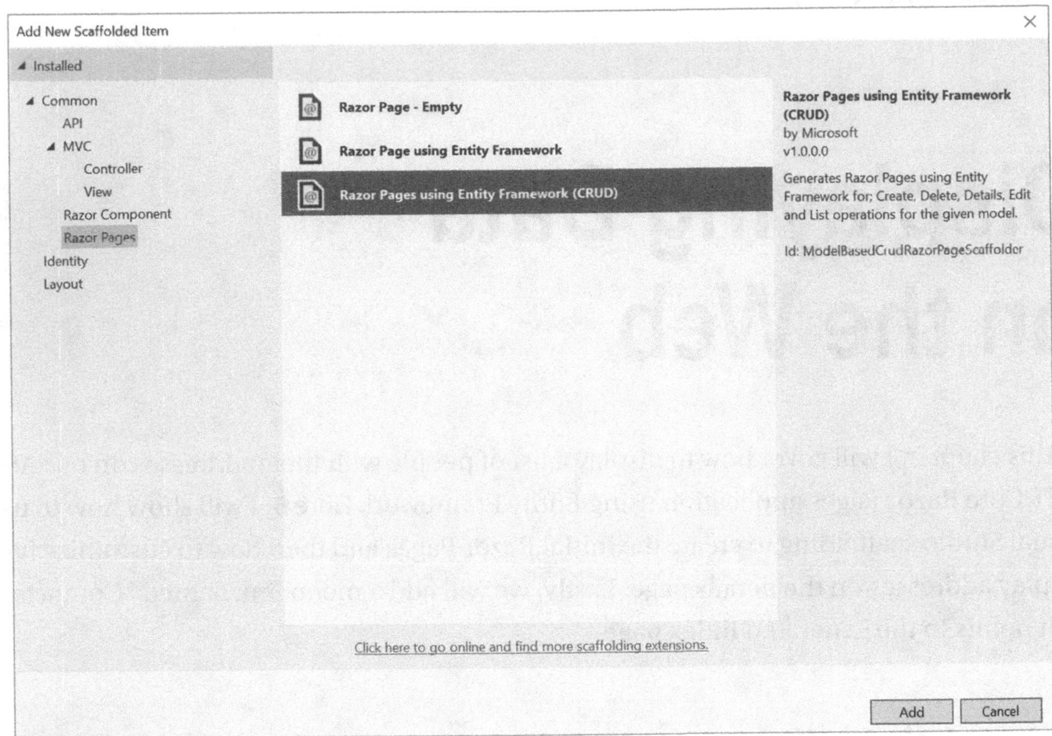

Figure 16-1. *Adding a Razor Pages EF Core Scaffold*

On the next screen, select the Person entity as the model class and AppDbContext as the data context class, and set the layout page to the Views/Shared/_Layout.cshtml view as seen in Figure 16-2.

Add Razor Pages using Entity Framework (CRUD)

Generates Razor Pages using Entity Framework for; Create, Delete, Details, Edit and List operations for the selected model.

Model class: Person (EFCore5WebApp.Core.Entities)

Data context class: AppDbContext (EFCOre5WebApp.DAL)

Options:

- [ ] Create as a partial view
- [x] Reference script libraries
- [x] Use a layout page:

~/Views/Shared/_Layout.cshtml

(Leave empty if it is set in a Razor _viewstart file)

Add Cancel

Figure 16-2. *Generating Razor Pages for the Person Entity*

You should now see the generated Razor Pages under the Contacts folder as seen in Figure 16-3.

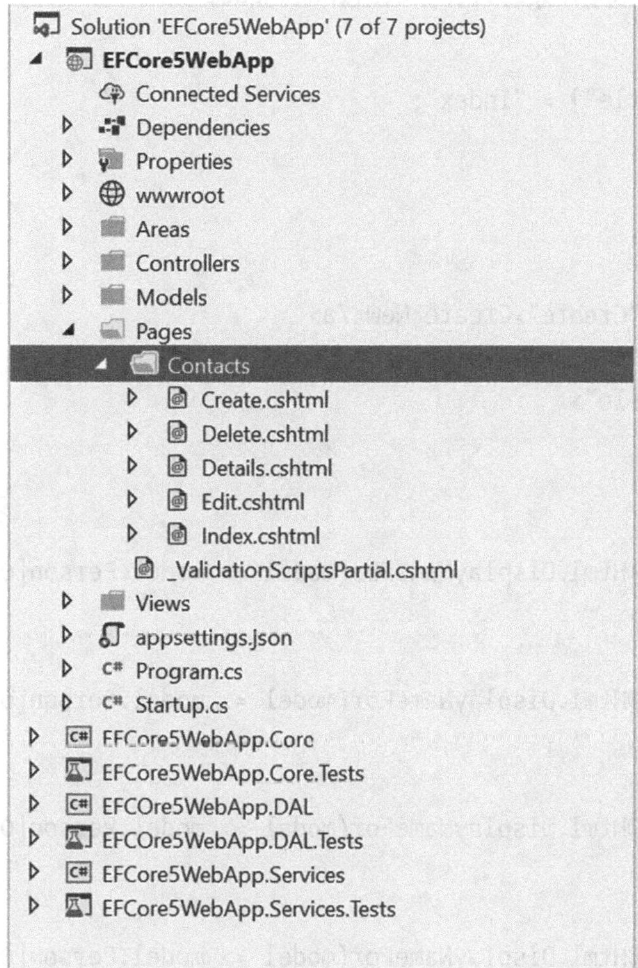

Figure 16-3. *Generated Razor Pages*

Generated List View and Model

The Person entity list view was generated as Index.cshtml and Index.cshtml.cs in the Contacts folder that we just created. The Index.cshtml is our view, and the Index.cshtml.cs is our page controller class. Your generated Index.cshtml file should look like Listing 16-1.

Listing 16-1. Person List View

```
@page
@model EFCore5WebApp.Pages.Contacts.IndexModel

@{
    ViewData["Title"] = "Index";
}

<h1>Index</h1>

<p>
    <a asp-page="Create">Create New</a>
</p>
<table class="table">
    <thead>
        <tr>
            <th>
                @Html.DisplayNameFor(model => model.Person[0].FirstName)
            </th>
            <th>
                @Html.DisplayNameFor(model => model.Person[0].LastName)
            </th>
            <th>
                @Html.DisplayNameFor(model => model.Person[0].EmailAddress)
            </th>
            <th>
                @Html.DisplayNameFor(model => model.Person[0].CreatedOn)
            </th>
            <th>
                @Html.DisplayNameFor(model => model.Person[0].Age)
            </th>
            <th></th>
        </tr>
    </thead>
    <tbody>
```

```
@foreach (var item in Model.Person) {
        <tr>
            <td>
                @Html.DisplayFor(modelItem => item.FirstName)
            </td>
            <td>
                @Html.DisplayFor(modelItem => item.LastName)
            </td>
            <td>
                @Html.DisplayFor(modelItem => item.EmailAddress)
            </td>
            <td>
                @Html.DisplayFor(modelItem => item.CreatedOn)
            </td>
            <td>
                @Html.DisplayFor(modelItem => item.Age)
            </td>
            <td>
                <a asp-page="./Edit" asp-route-id="@item.Id">Edit</a> |
                <a asp-page="./Details" asp-route-id="@item.Id">Details</a> |
                <a asp-page="./Delete" asp-route-id="@item.Id">Delete</a>
            </td>
        </tr>
}
    </tbody>
</table>
```

The table of Person entities will be rendered along with links to the Edit, Details, a nd Delete views. We are using a foreach loop in the Razor view to create the rows of the HTML table. Next, you will see the Index.cshtml.cs file that can be viewed by opening up the Index.cshtml file in Visual Studio. The Index.cshtml.cs file should look like Listing 16-2.

Listing 16-2. Person List Page Model

```
using System;
using System.Collections.Generic;
using System.Linq;
using System.Threading.Tasks;
using Microsoft.AspNetCore.Mvc;
using Microsoft.AspNetCore.Mvc.RazorPages;
using Microsoft.EntityFrameworkCore;
using EFCOre5WebApp.DAL;
using EFCore5WebApp.Core.Entities;

namespace EFCore5WebApp.Pages.Contacts
{
    public class IndexModel : PageModel
    {
        private readonly EFCOre5WebApp.DAL.AppDbContext _context;

        public IndexModel(EFCOre5WebApp.DAL.AppDbContext context)
        {
            _context = context;
        }

        public IList<Person> Person { get;set; }

        public async Task OnGetAsync()
        {
            Person = await _context.Persons.ToListAsync();
        }
    }
}
```

The Index model uses our AppDbContext class to get all Person entities in the database in the OnGetAsync() method. You will also notice that the generated code uses the async ToListAsync() method to retrieve the Person entities.

Generated Details View and Model

Now let us look at the generated Details Razor Page and page controller. The Details.cshtml should look like Listing 16-3.

Listing 16-3. Generated Details Razor Page View

```
@page
@model EFCore5WebApp.Pages.Contacts.DetailsModel

@{
    ViewData["Title"] = "Details";
}

<h1>Details</h1>

<div>
    <h4>Person</h4>
    <hr />
    <dl class="row">
        <dt class="col-sm-2">
            @Html.DisplayNameFor(model => model.Person.FirstName)
        </dt>
        <dd class="col-sm-10">
            @Html.DisplayFor(model => model.Person.FirstName)
        </dd>
        <dt class="col-sm-2">
            @Html.DisplayNameFor(model => model.Person.LastName)
        </dt>
        <dd class="col-sm-10">
            @Html.DisplayFor(model => model.Person.LastName)
        </dd>
        <dt class="col-sm-2">
            @Html.DisplayNameFor(model => model.Person.EmailAddress)
        </dt>
        <dd class="col-sm-10">
            @Html.DisplayFor(model => model.Person.EmailAddress)
        </dd>
```

```
        <dt class="col-sm-2">
            @Html.DisplayNameFor(model => model.Person.CreatedOn)
        </dt>
        <dd class="col-sm-10">
            @Html.DisplayFor(model => model.Person.CreatedOn)
        </dd>
        <dt class="col-sm-2">
            @Html.DisplayNameFor(model => model.Person.Age)
        </dt>
        <dd class="col-sm-10">
            @Html.DisplayFor(model => model.Person.Age)
        </dd>
    </dl>
</div>
<div>
    <a asp-page="./Edit" asp-route-id="@Model.Person.Id">Edit</a> |
    <a asp-page="./Index">Back to List</a>
</div>
```

The Details view displays all the properties of the Person entity. The Details page controller class is in Details.cshtml.cs and should look like Listing 16-4.

Listing 16-4. Generated Details Page Controller

```
using System;
using System.Collections.Generic;
using System.Linq;
using System.Threading.Tasks;
using Microsoft.AspNetCore.Mvc;
using Microsoft.AspNetCore.Mvc.RazorPages;
using Microsoft.EntityFrameworkCore;
using EFCOre5WebApp.DAL;
using EFCore5WebApp.Core.Entities;
```

```
namespace EFCore5WebApp.Pages.Contacts
{
    public class DetailsModel : PageModel
    {
        private readonly EFCOre5WebApp.DAL.AppDbContext _context;
        public DetailsModel(EFCOre5WebApp.DAL.AppDbContext context)
        {
            _context = context;
        }

        public Person Person { get; set; }

        public async Task<IActionResult> OnGetAsync(int? id)
        {
            if (id == null)
            {
                return NotFound();
            }

            Person = await _context.Persons.FirstOrDefaultAsync(m => m.Id
            == id);

            if (Person == null)
            {
                return NotFound();
            }
            return Page();
        }
    }
}
```

The Details page controller retrieves a Person entity by its Id. It has a guard check if the Id value is null and also checks if the Id is valid, but no person record exists for that Id. The FirstOrDefaultAsync() method is used to actually retrieve the person record through Entity Framework.

Adding Addresses to the Details View

Our Details Razor Page does not currently display the addresses for a person record. We will change that by updating the Details.cshtml Razor Page view to display addresses. To accomplish this, we will be building an HTML table using Razor C# syntax. First, we create a <table> tag, and then we use a foreach loop to generate the table headers. After that, we generate the table body using another foreach loop over the Addresses collection in Model.Person as seen in Listing 16-5.

Listing 16-5. Updated Person Details View

```
@page
@model EFCore5WebApp.Pages.Contacts.DetailsModel

@{
    ViewData["Title"] = "Details";
}

<h1>Details</h1>

<div>
    <h4>Person</h4>
    <hr />
    <dl class="row">
        <dt class="col-sm-2">
            @Html.DisplayNameFor(model => model.Person.FirstName)
        </dt>
        <dd class="col-sm-10">
            @Html.DisplayFor(model => model.Person.FirstName)
        </dd>
        <dt class="col-sm-2">
            @Html.DisplayNameFor(model => model.Person.LastName)
        </dt>
        <dd class="col-sm-10">
            @Html.DisplayFor(model => model.Person.LastName)
        </dd>
```

```
    <dt class="col-sm-2">
        @Html.DisplayNameFor(model => model.Person.EmailAddress)
    </dt>
    <dd class="col-sm-10">
        @Html.DisplayFor(model => model.Person.EmailAddress)
    </dd>
    <dt class="col-sm-2">
        @Html.DisplayNameFor(model => model.Person.CreatedOn)
    </dt>
    <dd class="col-sm-10">
        @Html.DisplayFor(model => model.Person.CreatedOn)
    </dd>
    <dt class="col-sm-2">
        @Html.DisplayNameFor(model => model.Person.Age)
    </dt>
    <dd class="col-sm-10">
        @Html.DisplayFor(model => model.Person.Age)
    </dd>
</dl>
<table class="table">
    <thead>
        <tr>
            <th>
                @Html.DisplayNameFor(model => model.Person.Addresses.
                First().AddressLine1)
            </th>
            <th>
                @Html.DisplayNameFor(model => model.Person.Addresses.
                First().AddressLine2)
            </th>
            <th>
                @Html.DisplayNameFor(model => model.Person.Addresses.
                First().City)
            </th>
```

```
            <th>
                @Html.DisplayNameFor(model => model.Person.Addresses.
                First().State)
            </th>
            <th>
                @Html.DisplayNameFor(model => model.Person.Addresses.
                First().Country)
            </th>
            <th>
                @Html.DisplayNameFor(model => model.Person.Addresses.
                First().ZipCode)
            </th>
            <th></th>
        </tr>
    </thead>
    <tbody>
        @foreach (var item in Model.Person.Addresses)
        {
        <tr>
            <td>
                @Html.DisplayFor(modelItem => item.AddressLine1)
            </td>
            <td>
                @Html.DisplayFor(modelItem => item.AddressLine2)
            </td>
            <td>
                @Html.DisplayFor(modelItem => item.City)
            </td>
            <td>
                @Html.DisplayFor(modelItem => item.State)
            </td>
            <td>
                @Html.DisplayFor(modelItem => item.Country)
            </td>
```

```
                <td>
                    @Html.DisplayFor(modelItem => item.ZipCode)
                </td>
            </tr>
            }
        </tbody>
    </table>
</div>
<div>
    <a asp-page="./Edit" asp-route-id="@Model.Person.Id">Edit</a> |
    <a asp-page="./Index">Back to List</a>
</div>
```

We also need to update the Details page controller to eager load the addresses for a person record like this:

```
Person = await _context.Persons.Include(nameof(Person.Addresses)).
FirstOrDefaultAsync(m => m.Id == id);
```

Eager loading means that when the person record is retrieved from the database, the addresses will be retrieved at the same time. We use the Include() method to specify that we want to eager load data passing in the path of the navigation property to eager load. Update the Details page controller to match Listing 16-6.

Listing 16-6. Updated Details Page Controller to Load Addresses

```
using System.Threading.Tasks;
using Microsoft.AspNetCore.Mvc;
using Microsoft.AspNetCore.Mvc.RazorPages;
using Microsoft.EntityFrameworkCore;
using EFCore5WebApp.Core.Entities;

namespace EFCore5WebApp.Pages.Contacts
{
    public class DetailsModel : PageModel
    {
        private readonly EFCOre5WebApp.DAL.AppDbContext _context;

        public DetailsModel(EFCOre5WebApp.DAL.AppDbContext context)
```

```
        {
            _context = context;
        }

        public Person Person { get; set; }

        public async Task<IActionResult> OnGetAsync(int? id)
        {
            if (id == null)
            {
                return NotFound();
            }

            Person = await _context.Persons.Include(nameof(Person.
            Addresses)).FirstOrDefaultAsync(m => m.Id == id);

            if (Person == null)
            {
                return NotFound();
            }
            return Page();
        }
    }
}
```

Adding Contacts to Navigation

Now it is time to add our Contacts menu item and test out our app. One thing you might need to fix first is to copy the Views/_ViewImports.cshtml file into the Pages folder if it is missing. This will ensure that custom tag helpers will work. Now let's add the Contacts menu item to our site navigation. We will do this by adding an HTML list item that has a link that points to our Contacts list page like this:

```
<li class="nav-item">
    <a class="nav-link text-dark" asp-page="/Contacts/Index">Contacts</a>
</li>
```

Open up the Views/Shared/_Layout.cshtml file and update it to match Listing 16-7.

Listing 16-7. Updated Layout Page with the Contacts Menu Item Added

```
<!DOCTYPE html>
<html lang="en">
<head>
    <meta charset="utf-8" />
    <meta name="viewport" content="width=device-width, initial-scale=1.0" />
    <title>@ViewData["Title"] - EFCore5WebApp</title>
    <link rel="stylesheet" href="~/lib/bootstrap/dist/css/bootstrap.min.css" />
    <link rel="stylesheet" href="~/css/site.css" />
</head>

<body>
    <header>
        <nav class="navbar navbar-expand-sm navbar-toggleable-sm navbar-
        light bg-white border-bottom box-shadow mb-3">
            <div class="container">
                <a class="navbar-brand" asp-area="" asp-controller="Home"
                asp-action="Index">EFCore5WebApp</a>
                <button class="navbar-toggler" type="button" data-
                toggle="collapse" data-target=".navbar-collapse" aria-
                controls="navbarSupportedContent"
                        aria-expanded="false" aria-label="Toggle
                        navigation">
                    <span class="navbar-toggler-icon"></span>
                </button>
                <div class="navbar-collapse collapse d-sm-inline-flex flex-
                sm-row-reverse">
                    <partial name="_LoginPartial" />
                    <ul class="navbar-nav flex-grow-1">
                        <li class="nav-item">
                            <a class="nav-link text-dark" asp-area="" asp-
                            controller="Home" asp-action="Index">Home</a>
                        </li>
```

```
                        <li class="nav-item">
                            <a class="nav-link text-dark"
                            asp-area="" asp-controller="Home"
                            asp-action="Privacy">Privacy</a>
                        </li>
                        <li class="nav-item">
                            <a class="nav-link text-dark" asp-page="/
                            Contacts/Index">Contacts</a>
                        </li>
                    </ul>
                </div>
            </div>
        </nav>
    </header>
    <div class="container">
        <main role="main" class="pb-3">
            @RenderBody()
        </main>
    </div>

    <footer class="border-top footer text-muted">
        <div class="container">
            &copy; 2020 - EFCore5WebApp - <a asp-area=""
            asp-controller="Home" asp-action="Privacy">Privacy</a>
        </div>
    </footer>
    <script src="~/lib/jquery/dist/jquery.min.js"></script>
    <script src="~/lib/bootstrap/dist/js/bootstrap.bundle.min.js"></script>
    <script src="~/js/site.js" asp-append-version="true"></script>
    @await RenderSectionAsync("Scripts", required: false)
</body>
</html>
```

Testing the App

You should now be able to run the app and see the new "Contacts" menu item as seen in Figure 16-4.

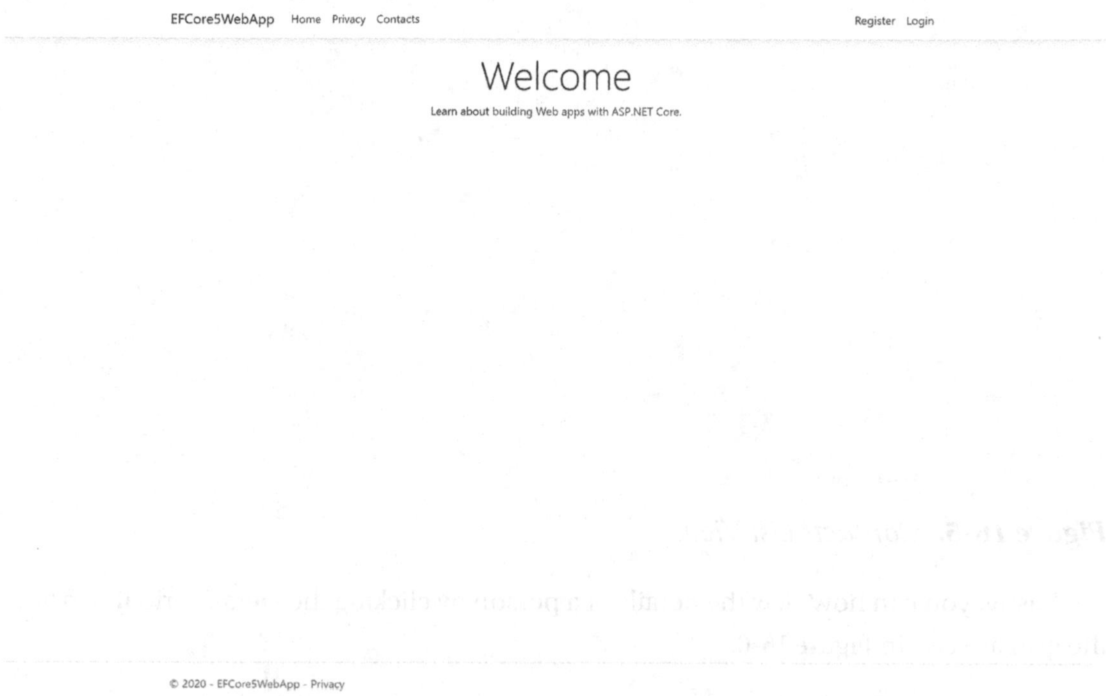

***Figure 16-4.** Contacts Menu Item Added*

When you click the "Contacts" menu item, you should now see a list of all Person entities in the database as seen in Figure 16-5.

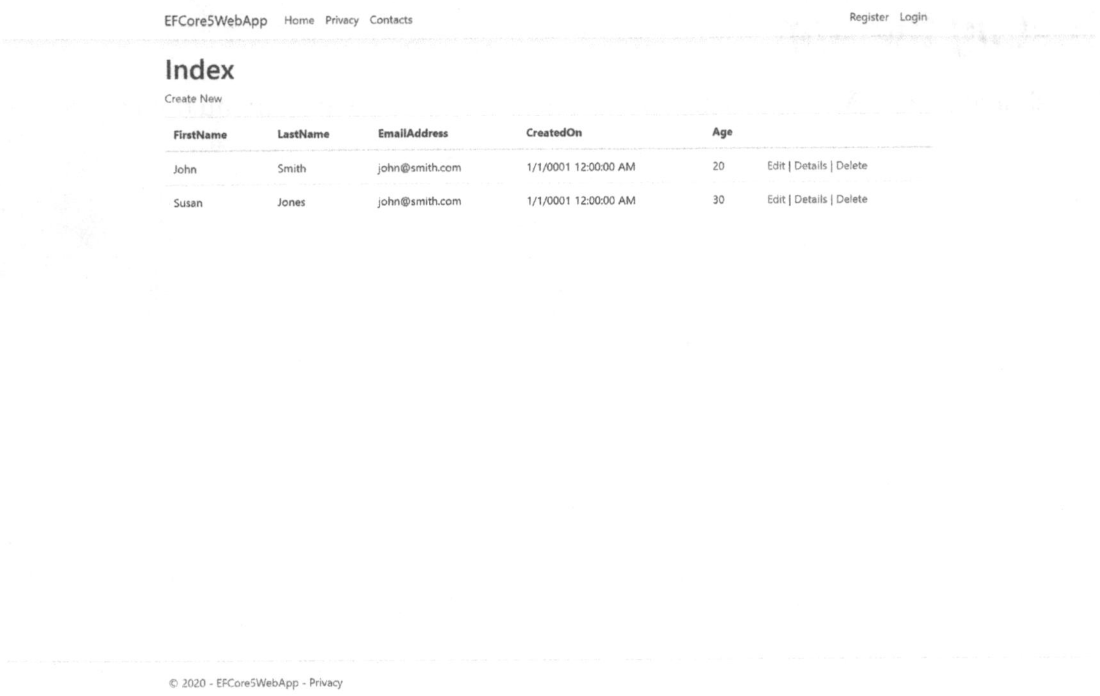

EFCore5WebApp Home Privacy Contacts Register Login

Index

Create New

FirstName	LastName	EmailAddress	CreatedOn	Age	
John	Smith	john@smith.com	1/1/0001 12:00:00 AM	20	Edit | Details | Delete
Susan	Jones	john@smith.com	1/1/0001 12:00:00 AM	30	Edit | Details | Delete

© 2020 - EFCore5WebApp - Privacy

Figure 16-5. *Contacts List View*

Lastly, you can now view the details of a person by clicking the Details grid link from the grid as seen in Figure 16-6.

Figure 16-6. *Details View with Addresses*

Adding Some Polish

You will notice that the generated Razor Pages display the grid column headers as the exact names of the properties on that entity for a person or a contact. We can easily fix that by using the Display attribute on our model classes.

Let us first update the Person model class with friendly names for the properties as seen in Listing 16-8.

Listing 16-8. Updated Person Entity with Display Names

```
using System;
using System.Collections.Generic;
using System.ComponentModel.DataAnnotations;
using System.ComponentModel.DataAnnotations.Schema;
```

```
namespace EFCore5WebApp.Core.Entities
{
    [Table("Persons")]
    public class Person
    {
        public int Id { get; set; }
        [Required]
        [MaxLength(255)]
        [Display(Name = "First Name")]
        public string FirstName { get; set; }
        [Required]
        [MaxLength(255)]
        [Display(Name = "Last Name")]
        public string LastName { get; set; }
        [Required]
        [Display(Name = "Email")]
        public string EmailAddress { get; set; }
        public List<Address> Addresses { get; set; } = new List<Address>();
        [NotMapped]
        [Display(Name = "Name")]
        public string FullName => $"{FirstName} {LastName}";
        [Display(Name = "Created On")]
        public DateTime CreatedOn { get; set; }

        public List<Person> Parents { get; set; } = new List<Person>();
        public List<Person> Children { get; set; } = new List<Person>();
        public int Age { get; set; }
    }
}
```

Next, we will update the Address entity to also have friendly display names. Update the Address entity class to match Listing 16-9.

Listing 16-9. Updated Address Entity with Display Names

```
using System.ComponentModel.DataAnnotations;

namespace EFCore5WebApp.Core.Entities
{
    public class Address
    {
        public int Id { get; set; }
        [Display(Name = "Address Line 1")]
        public string AddressLine1 { get; set; }
        [Display(Name = "Address Line 2")]
        public string AddressLine2 { get; set; }
        public string City { get; set; }
        public string State { get; set; }
        public string Country { get; set; }
        [Display(Name = "Zip Code")]
        public string ZipCode { get; set; }
        public int PersonId { get; set; }
        public Person Person { get; set; }
    }
}
```

You can now see Contacts displays with friendly names as seen in Figure 16-7.

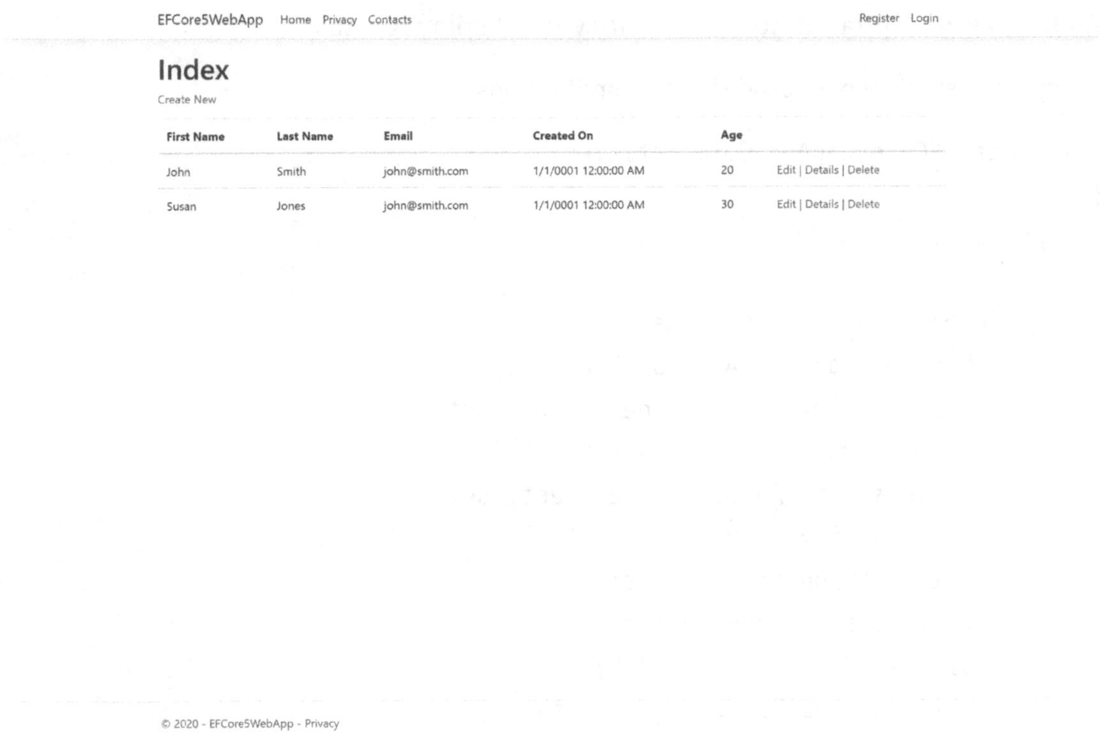

EFCore5WebApp Home Privacy Contacts Register Login

Index

Create New

First Name	Last Name	Email	Created On	Age	
John	Smith	john@smith.com	1/1/0001 12:00:00 AM	20	Edit | Details | Delete
Susan	Jones	john@smith.com	1/1/0001 12:00:00 AM	30	Edit | Details | Delete

© 2020 - EFCore5WebApp - Privacy

Figure 16-7. *Contacts with Friendly Grid Headers*

Also, the address records of a contact now look better as well as seen in Figure 16-8.

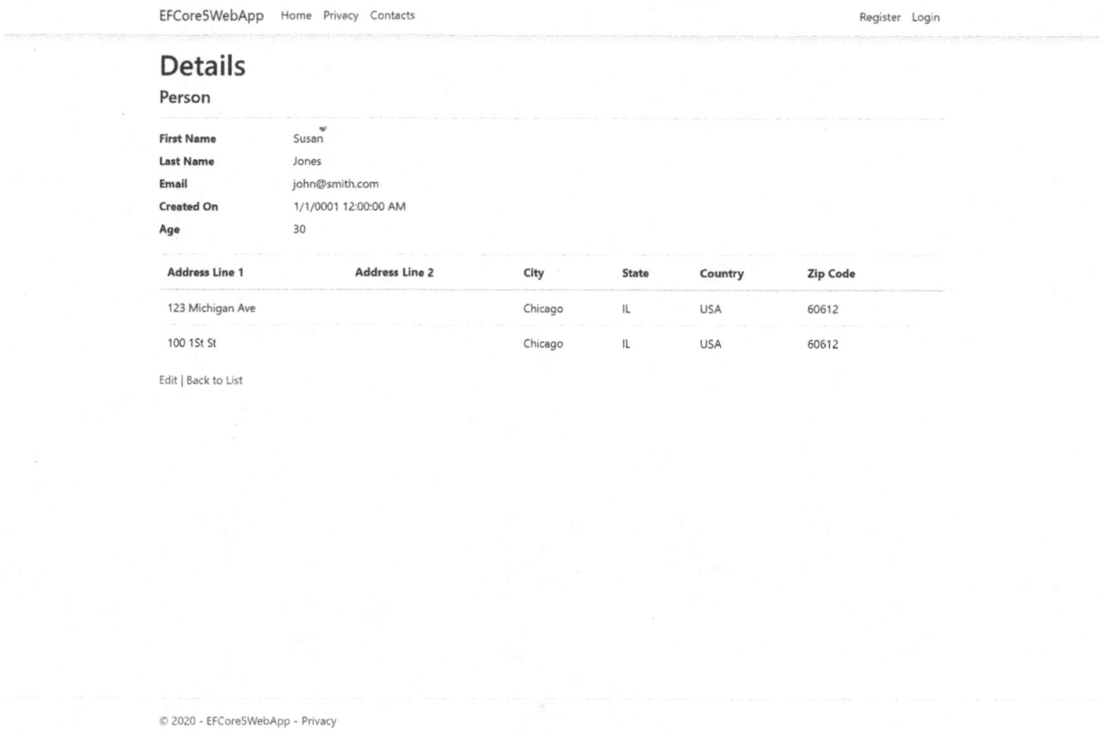

EFCore5WebApp Home Privacy Contacts Register Login

Details

Person

First Name Susan
Last Name Jones
Email john@smith.com
Created On 1/1/0001 12:00:00 AM
Age 30

Address Line 1	Address Line 2	City	State	Country	Zip Code
123 Michigan Ave		Chicago	IL	USA	60612
100 1St St		Chicago	IL	USA	60612

Edit | Back to List

© 2020 - EFCore5WebApp - Privacy

Figure 16-8. *Person Details with Friendly Address Grid Headers*

Summary

In this chapter, I covered how to use scaffolding to generate CRUD Razor Pages that use Entity Framework Core 5. Then we dived into how the list and details pages were generated. Then we updated the Details view to display address records. Lastly, we added some polish to the generated code. In the next chapter, I will cover how to insert data in the web app.

CHAPTER 17

Inserting Data on the Web

In this chapter, I will go over how to insert data in our database using Entity Framework Core 5 and ASP.NET Core Razor Pages. I will cover the generated Create Razor Page from the previous chapter. I will also show how to allow adding an address record.

Generated Create Razor Page

Visual Studio generated the Create.cshtml and Create.cshtml.cs files, which are the view and model, respectively. Let's now take a look at the generated Create Razor view and model classes. These files allow the user to create a new person record.

Generated View

The generated Create.cshtml Razorview displays text boxes for all of the Person properties with a Create button. The Create button calls the Post action on the Create model that I will go over soon. The generated Create.cshtml Razor view markup is in Listing 17-1.

Listing 17-1. Create Razor Page View

```
@page
@model EFCore5WebApp.Pages.Contacts.CreateModel

@{
    ViewData["Title"] = "Create";
    Layout = "~/Views/Shared/_Layout.cshtml";
}
```


E. Vogel, *Beginning Entity Framework Core 5*, https://doi.org/10.1007/978-1-4842-6882-7_17

```
<h1>Create</h1>

<h4>Person</h4>
<hr />
<div class="row">
    <div class="col-md-4">
        <form method="post">
            <div asp-validation-summary="ModelOnly" class="text-danger"></div>
            <div class="form-group">
                <label asp-for="Person.FirstName" class="control-label">
                </label>
                <input asp-for="Person.FirstName" class="form-control" />
                <span asp-validation-for="Person.FirstName" class="text-
                danger"></span>
            </div>
            <div class="form-group">
                <label asp-for="Person.LastName" class="control-label">
                </label>
                <input asp-for="Person.LastName" class="form-control" />
                <span asp-validation-for="Person.LastName" class="text-
                danger"></span>
            </div>
            <div class="form-group">
                <label asp-for="Person.EmailAddress" class="control-label">
                </label>
                <input asp-for="Person.EmailAddress" class="form-control" />
                <span asp-validation-for="Person.EmailAddress" class="text-
                danger"></span>
            </div>
            <div class="form-group">
                <label asp-for="Person.CreatedOn" class="control-label">
                </label>
                <input asp-for="Person.CreatedOn" class="form-control" />
                <span asp-validation-for="Person.CreatedOn" class="text-
                danger"></span>
            </div>
```

```
            <div class="form-group">
                <label asp-for="Person.Age" class="control-label"></label>
                <input asp-for="Person.Age" class="form-control" />
                <span asp-validation-for="Person.Age" class="text-danger">
                </span>
            </div>
            <div class="form-group">
                <input type="submit" value="Create" class="btn btn-primary" />
            </div>
        </form>
    </div>
</div>

<div>
    <a asp-page="Index">Back to List</a>
</div>

@section Scripts {
    @{await Html.RenderPartialAsync("_ValidationScriptsPartial");}
}
```

Generated Model

The generated Create model file named Create.cshtml.cs should look like Listing 17-2. The CreateModel class returns a view in OnGet and inserts the bound Person model in the OnPost method and then redirects the users to the Contacts list page.

Listing 17-2. Create Model

```
using System;
using System.Collections.Generic;
using System.Linq;
using System.Threading.Tasks;
using Microsoft.AspNetCore.Mvc;
using Microsoft.AspNetCore.Mvc.RazorPages;
using Microsoft.AspNetCore.Mvc.Rendering;
using EFCOre5WebApp.DAL;
```

```
using EFCore5WebApp.Core.Entities;

namespace EFCore5WebApp.Pages.Contacts
{
    public class CreateModel : PageModel
    {
        private readonly EFCOre5WebApp.DAL.AppDbContext _context;

        public CreateModel(EFCOre5WebApp.DAL.AppDbContext context)
        {
            _context = context;
        }

        public IActionResult OnGet()
        {
            return Page();
        }

        [BindProperty]
        public Person Person { get; set; }

        // To protect from overposting attacks, see https://aka.ms/
        RazorPagesCRUD
        public async Task<IActionResult> OnPostAsync()
        {
            if (!ModelState.IsValid)
            {
                return Page();
            }

            _context.Persons.Add(Person);
            await _context.SaveChangesAsync();

            return RedirectToPage("./Index");
        }
    }
}
```

As you can see, the page controller code looks very similar to our Add Unit Test except instead of calling SaveChanges(), the SaveChangesAsync() method is used.

Person Model Validation

You will also see that there is a guard check to see if the model state is valid. Have a look at our Person model, for example, in Listing 17-3.

Listing 17-3. Person Model Class

```
using System;
using System.Collections.Generic;
using System.ComponentModel.DataAnnotations;
using System.ComponentModel.DataAnnotations.Schema;

namespace EFCore5WebApp.Core.Entities
{
    [Table("Persons", Schema ="dbo")]
    public class Person
    {
        public int Id { get; set; }
        [Required]
        [MaxLength(255)]
        [Display(Name = "First Name")]
        public string FirstName { get; set; }
        [Required]
        [MaxLength(255)]
        [Display(Name = "Last Name")]
        public string LastName { get; set; }
        [Required]
        [Display(Name = "Email")]
        public string EmailAddress { get; set; }
        public List<Address> Addresses { get; set; } = new List<Address>();
        [NotMapped]
        [Display(Name = "Name")]
        public string FullName => $"{FirstName} {LastName}";
```

```
        [Display(Name = "Created On")]
        public DateTime CreatedOn { get; set; }
        public int Age { get; set; }
    }
}
```

You will notice the use of the Required and MaxLength attributes. The Required attribute will ensure that the associated property is not null. The MaxLength property will make sure the length of the associated property does not exceed the specified length, in this case 255 characters. This validation is enforced both in the database and in our code.

Adding Addresses

We'll now update the Create Razor Page to allow the user to add a single address record for that person. We will first update the Address entity validation, create a migration, and then update the UI.

Address Model Validation

We also want to ensure that address records have validation as well. To do this, we will update the Address model class to make Address Line 1, City, State, Country, and ZipCode properties to be required as seen in Listing 17-4.

Listing 17-4. Address Model with Validation

```
using System.ComponentModel.DataAnnotations;

namespace EFCore5WebApp.Core.Entities
{
    public class Address
    {
        public int Id { get; set; }
        [Display(Name = "Address Line 1")]
        [Required]
        public string AddressLine1 { get; set; }
        [Display(Name = "Address Line 2")]
```

```
        public string AddressLine2 { get; set; }
        [Required]
        public string City { get; set; }
        [Required]
        public string State { get; set;}
        [Required]
        public string Country { get; set; }
        [Display(Name = "Zip Code")]
        [Required]
        public string ZipCode { get; set; }
        public int PersonId { get; set; }
        public Person Person { get; set; }
    }
}
```

Enforce Address Validation in Database

In order to enforce the Address entity validation, we need to add and run a database migration. To do this, first run "Add-Migration AddedAddressValidation" from the Package Manager Console. Once the migration is created, run "Update-Database" from the Package Manager Console.

The generated migration should look like Listing 17-5.

Listing 17-5. Add Address Validation Migration

```
using Microsoft.EntityFrameworkCore.Migrations;

namespace EFCOre5WebApp.DAL.Migrations
{
    public partial class AddedAddressValidation : Migration
    {
        protected override void Up(MigrationBuilder migrationBuilder)
        {
            migrationBuilder.AlterColumn<string>(
                name: "ZipCode",
                table: "Addresses",
```

```
        type: "nvarchar(max)",
        nullable: false,
        defaultValue: "",
        oldClrType: typeof(string),
        oldType: "nvarchar(max)",
        oldNullable: true);

    migrationBuilder.AlterColumn<string>(
        name: "State",
        table: "Addresses",
        type: "nvarchar(max)",
        nullable: false,
        defaultValue: "",
        oldClrType: typeof(string),
        oldType: "nvarchar(max)",
        oldNullable: true);

    migrationBuilder.AlterColumn<string>(
        name: "Country",
        table: "Addresses",
        type: "nvarchar(max)",
        nullable: false,
        defaultValue: "",
        oldClrType: typeof(string),
        oldType: "nvarchar(max)",
        oldNullable: true);

    migrationBuilder.AlterColumn<string>(
        name: "City",
        table: "Addresses",
        type: "nvarchar(max)",
        nullable: false,
        defaultValue: "",
        oldClrType: typeof(string),
        oldType: "nvarchar(max)",
        oldNullable: true);
```

```
        migrationBuilder.AlterColumn<string>(
            name: "AddressLine1",
            table: "Addresses",
            type: "nvarchar(max)",
            nullable: false,
            defaultValue: "",
            oldClrType: typeof(string),
            oldType: "nvarchar(max)",
            oldNullable: true);
    }

    protected override void Down(MigrationBuilder migrationBuilder)
    {
        migrationBuilder.AlterColumn<string>(
            name: "ZipCode",
            table: "Addresses",
            type: "nvarchar(max)",
            nullable: true,
            oldClrType: typeof(string),
            oldType: "nvarchar(max)");

        migrationBuilder.AlterColumn<string>(
            name: "State",
            table: "Addresses",
            type: "nvarchar(max)",
            nullable: true,
            oldClrType: typeof(string),
            oldType: "nvarchar(max)");

        migrationBuilder.AlterColumn<string>(
            name: "Country",
            table: "Addresses",
            type: "nvarchar(max)",
            nullable: true,
            oldClrType: typeof(string),
            oldType: "nvarchar(max)");
```

```
            migrationBuilder.AlterColumn<string>(
                name: "City",
                table: "Addresses",
                type: "nvarchar(max)",
                nullable: true,
                oldClrType: typeof(string),
                oldType: "nvarchar(max)");

            migrationBuilder.AlterColumn<string>(
                name: "AddressLine1",
                table: "Addresses",
                type: "nvarchar(max)",
                nullable: true,
                oldClrType: typeof(string),
                oldType: "nvarchar(max)");
        }
    }
}
```

You will notice that most of the columns are nvarchar(max), which means they have the maximum length allowed by the target database because we didn't define a fixed length in our model. You will also note that the nullable value for our required fields was now set to true.

Updating UI

To keep things simple, we will allow the entry of a single address record per person. To get started, we will update the Razor Page view first. To do this, we are going to add labels and text boxes for each of the Addresses properties to the Create Razor view like this:

```
<div class="col-md-4">
    <div class="form-group">
        <label asp-for="Person.Addresses[0].AddressLine1"
        class="control-label"></label>
        <input asp-for="Person.Addresses[0].AddressLine1"
        class="form-control" />
```

```
        <span asp-validation-for="Person.Addresses[0].AddressLine1"
        class="text-danger"></span>
    </div>
    <div class="form-group">
        <label asp-for="Person.Addresses[0].AddressLine2"
        class="control-label"></label>
        <input asp-for="Person.Addresses[0].AddressLine2"
        class="form-control" />
        <span asp-validation-for="Person.Addresses[0].AddressLine2"
        class="text-danger"></span>
    </div>
    <div class="form-group">
        <label asp-for="Person.Addresses[0].City" class="control-
        label"></label>
        <input asp-for="Person.Addresses[0].City" class="form-
        control" />
        <span asp-validation-for="Person.Addresses[0].City"
        class="text-danger"></span>
    </div>
    <div class="form-group">
        <label asp-for="Person.Addresses[0].State" class="control-
        label"></label>
        <input asp-for="Person.Addresses[0].State" class="form-
        control" />
        <span asp-validation-for="Person.Addresses[0].State"
        class="text-danger"></span>
    </div>
    <div class="form-group">
        <label asp-for="Person.Addresses[0].Country"
        class="control-label"></label>
        <input asp-for="Person.Addresses[0].Country" class="form-
        control" />
        <span asp-validation-for="Person.Addresses[0].Country"
        class="text-danger"></span>
    </div>
```

```
        <div class="form-group">
            <label asp-for="Person.Addresses[0].ZipCode"
            class="control-label"></label>
            <input asp-for="Person.Addresses[0].ZipCode" class="form-
            control" />
            <span asp-validation-for="Person.Addresses[0].ZipCode"
            class="text-danger"></span>
        </div>
    </div>
```

We will soon update our CreateModel class to ensure that there is a single address available to edit that will be bound to the view. Your completed Create Razor view should now look like Listing 17-6.

Listing 17-6. Updated Create Razor View

```
@page
@model EFCore5WebApp.Pages.Contacts.CreateModel

@{
    ViewData["Title"] = "Create";
    Layout = "~/Views/Shared/_Layout.cshtml";
}

<h1>Create</h1>

<h4>Person</h4>
<hr />
<form method="post">
    <div class="row">
        <div class="col-md-4">
            <div asp-validation-summary="ModelOnly" class="text-danger"></div>
            <div class="form-group">
                <label asp-for="Person.FirstName" class="control-label">
                </label>
                <input asp-for="Person.FirstName" class="form-control" />
                <span asp-validation-for="Person.FirstName" class="text-
                danger"></span>
```

```
        </div>
        <div class="form-group">
            <label asp-for="Person.LastName" class="control-label">
            </label>
            <input asp-for="Person.LastName" class="form-control" />
            <span asp-validation-for="Person.LastName" class="text-
            danger"></span>
        </div>
        <div class="form-group">
            <label asp-for="Person.EmailAddress" class="control-
            label"></label>
            <input asp-for="Person.EmailAddress" class="form-control" />
            <span asp-validation-for="Person.EmailAddress" class="text-
            danger"></span>
        </div>
        <div class="form-group">
            <label asp-for="Person.Age" class="control-label"></label>
            <input asp-for="Person.Age" class="form-control" />
            <span asp-validation-for="Person.Age" class="text-
            danger"></span>
        </div>
    </div>
    <div class="col-md-4">
        <div class="form-group">
            <label asp-for="Person.Addresses[0].AddressLine1"
            class="control-label"></label>
            <input asp-for="Person.Addresses[0].AddressLine1"
            class="form-control" />
            <span asp-validation-for="Person.Addresses[0].AddressLine1"
            class="text-danger"></span>
        </div>
        <div class="form-group">
            <label asp-for="Person.Addresses[0].AddressLine2"
            class="control-label"></label>
```

```
        <input asp-for="Person.Addresses[0].AddressLine2"
        class="form-control" />
        <span asp-validation-for="Person.Addresses[0].AddressLine2"
        class="text-danger"></span>
    </div>
    <div class="form-group">
        <label asp-for="Person.Addresses[0].City" class="control-
        label"></label>
        <input asp-for="Person.Addresses[0].City" class="form-
        control" />
        <span asp-validation-for="Person.Addresses[0].City"
        class="text-danger"></span>
    </div>
    <div class="form-group">
        <label asp-for="Person.Addresses[0].State" class="control-
        label"></label>
        <input asp-for="Person.Addresses[0].State" class="form-
        control" />
        <span asp-validation-for="Person.Addresses[0].State"
        class="text-danger"></span>
    </div>
    <div class="form-group">
        <label asp-for="Person.Addresses[0].Country"
        class="control-label"></label>
        <input asp-for="Person.Addresses[0].Country" class="form-
        control" />
        <span asp-validation-for="Person.Addresses[0].Country"
        class="text-danger"></span>
    </div>
    <div class="form-group">
        <label asp-for="Person.Addresses[0].ZipCode"
        class="control-label"></label>
        <input asp-for="Person.Addresses[0].ZipCode" class="form-
        control" />
```

```
                <span asp-validation-for="Person.Addresses[0].ZipCode"
                    class="text-danger"></span>
            </div>
        </div>
    </div>
    <div class="row">
        <div class="form-group">
            <input type="submit" value="Create" class="btn btn-primary" />
        </div>
    </div>
</form>

<div>
    <a asp-page="Index">Back to List</a>
</div>

@section Scripts {
    @{await Html.RenderPartialAsync("_ValidationScriptsPartial");}
}
```

If you are familiar with Bootstrap, you will see that I am going with a two-column layout with the Person details on the left and Address details on the right side.

Update the Razor Page Model

The next step is to update the Razor model to allow for adding a single address record. Luckily for us, Razor Pages has built-in model binding. So we will make the binding support get and add an empty address record to the collection of addresses for the person in the OnGet() method like this:

```
public IActionResult OnGet()
{
    Person.Addresses.Add(new Address());
    return Page();
}
```

I also set the CreatedOn property value to the current date in the OnPostAsync() method like this:

```
public async Task<IActionResult> OnPostAsync()
{
    if (!ModelState.IsValid)
    {
        return Page();
    }

    Person.CreatedOn = DateTime.Now;
    _context.Persons.Add(Person);
    await _context.SaveChangesAsync();

    return RedirectToPage("./Index");
}
```

See the completed updated code in Listing 17-7. You will notice that I added SupportsGet to the Person model to make sure it is bound when the page is requested.

Listing 17-7. Updated Create Razor Page Controller

```
using System;
using System.Collections.Generic;
using System.Linq;
using System.Threading.Tasks;
using Microsoft.AspNetCore.Mvc;
using Microsoft.AspNetCore.Mvc.RazorPages;
using Microsoft.AspNetCore.Mvc.Rendering;
using EFCOre5WebApp.DAL;
using EFCore5WebApp.Core.Entities;

namespace EFCore5WebApp.Pages.Contacts
{
    public class CreateModel : PageModel
    {
        private readonly EFCOre5WebApp.DAL.AppDbContext _context;

        public CreateModel(EFCOre5WebApp.DAL.AppDbContext context)
```

```
        {
            _context = context;
        }

        public IActionResult OnGet()
        {
            Person.Addresses.Add(new Address());
            return Page();
        }

        [BindProperty(SupportsGet = true)]
        public Person Person { get; set; }

        // To protect from overposting attacks, see https://aka.ms/
        RazorPagesCRUD
        public async Task<IActionResult> OnPostAsync()
        {
            if (!ModelState.IsValid)
            {
                return Page();
            }

            Person.CreatedOn = DateTime.Now;
            _context.Persons.Add(Person);
            await _context.SaveChangesAsync();

            return RedirectToPage("./Index");
        }
    }
}
```

Running the App

You can now add a new person record with their very own address as seen in Figure 17-1.

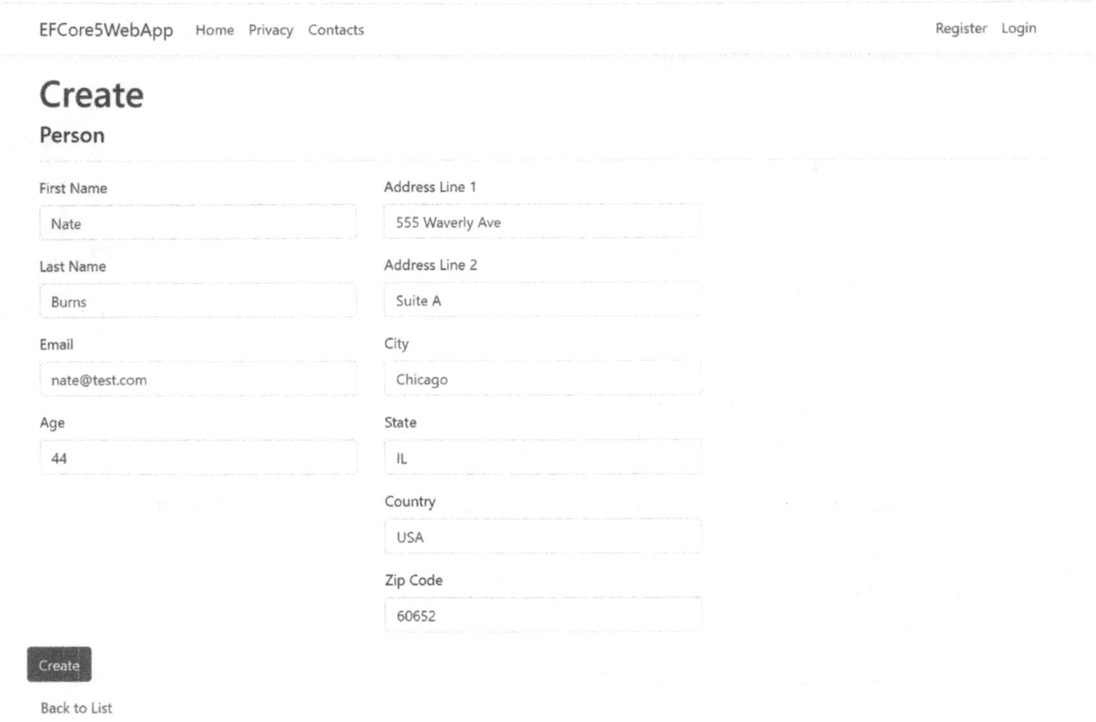

Figure 17-1. *Create Page with Address Entry*

You can verify that the person was added successfully by going back to the main Contact Details page for the newly added person record as seen in Figure 17-2.

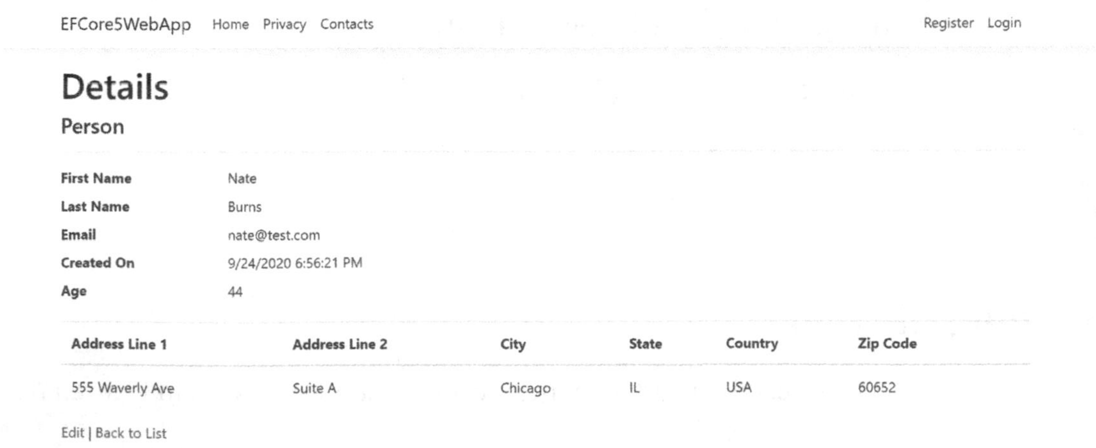

Figure 17-2. *Viewing the Added Person*

Adding Some Polish

We have a LookUps table, but so far, we have not put it to use. Now is the time to use it and add State and Country dropdowns to our Create form. It will take two steps to accomplish this task. First, we will update the model code to load and save the dropdowns; and second, we will update the UI to display the dropdowns.

Update the Model

The first step is to update the Create Razor page controller to have bound properties for states and countries. To accomplish this, we first add bound properties to our CreateModel class for the States and Countries select list items:

```
[BindProperty(SupportsGet = true)]
public List<SelectListItem> States { get; set; }

[BindProperty(SupportsGet = true)]
public List<SelectListItem> Countries { get; set; }
```

Then we populate States and Countries from their lookup records in the database in the OnGet() method:

```
public IActionResult OnGet()
{
    Person.Addresses.Add(new Address());

    States = _context.LookUps.Where(x => x.LookUpType == LookUpType.State).
    Select(x => new SelectListItem { Text = x.Description, Value = x.Code
    }).ToList();
    Countries = _context.LookUps.Where(x => x.LookUpType == LookUpType.
    Country).Select(x => new SelectListItem { Text = x.Description,
    Value = x.Code }).ToList();

    States.Insert(0, new SelectListItem { Text = "Select an item",
    Value = string.Empty });
    Countries.Insert(0, new SelectListItem { Text = "Select an item",
    Value = string.Empty });

    return Page();
}
```

We set the displayed text for the dropdowns to the Description property of the LookUp record and save the Code property value upon selection by the user. Your updated Create Razor view should now look like Listing 17-8.

Listing 17-8. Create Page Controller with States and Countries

```
using System;
using System.Collections.Generic;
using System.Linq;
using System.Threading.Tasks;
using Microsoft.AspNetCore.Mvc;
using Microsoft.AspNetCore.Mvc.RazorPages;
using Microsoft.AspNetCore.Mvc.Rendering;
using EFCOre5WebApp.DAL;
using EFCore5WebApp.Core.Entities;

namespace EFCore5WebApp.Pages.Contacts
{
    public class CreateModel : PageModel
    {
        private readonly EFCOre5WebApp.DAL.AppDbContext _context;

        [BindProperty(SupportsGet = true)]
        public List<SelectListItem> States { get; set; }

        [BindProperty(SupportsGet = true)]
        public List<SelectListItem> Countries { get; set; }

        public CreateModel(EFCOre5WebApp.DAL.AppDbContext context)
        {
            _context = context;
        }

        public IActionResult OnGet()
        {
            Person.Addresses.Add(new Address());

            States = _context.LookUps.Where(x => x.LookUpType ==
            LookUpType.State).Select(x => new SelectListItem { Text =
            x.Description, Value = x.Code  } ).ToList();
```

```
            Countries = _context.LookUps.Where(x => x.LookUpType ==
            LookUpType.Country).Select(x => new SelectListItem { Text =
            x.Description, Value = x.Code }).ToList();

            States.Insert(0, new SelectListItem { Text = "Select an item",
            Value = string.Empty });
            Countries.Insert(0, new SelectListItem { Text = "Select an
            item", Value = string.Empty });

            return Page();
        }

        [BindProperty(SupportsGet = true)]
        public Person Person { get; set; }

        // To protect from overposting attacks, see https://aka.ms/
        RazorPagesCRUD
        public async Task<IActionResult> OnPostAsync()
        {
            if (!ModelState.IsValid)
            {
                return Page();
            }

            Person.CreatedOn = DateTime.Now;
            _context.Persons.Add(Person);
            await _context.SaveChangesAsync();

            return RedirectToPage("./Index");
        }
    }
}
```

The tag helpers we will be using in the next step expect an IEnumerable<SelectListItem>, so I made sure both the States Countries properties are of that type for easy use. You can see that I am using LookUpType to determine the difference between country and state lookup values. Next, we will update the UI.

Update the UI

Now we will make a small change to the UI to change our text boxes for states and countries to be dropdowns. To do this, we change from using an "input" to a "select" tag for the state and country form elements, and we use the "asp-items" property to bind the State dropdown to the States property and the Country dropdown to the Countries property on the model as seen in the following:

```
<div class="form-group">
    <label asp-for="Person.Addresses[0].State" class="control-label">
    </label>
    <select asp-for="Person.Addresses[0].State" class="form-control"
    asp-items="Model.States"></select>
    <span asp-validation-for="Person.Addresses[0].State" class="text-
    danger"></span>
</div>
<div class="form-group">
    <label asp-for="Person.Addresses[0].Country" class="control-label">
    </label>
    <select asp-for="Person.Addresses[0].Country" class="form-control"
    asp-items="Model.Countries"></select>
    <span asp-validation-for="Person.Addresses[0].Country" class="text-
    danger"></span>
</div>
```

See the completed Create Razor view in Listing 17-9.

Listing 17-9. Updated Create Razor View

```
@page
@model EFCore5WebApp.Pages.Contacts.CreateModel

@{
    ViewData["Title"] = "Create";
    Layout = "~/Views/Shared/_Layout.cshtml";
}
```

```
<h1>Create</h1>

<h4>Person</h4>
<hr />
<form method="post">
    <div class="row">
        <div class="col-md-4">
            <div asp-validation-summary="ModelOnly" class="text-danger">
            </div>
            <div class="form-group">
                <label asp-for="Person.FirstName" class="control-label">
                </label>
                <input asp-for="Person.FirstName" class="form-control" />
                <span asp-validation-for="Person.FirstName" class="text-
                danger"></span>
            </div>
            <div class="form-group">
                <label asp-for="Person.LastName" class="control-label">
                </label>
                <input asp-for="Person.LastName" class="form-control" />
                <span asp-validation-for="Person.LastName" class="text-
                danger"></span>
            </div>
            <div class="form-group">
                <label asp-for="Person.EmailAddress" class="control-label">
                </label>
                <input asp-for="Person.EmailAddress" class="form-control" />
                <span asp-validation-for="Person.EmailAddress" class="text-
                danger"></span>
            </div>
            <div class="form-group">
                <label asp-for="Person.Age" class="control-label"></label>
                <input asp-for="Person.Age" class="form-control" />
                <span asp-validation-for="Person.Age" class="text-
                danger"></span>
            </div>
```

```
        </div>
        <div class="col-md-4">
            <div class="form-group">
                <label asp-for="Person.Addresses[0].AddressLine1"
                class="control-label"></label>
                <input asp-for="Person.Addresses[0].AddressLine1"
                class="form-control" />
                <span asp-validation-for="Person.Addresses[0].AddressLine1"
                class="text-danger"></span>
            </div>
            <div class="form-group">
                <label asp-for="Person.Addresses[0].AddressLine2"
                class="control-label"></label>
                <input asp-for="Person.Addresses[0].AddressLine2"
                class="form-control" />
                <span asp-validation-for="Person.Addresses[0].AddressLine2"
                class="text-danger"></span>
            </div>
            <div class="form-group">
                <label asp-for="Person.Addresses[0].City" class="control-
                label"></label>
                <input asp-for="Person.Addresses[0].City" class="form-
                control" />
                <span asp-validation-for="Person.Addresses[0].City"
                class="text-danger"></span>
            </div>
            <div class="form-group">
                <label asp-for="Person.Addresses[0].State" class="control-
                label"></label>
                <select asp-for="Person.Addresses[0].State" class="form-
                control" asp-items="Model.States"></select>
                <span asp-validation-for="Person.Addresses[0].State"
                class="text-danger"></span>
            </div>
```

```
            <div class="form-group">
                <label asp-for="Person.Addresses[0].Country"
                class="control-label"></label>
                <select asp-for="Person.Addresses[0].Country" class="form-
                control" asp-items="Model.Countries"></select>
                <span asp-validation-for="Person.Addresses[0].Country"
                class="text-danger"></span>
            </div>
            <div class="form-group">
                <label asp-for="Person.Addresses[0].ZipCode"
                class="control-label"></label>
                <input asp-for="Person.Addresses[0].ZipCode" class="form-
                control" />
                <span asp-validation-for="Person.Addresses[0].ZipCode"
                class="text-danger"></span>
            </div>
        </div>
    </div>
    <div class="row">
        <div class="form-group">
            <input type="submit" value="Create" class="btn btn-primary" />
        </div>
    </div>
</form>

<div>
    <a asp-page="Index">Back to List</a>
</div>

@section Scripts {
    @{await Html.RenderPartialAsync("_ValidationScriptsPartial");}
}
```

Now you can run the app to see that the State and Country dropdowns are working correctly as seen in Figure 17-3.

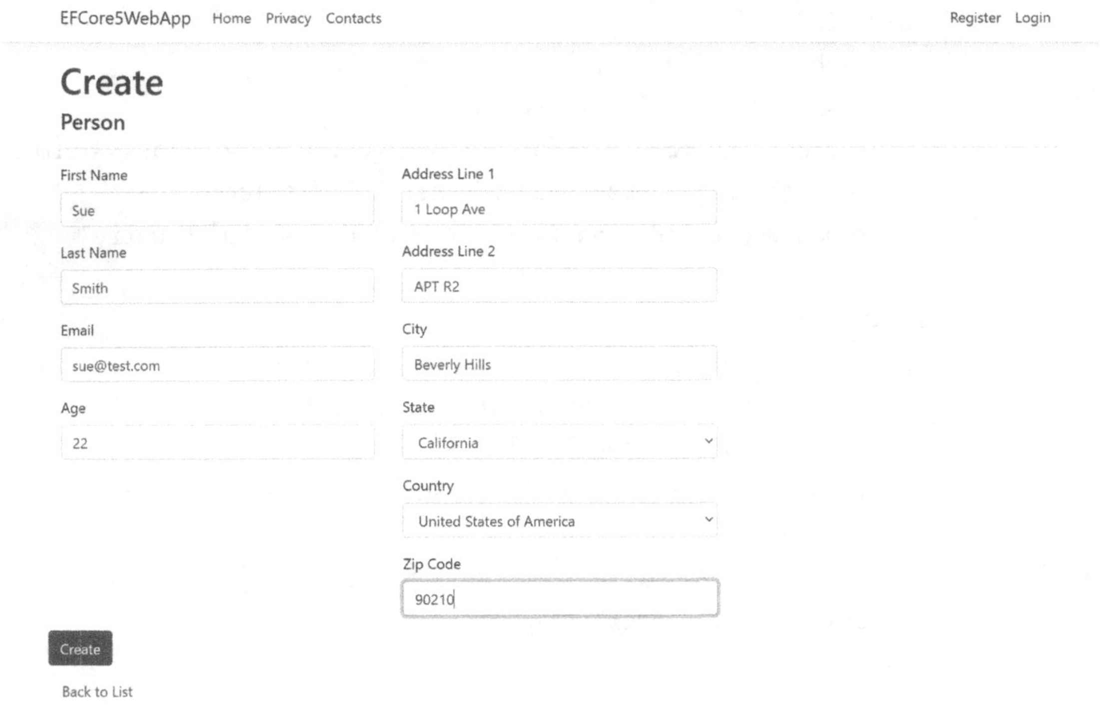

Figure 17-3. *Person View with Address Dropdowns*

After you add your person record, you can view the dropdowns as seen in Figure 17-4.

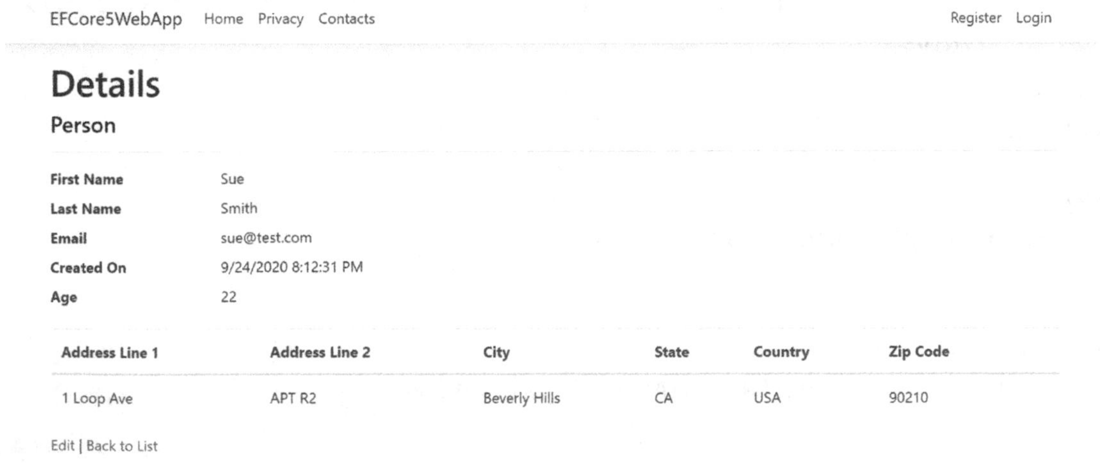

Figure 17-4. *Verify the Dropdowns Worked*

You can see that the Value property value was correctly saved into the State and Country Addresses properties.

Summary

In this chapter, I have shown what the generated Create Razor Page and page controller code looks like. I also went over some basics of model validation. We then added some extra model validation to the Address entity. Next, we updated the Create Razor Page to allow for the entry of an address record and verified that it worked through the details page. Lastly, we put our lookup items to use for State and Country dropdowns. In the next chapter, I will show how the Edit Razor Page works and how to update it to allow editing an address record.

Summary

[illegible]

CHAPTER 18

Updating Data on the Web

In this chapter, I will cover how to update data using Entity Framework Core 5 and Razor Pages in ASP.NET Core. First, I will go over the generated Edit Razor Page and model that were previously created. After that, I will cover how to update the Edit Razor Page to edit an address record for our edited person.

Generated Edit Razor Page View

The Edit Razor Page view is in the Edit.cshtml file under Pages ➤ Contacts and should look like Listing 18-1.

Listing 18-1. Generated Edit Razor Page View

```
@page
@model EFCore5WebApp.Pages.Contacts.EditModel
@{
    ViewData["Title"] = "Edit";
    Layout = "~/Views/Shared/_Layout.cshtml";
}

<h1>Edit</h1>

<h4>Person</h4>
<hr />
<div class="row">
    <div class="col-md-4">
        <form method="post">
            <div asp-validation-summary="ModelOnly" class="text-danger"></div>
            <input type="hidden" asp-for="Person.Id" />
            <div class="form-group">
```


E. Vogel, *Beginning Entity Framework Core 5*, https://doi.org/10.1007/978-1-4842-6882-7_18

```
        <label asp-for="Person.FirstName" class="control-label">
        </label>
        <input asp-for="Person.FirstName" class="form-control" />
        <span asp-validation-for="Person.FirstName" class="text-
        danger"></span>
    </div>
    <div class="form-group">
        <label asp-for="Person.LastName" class="control-label">
        </label>
        <input asp-for="Person.LastName" class="form-control" />
        <span asp-validation-for="Person.LastName" class="text-
        danger"></span>
    </div>
    <div class="form-group">
        <label asp-for="Person.EmailAddress" class="control-
        label"></label>
        <input asp-for="Person.EmailAddress" class="form-control" />
        <span asp-validation-for="Person.EmailAddress" class="text-
        danger"></span>
    </div>
    <div class="form-group">
        <label asp-for="Person.CreatedOn" class="control-label">
        </label>
        <input asp-for="Person.CreatedOn" class="form-control" />
        <span asp-validation-for="Person.CreatedOn" class="text-
        danger"></span>
    </div>
    <div class="form-group">
        <label asp-for="Person.Age" class="control-label"></label>
        <input asp-for="Person.Age" class="form-control" />
        <span asp-validation-for="Person.Age" class="text-
        danger"></span>
    </div>
```

```
            <div class="form-group">
                <input type="submit" value="Save" class="btn btn-primary" />
            </div>
        </form>
    </div>
</div>

<div>
    <a asp-page="./Index">Back to List</a>
</div>

@section Scripts {
    @{await Html.RenderPartialAsync("_ValidationScriptsPartial");}
}
```

As you can see, the generated view contains a form with text boxes for all the Person entity properties.

Generated Edit Razor Model

The generated Edit Razor Page model is in Pages ➤ Contacts ➤ Edit.cshtmlcs and should look like Listing 18-2.

Listing 18-2. Generated Edit Razor Model

```
using System;
using System.Collections.Generic;
using System.Linq;
using System.Threading.Tasks;
using Microsoft.AspNetCore.Mvc;
using Microsoft.AspNetCore.Mvc.RazorPages;
using Microsoft.AspNetCore.Mvc.Rendering;
using Microsoft.EntityFrameworkCore;
using EFCOre5WebApp.DAL;
using EFCore5WebApp.Core.Entities;
```

```
namespace EFCore5WebApp.Pages.Contacts
{
    public class EditModel : PageModel
    {
        private readonly EFCOre5WebApp.DAL.AppDbContext _context;

        public EditModel(EFCOre5WebApp.DAL.AppDbContext context)
        {
            _context = context;
        }

        [BindProperty]
        public Person Person { get; set; }

        public async Task<IActionResult> OnGetAsync(int? id)
        {
            if (id == null)
            {
                return NotFound();
            }

            Person = await _context.Persons.FirstOrDefaultAsync(m => m.Id
            == id);

            if (Person == null)
            {
                return NotFound();
            }
            return Page();
        }

        // To protect from overposting attacks, enable the specific
        properties you want to bind to.
        // For more details, see https://aka.ms/RazorPagesCRUD.
        public async Task<IActionResult> OnPostAsync()
        {
            if (!ModelState.IsValid)
```

```
            {
                return Page();
            }

            _context.Attach(Person).State = EntityState.Modified;

            try
            {
                await _context.SaveChangesAsync();
            }
            catch (DbUpdateConcurrencyException)
            {
                if (!PersonExists(Person.Id))
                {
                    return NotFound();
                }
                else
                {
                    throw;
                }
            }

            return RedirectToPage("./Index");
        }

        private bool PersonExists(int id)
        {
            return _context.Persons.Any(e => e.Id == id);
        }
    }
}
```

The Edit Razor Page model is very similar to the Create page model, but instead of adding a new Person entity, we are retrieving the existing Person entity by its primary key in the OnGetAsync() method for use by the view in this code:

```
Person = await _context.Persons.FirstOrDefaultAsync(m => m.Id == id);
```

The FirstOrDefaultAsync method finds the first record by finding the first item in the Persons collection that has a matching Id value and returns null if the person record isn't found.

In the OnPostAsync() method, we are validating that the model is valid and then updating all properties on the entity by attaching it to the database context and setting the state to modified. This is done in the following code:

```
_context.Attach(Person).State = EntityState.Modified;
```

The Attach() method tells the context that the Person object will be fully modified with the same primary key Id value. This is a quicker way to update a record if you want to update every property value on the record. Then the entity is attempted to be saved, and we check for a concurrency error. This could happen if two users try to edit the person record at the same time or if the person was deleted before the person was attempted to be updated.

Add a Friendly Address Update

Like the Create view, we would like our users to be able to update an address for a Person entity as well. Also, like the Create view, we will use dropdowns for the States and Countries Person properties for a nice user experience. To accomplish this, we will first update the Edit page model and then the Edit view.

Update the Model

Now it is time to update the Edit Razor Page model to load the person's address and populate the model properties for the State and Country dropdowns. First, we add the States and Countries properties and bind them to the model:

```
[BindProperty(SupportsGet = true)]
public List<SelectListItem> States { get; set; }

[BindProperty(SupportsGet = true)]
public List<SelectListItem> Countries { get; set; }
```

Next, we load the States and Countries properties in the OnGetAsync() method:

```
public async Task<IActionResult> OnGetAsync(int? id)
{
    if (id == null)
    {
        return NotFound();
    }

    Person = await _context.Persons.Include(nameof(Person.Addresses)).
    FirstOrDefaultAsync(m => m.Id == id);

    if (Person == null)
    {
        return NotFound();
    }

    var lookups = _context.LookUps.Where(x => new List<LookUpType> {
    LookUpType.State, LookUpType.State }.Contains(x.LookUpType)).ToList();

    States = lookups.Where(x => x.LookUpType == LookUpType.State).
    Select(x => new SelectListItem { Text = x.Description, Value = x.Code
    }).ToList();
    Countries = lookups.Where(x => x.LookUpType == LookUpType.Country).
    Select(x => new SelectListItem { Text = x.Description, Value = x.Code
    }).ToList();

    States.Insert(0, new SelectListItem { Text = "Select an item", Value =
    string.Empty });
    Countries.Insert(0, new SelectListItem { Text = "Select an item", Value
    = string.Empty });

    return Page();
}
```

I used the Contains method to retrieve both the state and country lookups in one database call and then filter down in memory both collections. See Listing 18-3 for the completed Edit model code.

Listing 18-3. Updated Edit Razor Page Model

```
using System;
using System.Collections.Generic;
using System.Linq;
using System.Threading.Tasks;
using Microsoft.AspNetCore.Mvc;
using Microsoft.AspNetCore.Mvc.RazorPages;
using Microsoft.AspNetCore.Mvc.Rendering;
using Microsoft.EntityFrameworkCore;
using EFCOre5WebApp.DAL;
using EFCore5WebApp.Core.Entities;

namespace EFCore5WebApp.Pages.Contacts
{
    public class EditModel : PageModel
    {
        private readonly EFCOre5WebApp.DAL.AppDbContext _context;

        [BindProperty(SupportsGet = true)]
        public List<SelectListItem> States { get; set; }

        [BindProperty(SupportsGet = true)]
        public List<SelectListItem> Countries { get; set; }

        public EditModel(EFCOre5WebApp.DAL.AppDbContext context)
        {
            _context = context;
        }

        [BindProperty]
        public Person Person { get; set; }

        public async Task<IActionResult> OnGetAsync(int? id)
        {
            if (id == null)
            {
                return NotFound();
            }
```

```
        Person = await _context.Persons.Include("Addresses").
        FirstOrDefaultAsync(m => m.Id == id);

        if (Person == null)
        {
            return NotFound();
        }

        States = _context.LookUps.Where(x => x.LookUpType ==
        LookUpType.State).Select(x => new SelectListItem { Text =
        x.Description, Value = x.Code }).ToList();
        Countries = _context.LookUps.Where(x => x.LookUpType ==
        LookUpType.Country).Select(x => new SelectListItem { Text =
        x.Description, Value = x.Code }).ToList();

        States.Insert(0, new SelectListItem { Text = "Select an item",
        Value = string.Empty });
        Countries.Insert(0, new SelectListItem { Text = "Select an
        item", Value = string.Empty });

        return Page();
    }

    // To protect from overposting attacks, enable the specific
    properties you want to bind to.
    // For more details, see https://aka.ms/RazorPagesCRUD.
    public async Task<IActionResult> OnPostAsync()
    {
        if (!ModelState.IsValid)
        {
            return Page();
        }

        _context.Attach(Person).State = EntityState.Modified;

        try
        {
            await _context.SaveChangesAsync();
        }
```

```
            catch (DbUpdateConcurrencyException)
            {
                if (!PersonExists(Person.Id))
                {
                    return NotFound();
                }
                else
                {
                    throw;
                }
            }

            return RedirectToPage("./Index");
        }

        private bool PersonExists(int id)
        {
            return _context.Persons.Any(e => e.Id == id);
        }
    }
}
```

Update the UI

Now it is time to update the Edit Razor Page view to allow editing an address using dropdowns for the States and Countries properties on the address:

```
<div class="col-md-4">
    <div class="form-group">
        <label asp-for="Person.Addresses[0].AddressLine1" class="control-
        label"></label>
        <input asp-for="Person.Addresses[0].AddressLine1" class="form-
        control" />
        <span asp-validation-for="Person.Addresses[0].AddressLine1"
        class="text-danger"></span>
    </div>
    <div class="form-group">
```

```
        <label asp-for="Person.Addresses[0].AddressLine2" class="control-
        label"></label>
        <input asp-for="Person.Addresses[0].AddressLine2" class="form-
        control" />
        <span asp-validation-for="Person.Addresses[0].AddressLine2"
        class="text-danger"></span>
    </div>
    <div class="form-group">
        <label asp-for="Person.Addresses[0].City" class="control-label">
        </label>
        <input asp-for="Person.Addresses[0].City" class="form-control" />
        <span asp-validation-for="Person.Addresses[0].City" class="text-
        danger"></span>
    </div>
    <div class="form-group">
        <label asp-for="Person.Addresses[0].State" class="control-label">
        </label>
        <select asp-for="Person.Addresses[0].State" class="form-control"
        asp-items="Model.States"></select>
        <span asp-validation-for="Person.Addresses[0].State" class="text-
        danger"></span>
    </div>
    <div class="form-group">
        <label asp-for="Person.Addresses[0].Country" class="control-label">
        </label>
        <select asp-for="Person.Addresses[0].Country" class="form-control"
        asp-items="Model.Countries"></select>
        <span asp-validation-for="Person.Addresses[0].Country" class="text-
        danger"></span>
    </div>
    <div class="form-group">
        <label asp-for="Person.Addresses[0].ZipCode" class="control-label">
        </label>
        <input asp-for="Person.Addresses[0].ZipCode" class="form-control" />
```

```
        <span asp-validation-for="Person.Addresses[0].ZipCode" class="text-
        danger"></span>
    </div>
</div>
```

See Listing 18-4 for the completed Edit Razor Page view.

Listing 18-4. Updated Edit Razor Page View

```
@page
@model EFCore5WebApp.Pages.Contacts.EditModel

@{
    ViewData["Title"] = "Edit";
    Layout = "~/Views/Shared/_Layout.cshtml";
}

<h1>Edit</h1>

<h4>Person</h4>
<hr />
<form method="post">
    <div class="row">
        <div class="col-md-4">
            <div asp-validation-summary="ModelOnly" class="text-danger"></div>
            <input type="hidden" asp-for="Person.Id" />
            <div class="form-group">
                <label asp-for="Person.FirstName" class="control-label">
                </label>
                <input asp-for="Person.FirstName" class="form-control" />
                <span asp-validation-for="Person.FirstName" class="text-
                danger"></span>
            </div>
            <div class="form-group">
                <label asp-for="Person.LastName" class="control-label">
                </label>
                <input asp-for="Person.LastName" class="form-control" />
```

```
            <span asp-validation-for="Person.LastName" class="text-
                danger"></span>
        </div>
        <div class="form-group">
            <label asp-for="Person.EmailAddress" class="control-label">
            </label>
            <input asp-for="Person.EmailAddress" class="form-control" />
            <span asp-validation-for="Person.EmailAddress" class="text-
            danger"></span>
        </div>
        <div class="form-group">
            <label asp-for="Person.Age" class="control-label"></label>
            <input asp-for="Person.Age" class="form-control" />
            <span asp-validation-for="Person.Age" class="text-danger">
            </span>
        </div>
    </div>
    <div class="col-md-4">
        <div class="form-group">
            <label asp-for="Person.Addresses[0].AddressLine1"
            class="control-label"></label>
            <input asp-for="Person.Addresses[0].AddressLine1"
            class="form-control" />
            <span asp-validation-for="Person.Addresses[0].AddressLine1"
            class="text-danger"></span>
        </div>
        <div class="form-group">
            <label asp-for="Person.Addresses[0].AddressLine2"
            class="control-label"></label>
            <input asp-for="Person.Addresses[0].AddressLine2"
            class="form-control" />
            <span asp-validation-for="Person.Addresses[0].AddressLine2"
            class="text-danger"></span>
        </div>
        <div class="form-group">
```

```
            <label asp-for="Person.Addresses[0].City" class="control-
            label"></label>
            <input asp-for="Person.Addresses[0].City" class="form-
            control" />
            <span asp-validation-for="Person.Addresses[0].City"
            class="text-danger"></span>
        </div>
        <div class="form-group">
            <label asp-for="Person.Addresses[0].State" class="control-
            label"></label>
            <select asp-for="Person.Addresses[0].State" class="form-
            control" asp-items="Model.States"></select>
            <span asp-validation-for="Person.Addresses[0].State"
            class="text-danger"></span>
        </div>
        <div class="form-group">
            <label asp-for="Person.Addresses[0].Country"
            class="control-label"></label>
            <select asp-for="Person.Addresses[0].Country" class="form-
            control" asp-items="Model.Countries"></select>
            <span asp-validation-for="Person.Addresses[0].Country"
            class="text-danger"></span>
        </div>
        <div class="form-group">
            <label asp-for="Person.Addresses[0].ZipCode"
            class="control-label"></label>
            <input asp-for="Person.Addresses[0].ZipCode" class="form-
            control" />
            <span asp-validation-for="Person.Addresses[0].ZipCode"
            class="text-danger"></span>
        </div>
    </div>
</div>
```

```
    <div class="row">
        <div class="form-group">
            <input type="submit" value="Edit" class="btn btn-primary" />
        </div>
    </div>
</form>

<div>
    <a asp-page="./Index">Back to List</a>
</div>

@section Scripts {
    @{await Html.RenderPartialAsync("_ValidationScriptsPartial");}
}
```

Running the App

Now it is time to test our Edit form. Run the app and use the Edit link on the main Contacts page to edit a contact record. You should now see the completed Edit as seen in Figure 18-1.

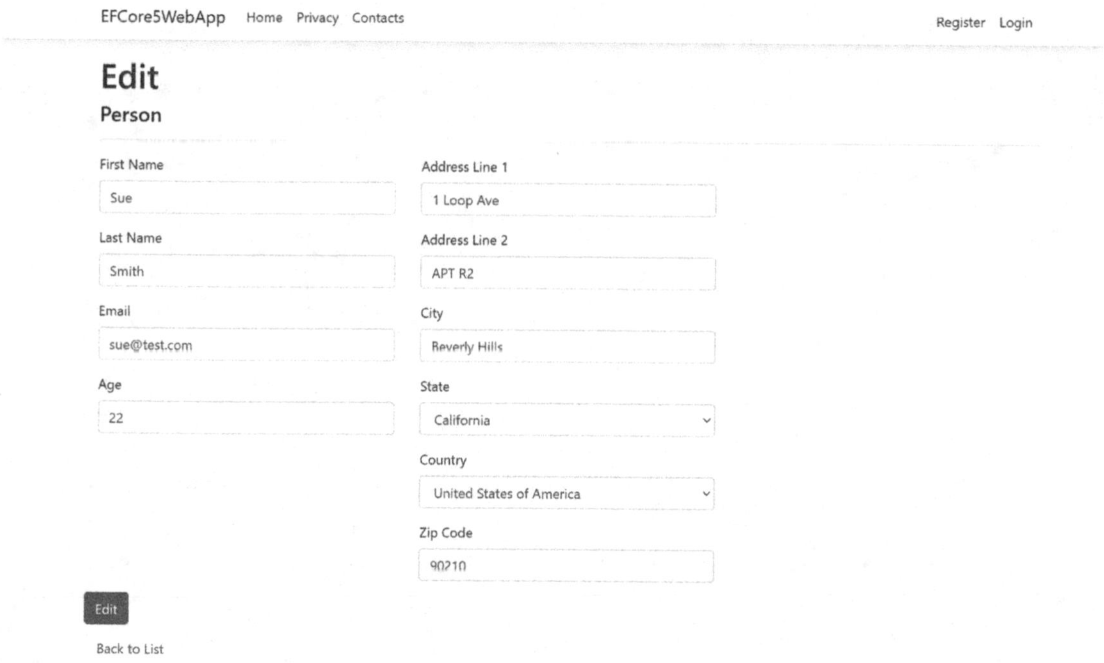

Figure 18-1. *Completed Edit Page*

Summary

In this chapter, I covered how to edit a person record and an associated address record for them. In the next chapter, I will cover how to delete a person record and their associated address records.

CHAPTER 19

Deleting Data on the Web

In this chapter, I will cover how to delete a person record and their associated address record by updating the generated Delete Razor page controller code. There will be no UI changes needed.

Generated Delete Razor Page View

First, let us look at the generated Delete Razor Page view in Pages ➤ Contacts ➤ Delete.cshtml. Your view should look like Listing 19-1.

Listing 19-1. Generated Delete Razor Page View

```
@page
@model EFCore5WebApp.Pages.Contacts.DeleteModel

@{
    ViewData["Title"] = "Delete";
    Layout = "~/Views/Shared/_Layout.cshtml";
}

<h1>Delete</h1>

<h3>Are you sure you want to delete this?</h3>
<div>
    <h4>Person</h4>
    <hr />
    <dl class="row">
        <dt class="col-sm-2">
            @Html.DisplayNameFor(model => model.Person.FirstName)
        </dt>
```


E. Vogel, *Beginning Entity Framework Core 5*, https://doi.org/10.1007/978-1-4842-6882-7_19

```
        <dd class="col-sm-10">
            @Html.DisplayFor(model => model.Person.FirstName)
        </dd>
        <dt class="col-sm-2">
            @Html.DisplayNameFor(model => model.Person.LastName)
        </dt>
        <dd class="col-sm-10">
            @Html.DisplayFor(model => model.Person.LastName)
        </dd>
        <dt class="col-sm-2">
            @Html.DisplayNameFor(model => model.Person.EmailAddress)
        </dt>
        <dd class="col-sm-10">
            @Html.DisplayFor(model => model.Person.EmailAddress)
        </dd>
        <dt class="col-sm-2">
            @Html.DisplayNameFor(model => model.Person.CreatedOn)
        </dt>
        <dd class="col-sm-10">
            @Html.DisplayFor(model => model.Person.CreatedOn)
        </dd>
        <dt class="col-sm-2">
            @Html.DisplayNameFor(model => model.Person.Age)
        </dt>
        <dd class="col-sm-10">
            @Html.DisplayFor(model => model.Person.Age)
        </dd>
    </dl>

    <form method="post">
        <input type="hidden" asp-for="Person.Id" />
        <input type="submit" value="Delete" class="btn btn-danger" /> |
        <a asp-page="./Index">Back to List</a>
    </form>
</div>
```

You can see the user will get the person record details and have a Delete button on the bottom of the page.

Generated Model

You will also see the generated Delete Razor page controller code in Pages ➤ Contacts ➤ Delete.cshtml.cs as seen in Listing 19-2.

Listing 19-2. Generated Delete Razor Model

```
using System;
using System.Collections.Generic;
using System.Linq;
using System.Threading.Tasks;
using Microsoft.AspNetCore.Mvc;
using Microsoft.AspNetCore.Mvc.RazorPages;
using Microsoft.EntityFrameworkCore;
using EFCOre5WebApp.DAL;
using EFCore5WebApp.Core.Entities;

namespace EFCore5WebApp.Pages.Contacts
{
    public class DeleteModel : PageModel
    {
        private readonly EFCOre5WebApp.DAL.AppDbContext _context;

        public DeleteModel(EFCOre5WebApp.DAL.AppDbContext context)
        {
            _context = context;
        }

        [BindProperty]
        public Person Person { get; set; }

        public async Task<IActionResult> OnGetAsync(int? id)
        {
            if (id == null)
```

```
            {
                return NotFound();
            }

            Person = await _context.Persons.FirstOrDefaultAsync(m => m.Id
            == id);

            if (Person == null)
            {
                return NotFound();
            }
            return Page();
        }

        public async Task<IActionResult> OnPostAsync(int? id)
        {
            if (id == null)
            {
                return NotFound();
            }

            Person = await _context.Persons.FindAsync(id);

            if (Person != null)
            {
                _context.Persons.Remove(Person);
                await _context.SaveChangesAsync();
            }

            return RedirectToPage("./Index");
        }
    }
}
```

If you try to run the generated Delete page and try to delete a person, you will get an error saying that there is a foreign key constraint violation on the Addresses table PersonId column. Let us fix that now.

Updating Page Controller Code to Delete Addresses

The error is caused by a foreign key constraint in the database on the person's address records. When we are deleting the person record, we aren't deleting their associated address records. We will delete the person's address records in the Delete Razor model by eager loading the person's addresses in the OnPostAsync() method. This will cause a cascade delete to be performed on the associated address records for the person as seen in the following:

```
public async Task<IActionResult> OnPostAsync(int? id)
{
    if (id == null)
    {
        return NotFound();
    }

    Person = await _context.Persons.Include(nameof(Person.Addresses)).
    SingleOrDefaultAsync(x => x.Id == id);

    if (Person != null)
    {
        _context.Persons.Remove(Person);
        await _context.SaveChangesAsync();
    }

    return RedirectToPage("./Index");
}
```

See the completed Delete model class in Listing 19-3.

Listing 19-3. Fixed Delete Razor Page Controller

```
using System;
using System.Collections.Generic;
using System.Linq;
using System.Threading.Tasks;
using Microsoft.AspNetCore.Mvc;
using Microsoft.AspNetCore.Mvc.RazorPages;
using Microsoft.EntityFrameworkCore;
using EFCOre5WebApp.DAL;
using EFCore5WebApp.Core.Entities;

namespace EFCore5WebApp.Pages.Contacts
{
    public class DeleteModel : PageModel
    {
        private readonly EFCOre5WebApp.DAL.AppDbContext _context;

        public DeleteModel(EFCOre5WebApp.DAL.AppDbContext context)
        {
            _context = context;
        }

        [BindProperty]
        public Person Person { get; set; }

        public async Task<IActionResult> OnGetAsync(int? id)
        {
            if (id == null)
            {
                return NotFound();
            }

            Person = await _context.Persons.FirstOrDefaultAsync(m => m.Id
            == id);
```

```
            if (Person == null)
            {
                return NotFound();
            }
            return Page();
        }

        public async Task<IActionResult> OnPostAsync(int? id)
        {
            if (id == null)
            {
                return NotFound();
            }

            Person = await _context.Persons.Include(nameof(Person.
            Addresses)).SingleOrDefaultAsync(x => x.Id == id);

            if (Person != null)
            {
                _context.Persons.Remove(Person);
                await _context.SaveChangesAsync();
            }

            return RedirectToPage("./Index");
        }
    }
}
```

Running the App

You can now run the app and see the Delete form as seen in Figure 19-1.

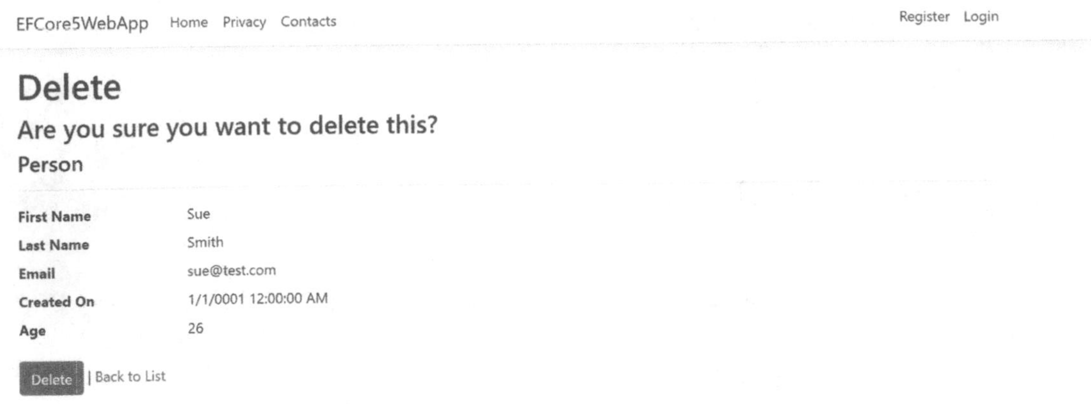

Figure 19-1. Delete Razor Page

After you delete the person, you will now see them removed from the main Contacts form as seen in Figure 19-2.

EFCore5WebApp Home Privacy Contacts Register Login

Index

Create New

First Name	Last Name	Email	Created On	Age	
John	Smith	john@smith.com	1/1/0001 12:00:00 AM	20	Edit | Details | Delete
Susan	Jones	john@smith.com	1/1/0001 12:00:00 AM	30	Edit | Details | Delete
Nate	Burns	nate@test.com	9/24/2020 6:56:21 PM	44	Edit | Details | Delete

Figure 19-2. Person Was Deleted

Showing a Person's Address on the Delete Form

To keep our app consistent, we will also update the Delete form to display the person's addresses. We will first update the Delete model to eager load the person's addresses and then update the UI to display them.

Update the Page Controller

To eager load the person's address records, all we need to do is use the Include method in the FirstOrDefaultAsync() call in the OnGetAsync() Delete page controller as seen in Listing 19-4.

Listing 19-4. Eager Loading Addresses in the Delete Page Controller

```
public async Task<IActionResult> OnGetAsync(int? id)
{
    if (id == null)
    {
        return NotFound();
    }

    Person = await _context.Persons.Include(nameof(Person.Addresses)).
    FirstOrDefaultAsync(m => m.Id == id);

    if (Person == null)
    {
        return NotFound();
    }
    return Page();
}
```

Update the UI

Now we will update the Delete UI to display any address records for the person being removed by adding an HTML table in our Razor view:

```
<table class="table">
    <thead>
        <tr>
            <th>
                @Html.DisplayNameFor(model => model.Person.Addresses.
                First().AddressLine1)
            </th>
            <th>
                @Html.DisplayNameFor(model => model.Person.Addresses.
                First().AddressLine2)
            </th>
```

```
            <th>
                @Html.DisplayNameFor(model => model.Person.Addresses.
                First().City)
            </th>
            <th>
                @Html.DisplayNameFor(model => model.Person.Addresses.
                First().State)
            </th>
            <th>
                @Html.DisplayNameFor(model => model.Person.Addresses.
                First().Country)
            </th>
            <th>
                @Html.DisplayNameFor(model => model.Person.Addresses.
                First().ZipCode)
            </th>
            <th></th>
        </tr>
    </thead>
    <tbody>
        @foreach (var item in Model.Person.Addresses)
        {
            <tr>
                <td>
                    @Html.DisplayFor(modelItem => item.AddressLine1)
                </td>
                <td>
                    @Html.DisplayFor(modelItem => item.AddressLine2)
                </td>
                <td>
                    @Html.DisplayFor(modelItem => item.City)
                </td>
                <td>
                    @Html.DisplayFor(modelItem => item.State)
                </td>
```

```
                <td>
                    @Html.DisplayFor(modelItem => item.Country)
                </td>
                <td>
                    @Html.DisplayFor(modelItem => item.ZipCode)
                </td>
            </tr>
        }
    </tbody>
</table>
```

See the completed Delete Razor view in Listing 19-5.

Listing 19-5. Delete Razor View with Addresses

```
@page
@model EFCore5WebApp.Pages.Contacts.DeleteModel

@{
    ViewData["Title"] = "Delete";
    Layout = "~/Views/Shared/_Layout.cshtml";
}

<h1>Delete</h1>

<h3>Are you sure you want to delete this?</h3>
<div>
    <h4>Person</h4>
    <hr />
    <dl class="row">
        <dt class="col-sm-2">
            @Html.DisplayNameFor(model => model.Person.FirstName)
        </dt>
        <dd class="col-sm-10">
            @Html.DisplayFor(model => model.Person.FirstName)
        </dd>
```

```
        <dt class="col-sm-2">
            @Html.DisplayNameFor(model => model.Person.LastName)
        </dt>
        <dd class="col-sm-10">
            @Html.DisplayFor(model => model.Person.LastName)
        </dd>
        <dt class="col-sm-2">
            @Html.DisplayNameFor(model => model.Person.EmailAddress)
        </dt>
        <dd class="col-sm-10">
            @Html.DisplayFor(model => model.Person.EmailAddress)
        </dd>
        <dt class="col-sm-2">
            @Html.DisplayNameFor(model => model.Person.CreatedOn)
        </dt>
        <dd class="col-sm-10">
            @Html.DisplayFor(model => model.Person.CreatedOn)
        </dd>
        <dt class="col-sm-2">
            @Html.DisplayNameFor(model => model.Person.Age)
        </dt>
        <dd class="col-sm-10">
            @Html.DisplayFor(model => model.Person.Age)
        </dd>
    </dl>

    <table class="table">
        <thead>
            <tr>
                <th>
                    @Html.DisplayNameFor(model => model.Person.Addresses.
                    First().AddressLine1)
                </th>
                <th>
                    @Html.DisplayNameFor(model => model.Person.Addresses.
                    First().AddressLine2)
                </th>
```

```
            <th>
                @Html.DisplayNameFor(model => model.Person.Addresses.
                First().City)
            </th>
            <th>
                @Html.DisplayNameFor(model => model.Person.Addresses.
                First().State)
            </th>
            <th>
                @Html.DisplayNameFor(model => model.Person.Addresses.
                First().Country)
            </th>
            <th>
                @Html.DisplayNameFor(model => model.Person.Addresses.
                First().ZipCode)
            </th>
            <th></th>
        </tr>
    </thead>
    <tbody>
        @foreach (var item in Model.Person.Addresses)
        {
            <tr>
                <td>
                    @Html.DisplayFor(modelItem => item.AddressLine1)
                </td>
                <td>
                    @Html.DisplayFor(modelItem => item.AddressLine2)
                </td>
                <td>
                    @Html.DisplayFor(modelItem => item.City)
                </td>
                <td>
                    @Html.DisplayFor(modelItem => item.State)
                </td>
```

```
                <td>
                    @Html.DisplayFor(modelItem => item.Country)
                </td>
                <td>
                    @Html.DisplayFor(modelItem => item.ZipCode)
                </td>
            </tr>
        }
    </tbody>
</table>

<form method="post">
    <input type="hidden" asp-for="Person.Id" />
    <input type="submit" value="Delete" class="btn btn-danger" /> |
    <a asp-page="./Index">Back to List</a>
</form>
</div>
```

You can now see the fruits of your labor in Figure 19-3.

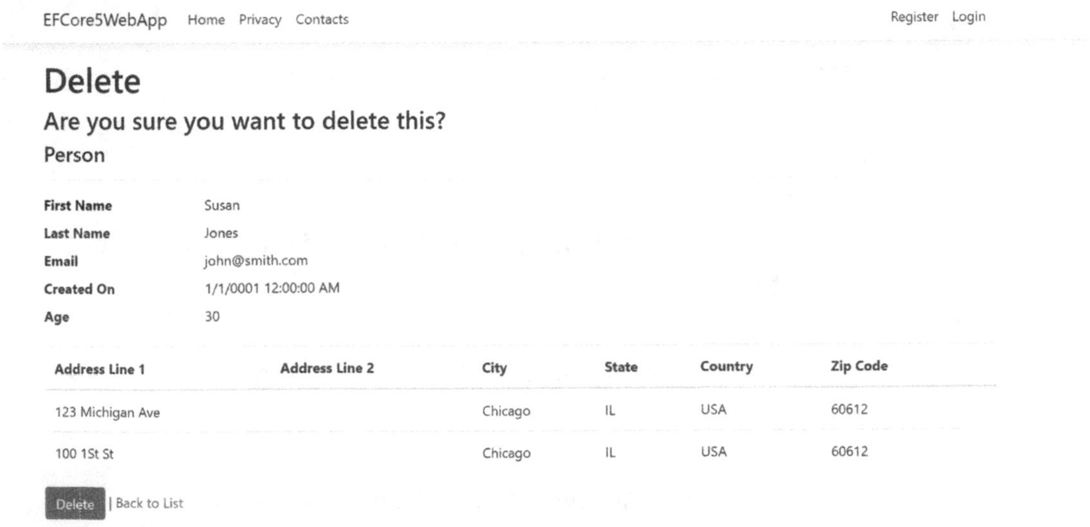

Figure 19-3. *Delete Form with Addresses*

Summary

In this chapter, I covered how to delete a person record and their associated address record by updating the generated Delete Razor page controller code. I also showed how to update the generated Delete view to load and display addresses for the person. In the next chapter, I will go over how to create and view reports that gather data via Entity Framework Core 5 and display them using ASP.NET Core Razor Pages.

CHAPTER 20

Reporting on the Web

In this chapter, I will show how to create a simple report that displays all person records in the database sorted by last name and then first name. We will be using Entity Framework Core 5 to aggregate the data and a custom Razor Page to display the report as an HTML table. After we have the report working, we'll add pagination to it.

Creating the Razor Page

To get started, add a new folder under the Pages directory in your web project named "Reports". Then add a new Razor Page template file named "PeopleReport.cshtml" as seen in Figure 20-1.

E. Vogel, *Beginning Entity Framework Core 5*, https://doi.org/10.1007/978-1-4842-6882-7_20

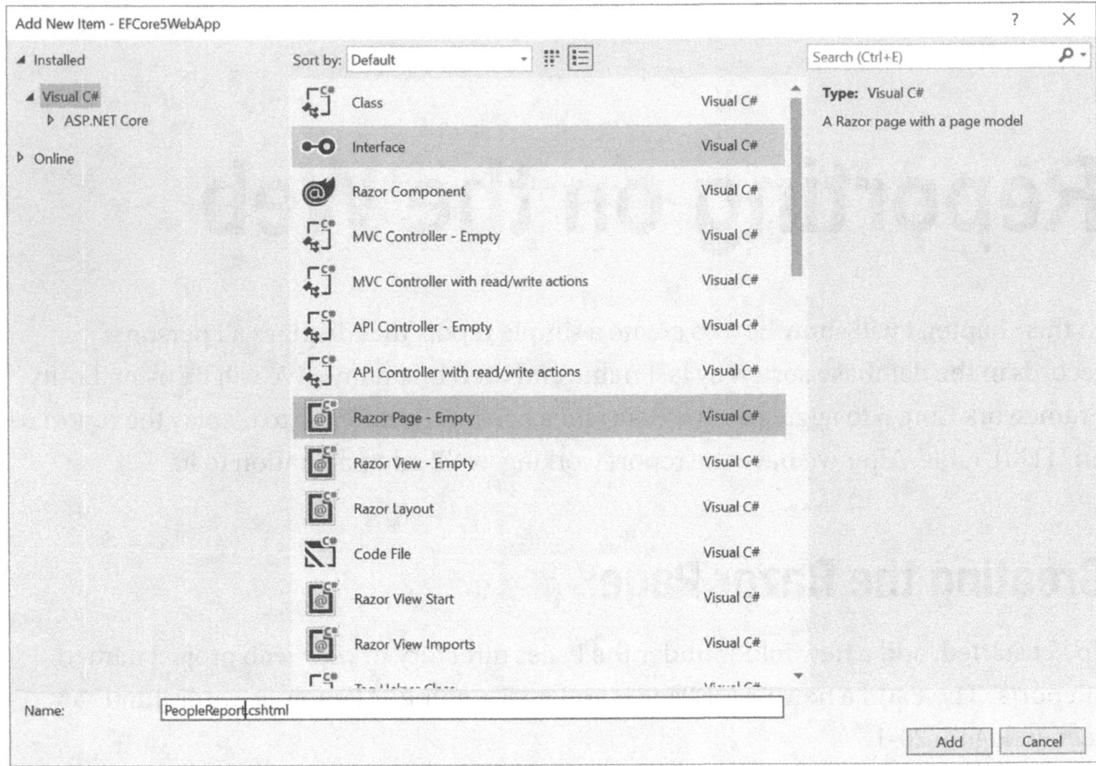

Figure 20-1. *Adding a People Razor Page*

This will add empty PeopleReport.cshtml and PeopleReport.cshtml.cs files under the Pages ➤ Reports folder.

Updating the Razor Model

Now let's update the PeopleReport.cshtml.cs model file to retrieve all person records in the database ordered by last name and then first name as seen in Listing 20-1.

Listing 20-1. People Report Razor Model

```
using System.Collections.Generic;
using System.Linq;
using System.Threading.Tasks;
using Microsoft.AspNetCore.Mvc.RazorPages;
using EFCore5WebApp.Core.Entities;
using Microsoft.EntityFrameworkCore;
```

```
namespace EFCore5WebApp.Pages.Reports
{
    public class PeopleReportModel : PageModel
    {
        private readonly EFCOre5WebApp.DAL.AppDbContext _context;

        public List<Person> ReportData { get; set; }

        public PeopleReportModel(EFCOre5WebApp.DAL.AppDbContext context)
        {
            _context = context;
        }

        public async Task OnGetAsync(int? pageIndex)
        {
            var persons = await (from p in _context.Persons
                                 orderby p.LastName, p.FirstName
                                 select p).ToListAsync();

            ReportData = persons;
        }
    }
}
```

We sort the person records using the LINQ syntax like this:

```
var persons = await (from p in _context.Persons
                     orderby p.LastName, p.FirstName
                     select p).ToListAsync();
```

The ReportData property will be bound to the Razor view next.

Updating the Razor View

Now we will update the Razor Page view to display a list of person records in an HTML table as seen in Listing 20-2.

Listing 20-2. People Report Razor View

```
@page
@model EFCore5WebApp.Pages.Reports.PeopleReportModel

@{
    ViewData["Title"] = "PeopleByState";
    Layout = "~/Views/Shared/_Layout.cshtml";
}

<h1>People</h1>

<table class="table">
    <thead>
        <tr>
            <th>
                @Html.DisplayNameFor(model => Model.ReportData.First().
                LastName)
            </th>
            <th>
                @Html.DisplayNameFor(model => Model.ReportData.First().
                FirstName)
            </th>
            <th>
                @Html.DisplayNameFor(model => Model.ReportData.First().
                EmailAddress)
            </th>
            <th>
                @Html.DisplayNameFor(model => Model.ReportData.First().Age)
            </th>
            <th></th>
        </tr>
    </thead>
    <tbody>
        @foreach (var record in Model.ReportData)
```

```
        {
            <tr>
                <td>
                    @Html.DisplayFor(modelItem => record.LastName)
                </td>
                <td>
                    @Html.DisplayFor(modelItem => record.FirstName)
                </td>
                <td>
                    @Html.DisplayFor(modelItem => record.EmailAddress)
                </td>
                <td>
                    @Html.DisplayFor(modelItem => record.Age)
                </td>
            </tr>
        }
    </tbody>
</table>
```

The HTML is fairly basic; and we display the person's last name, first name, email address, and age in the table.

Add a Link to Navigation

Now we will make our report easily accessible from the main menu of the site in the Views/Shared/_Layout.cshtml file layout Razor partial view. We simply add a new list item to display a link to our report in the nav bar ul list:

```
<li class="nav-item">
    <a class="nav-link text-dark" asp-page="/Reports/PeopleReport">Report
    </a>
</li>
```

See Listing 20-3 for the updated _Layout.cshtml Razor view.

Listing 20-3. Report Menu Item Added to Layout Template

```
<!DOCTYPE html>
<html lang="en">
<head>
    <meta charset="utf-8" />
    <meta name="viewport" content="width=device-width, initial-scale=1.0" />
    <title>@ViewData["Title"] - EFCore5WebApp</title>
    <link rel="stylesheet" href="~/lib/bootstrap/dist/css/bootstrap.min.
    css" />
    <link rel="stylesheet" href="~/css/site.css" />
</head>

<body>
    <header>
        <nav class="navbar navbar-expand-sm navbar-toggleable-sm navbar-
        light bg-white border-bottom box-shadow mb-3">
            <div class="container">
                <a class="navbar-brand" asp-area="" asp-controller="Home"
                asp-action="Index">EFCore5WebApp</a>
                <button class="navbar-toggler" type="button" data-
                toggle="collapse" data-target=".navbar-collapse" aria-
                controls="navbarSupportedContent"
                        aria-expanded="false" aria-label="Toggle
                        navigation">
                    <span class="navbar-toggler-icon"></span>
                </button>
                <div class="navbar-collapse collapse d-sm-inline-flex flex-
                sm-row-reverse">
                    <partial name="_LoginPartial" />
                    <ul class="navbar-nav flex-grow-1">
                        <li class="nav-item">
                            <a class="nav-link text-dark" asp-area="" asp-
                            controller="Home" asp-action="Index">Home</a>
                        </li>
                        <li class="nav-item">
```

```
                        <a class="nav-link text-dark" asp-
                        area="" asp-controller="Home" asp-
                        action="Privacy">Privacy</a>
                    </li>
                    <li class="nav-item">
                        <a class="nav-link text-dark" asp-page="/
                       Contacts/Index">Contacts</a>
                    </li>
                    <li class="nav-item">
                        <a class="nav-link text-dark" asp-page="/
                        Reports/PeopleReport">Report</a>
                    </li>
                </ul>
            </div>
        </div>
    </nav>
</header>
<div class="container">
    <main role="main" class="pb-3">
        @RenderBody()
    </main>
</div>
<footer class="border-top footer text-muted">
    <div class="container">
        &copy; 2020 - EFCore5WebApp - <a asp-area="" asp-
        controller="Home" asp-action="Privacy">Privacy</a>
    </div>
</footer>
<script src="~/lib/jquery/dist/jquery.min.js"></script>
<script src="~/lib/bootstrap/dist/js/bootstrap.bundle.min.js"></script>
<script src="~/js/site.js" asp-append-version="true"></script>
@await RenderSectionAsync("Scripts", required: false)
</body>
</html>
```

Running the Report

You can now run the report by clicking the Report menu item. The current report should look like Figure 20-2.

EFCore5WebApp Home Privacy Contacts Report
Register Login
People
Last Name First Name Email Age
Jones Susan john@smith.com 30
Smith John john@smith.com 20
© 2020 - EFCore5WebApp - Privacy

***Figure 20-2.** People Report Page*

Adding Pagination

Now it is time to add pagination to the report. We will allow the user to navigate using previous and next buttons. When there isn't a previous or next page, the appropriate button will be disabled. We will first add some more test data to the database; then we will update the Razor model and Razor view to have pagination.

Adding Sample Data

Open the AppDbContext class file in the DAL project. In the OnModelCreating code, find this block toward the end of the method:

```
modelBuilder.Entity<Person>().HasData(new List<Person>()
{
    new Person(){ Id = 1, FirstName = "John", LastName = "Smith",
    EmailAddress = "john@smith.com", Age = 20 },
    new Person(){ Id = 2, FirstName = "Susan", LastName = "Jones",
    EmailAddress = "john@smith.com", Age = 30 }
});
```

We are using the HasData() method to see data in the database. We will now update this code block to match Listing 20-4.

Listing 20-4. Seed Person Data for Pagination

```
modelBuilder.Entity<Person>().HasData(new List<Person>()
{
    new Person(){ Id = 1, FirstName = "John", LastName = "Smith",
    EmailAddress = "john@smith.com", Age = 20 },
    new Person(){ Id = 2, FirstName = "Susan", LastName = "Jones",
    EmailAddress = "john@smith.com", Age = 30 },
    new Person(){ Id = 3, FirstName = "Jane", LastName = "Foster",
    EmailAddress = "john@smith.com", Age = 31 },
    new Person(){ Id = 4, FirstName = "Burt", LastName = "Reynolds",
    EmailAddress = "john@smith.com", Age = 32 },
    new Person(){ Id = 5, FirstName = "Maisie", LastName = "Williams",
    EmailAddress = "john@smith.com", Age = 33 },
    new Person(){ Id = 6, FirstName = "Kit", LastName = "Harrington",
    EmailAddress = "john@smith.com", Age = 34 },
    new Person(){ Id = 7, FirstName = "Sophie", LastName = "Turner",
    EmailAddress = "john@smith.com", Age = 35 },
    new Person(){ Id = 8, FirstName = "Lena", LastName = "Headey",
    EmailAddress = "john@smith.com", Age = 36 },
    new Person(){ Id = 9, FirstName = "Peter", LastName = "Dinklage",
    EmailAddress = "john@smith.com", Age = 37 },
    new Person(){ Id = 10, FirstName = "Nikolaj", LastName = "Coster-
    Waldau", EmailAddress = "john@smith.com", Age = 38 },
    new Person(){ Id = 11, FirstName = "Gwendoline", LastName = "Christie",
    EmailAddress = "john@smith.com", Age = 39 },
```

```
new Person(){ Id = 12, FirstName = "Isac", LastName = "Hempstead",
EmailAddress = "john@smith.com", Age = 40 },
new Person(){ Id = 13, FirstName = "Iain", LastName = "Glen",
EmailAddress = "john@smith.com", Age = 20 },
new Person(){ Id = 14, FirstName = "Alfie", LastName = "Allen",
EmailAddress = "john@smith.com", Age = 21 },
new Person(){ Id = 15, FirstName = "Nathalie", LastName = "Emmanuel",
EmailAddress = "john@smith.com", Age = 22 },
new Person(){ Id = 16, FirstName = "Carice", LastName = "van Houten",
EmailAddress = "john@smith.com", Age = 23 },
new Person(){ Id = 17, FirstName = "Conleth", LastName = "Hil",
EmailAddress = "john@smith.com", Age = 24 },
new Person(){ Id = 18, FirstName = "John", LastName = "Bradley",
EmailAddress = "john@smith.com", Age = 25 },
new Person(){ Id = 19, FirstName = "Liam", LastName = "Cunningham",
EmailAddress = "john@smith.com", Age = 26 },
new Person(){ Id = 20, FirstName = "Aidan", LastName = "Gillen",
EmailAddress = "john@smith.com", Age = 27 },
new Person(){ Id = 21, FirstName = "Jason", LastName = "Mamoa",
EmailAddress = "john@smith.com", Age = 28 },
new Person(){ Id = 22, FirstName = "Natalie", LastName = "Dormer",
EmailAddress = "john@smith.com", Age = 29 },
new Person(){ Id = 23, FirstName = "Richard", LastName = "Madden",
EmailAddress = "john@smith.com", Age = 30 },
new Person(){ Id = 24, FirstName = "Rosie", LastName = "Leslie",
EmailAddress = "john@smith.com", Age = 31 },
new Person(){ Id = 25, FirstName = "Jerome", LastName = "Flynn",
EmailAddress = "john@smith.com", Age = 32 },
new Person(){ Id = 26, FirstName = "Kristofer", LastName = "Hivju",
EmailAddress = "john@smith.com", Age = 33 },
new Person(){ Id = 27, FirstName = "Jacob", LastName = "Anderson",
EmailAddress = "john@smith.com", Age = 34 },
new Person(){ Id = 28, FirstName = "Jack", LastName = "Gleeson",
EmailAddress = "john@smith.com", Age = 35 },
```

```
        new Person(){ Id = 29, FirstName = "Hannah", LastName = "Murray",
        EmailAddress = "john@smith.com", Age = 36 },
        new Person(){ Id = 30, FirstName = "Sean", LastName = "Bean",
        EmailAddress = "john@smith.com", Age = 37 },
        new Person(){ Id = 31, FirstName = "Charles", LastName = "Dance",
        EmailAddress = "john@smith.com", Age = 38 },
        new Person(){ Id = 32, FirstName = "Michelle", LastName = "Fairley",
        EmailAddress = "john@smith.com", Age = 39 },
});
```

Now add a migration named "MorePersonData" by typing "Add-Migration MorePersonData" in the NuGet Package Manager Console. Next, run the migration by running "Update-Database" in the NuGet Package Manager Console.

Adding Pagination Support

Now it is time to add a generic pagination class to our DAL project named PaginatedList as seen in Listing 20-5. You can find the full details of the class at `https://docs.microsoft.com/en-us/aspnet/core/data/ef-rp/sort-filter-page?view=aspnetcore-5.0` in the Microsoft sample docs for Entity Framework Core 5.

Listing 20-5. PaginatedList Class

```
using Microsoft.EntityFrameworkCore;
using System;
using System.Collections.Generic;
using System.Linq;
using System.Text;
using System.Threading.Tasks;

namespace EFCore5WebApp.DAL
{
    public class PaginatedList<T> : List<T>
    {
        public int PageIndex { get; private set; }
        public int TotalPages { get; private set; }
```

```
        public PaginatedList(List<T> items, int count, int pageIndex, int
        pageSize)
        {
            PageIndex = pageIndex;
            TotalPages = (int)Math.Ceiling(count / (double)pageSize);

            this.AddRange(items);
        }

        public bool HasPreviousPage
        {
            get
            {
                return (PageIndex > 1);
            }
        }

        public bool HasNextPage
        {
            get
            {
                return (PageIndex < TotalPages);
            }
        }

        public static async Task<PaginatedList<T>> CreateAsync(
            IQueryable<T> source, int pageIndex, int pageSize)
        {
            var count = await source.CountAsync();
            var items = await source.Skip(
                (pageIndex - 1) * pageSize)
                .Take(pageSize).ToListAsync();
            return new PaginatedList<T>(items, count, pageIndex, pageSize);
        }
    }
}
```

Updating the Model for Pagination

Now we are going to update the PeopleReportModel class to use our PaginatedList class to support pagination. First, we change our ReportData property to be of type PaginatedList<Person>:

```
public PaginatedList<Person> ReportData { get; set; }
```

Next, we update the OnGetAsync() method to call the PaginatedList<T>. CreateAsync() method with a page size of 10 and defaulting to page 1. We also pass in the current page to the OnGetAsync() method:

```
public async Task OnGetAsync(int? pageIndex)
{
    int pageSize = 10;

    var persons = from p in _context.Persons
                  orderby p.LastName, p.FirstName
                  select p;

    ReportData = await PaginatedList<Person>.CreateAsync(
        persons, pageIndex ?? 1, pageSize);
}
```

Your completed PeopleReportModel should now look like Listing 20-6.

Listing 20-6. Completed PeopleReportModel Class

```
using System.Linq;
using System.Threading.Tasks;
using Microsoft.AspNetCore.Mvc.RazorPages;
using EFCore5WebApp.Core.Entities;
using EFCore5WebApp.DAL;

namespace EFCore5WebApp.Pages.Reports
{
    public class PeopleReportModel : PageModel
    {
        private readonly EFCOre5WebApp.DAL.AppDbContext _context;

        public PaginatedList<Person> ReportData { get; set; }
```

```
        public PeopleReportModel(EFCOre5WebApp.DAL.AppDbContext context)
        {
            _context = context;
        }

        public async Task OnGetAsync(int? pageIndex)
        {
            int pageSize = 10;

            var persons = from p in _context.Persons
                          orderby p.LastName, p.FirstName
                          select p;

            ReportData = await PaginatedList<Person>.CreateAsync(
                persons, pageIndex ?? 1, pageSize);
        }
    }
}
```

Add Pagination to the Razor View

The last step is to add pagination buttons to our Report Razor view. We will be adding the following code to the end of the view:

```
@{
    var prevDisabled = !Model.ReportData.HasPreviousPage ? "disabled" : "";
    var nextDisabled = !Model.ReportData.HasNextPage ? "disabled" : "";
}

<a asp-page="/Reports/PeopleReport"
   asp-route-pageIndex="@(Model.ReportData.PageIndex - 1)"
   class="btn btn-primary @prevDisabled">
    Previous
</a>
<a asp-page="/Reports/PeopleReport"
   asp-route-pageIndex="@(Model.ReportData.PageIndex + 1)"
   class="btn btn-primary @nextDisabled">
    Next
</a>
```

The prevDisabled and nextDisabled variables indicate if the previous and next buttons should be disabled accordingly. After that, we add the previous button that links to the report and passes in the pageIndex variable as the current page minus one. Lastly, we add the next button that points to the report page and passes in the current page index plus one as its value.

Running the Finished Report

You should now be able to run the report and use pagination as seen in Figure 20-3.

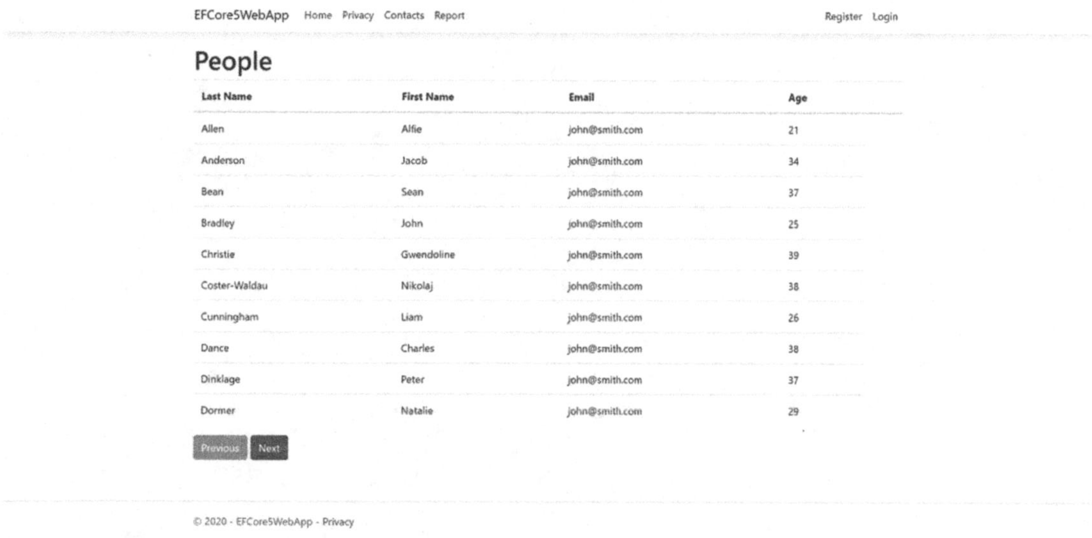

EFCore5WebApp Home Privacy Contacts Report Register Login

People

Last Name	First Name	Email	Age
Allen	Alfie	john@smith.com	21
Anderson	Jacob	john@smith.com	34
Bean	Sean	john@smith.com	37
Bradley	John	john@smith.com	25
Christie	Gwendoline	john@smith.com	39
Coster-Waldau	Nikolaj	john@smith.com	38
Cunningham	Liam	john@smith.com	26
Dance	Charles	john@smith.com	38
Dinklage	Peter	john@smith.com	37
Dormer	Natalie	john@smith.com	29

Previous Next

© 2020 - EFCore5WebApp - Privacy

Figure 20-3. *Report with Pagination*

Summary

In this chapter, I have shown how to put our knowledge of querying data with Entity Framework Core 5 with our knowledge of Razor Pages learned in the past few chapters together to create a web report. In the next chapter, I will cover authorization on the Web using Entity Framework Core 5.

CHAPTER 21

Authorization on the Web

In this chapter, I will cover how to enforce authentication and enable role-based security in our web app. I will first cover how to enable roles. Then we will create two roles and create two test users that each have a role. Lastly, we will update the app to enforce these roles. We will create a view role and an admin role. The view role will allow the user to view contacts, and the admin role will allow everything.

Enable Roles

The first step is to enable roles within our web app. This is simple enough. Open up the Startup class and find this statement:

```
services.AddDefaultIdentity<IdentityUser>(options => options.SignIn.
RequireConfirmedAccount = true)
    .AddEntityFrameworkStores<AppDbContext>();
```

Now we will update Identity configuration to add roles like this:

```
services.AddDefaultIdentity<IdentityUser>(options => options.SignIn.
RequireConfirmedAccount = true)
    .AddRoles<IdentityRole>()
   .AddEntityFrameworkStores<AppDbContext>();
```

Add Test Users

Run the app and register two users; the first will be the view-only user, and the second will be the admin user. Create two users with the email addresses viewonly@test.com and admin@test.com, respectively.

E. Vogel, *Beginning Entity Framework Core 5*, https://doi.org/10.1007/978-1-4842-6882-7_21

Add and Assign Roles on Startup

Due to the asynchronous nature of the RoleManager and UserManager classes, we will be adding and assigning roles in the Program class on the app rather than directly in the Startup class. First, let us look over the full code in Listing 21-1, and then I will break it down.

Listing 21-1. Adding and Assigning Roles on Program Startup

```
using System;
using System.Threading.Tasks;
using Microsoft.AspNetCore.Hosting;
using Microsoft.AspNetCore.Identity;
using Microsoft.Extensions.DependencyInjection;
using Microsoft.Extensions.Hosting;

namespace EFCore5WebApp
{
    public static class Roles
    {
        public const string ViewOnlyRoleName = "View Only";
        public const string AdminRoleName = "Admin";
    }

    public class Program
    {
        public static async Task Main(string[] args)
        {
            var webHost = CreateHostBuilder(args).Build();

            using (var scope = webHost.Services.CreateScope())
            {
                await AddAppRoles(scope.ServiceProvider);
            }

            await webHost.RunAsync();
        }
```

```
public static IHostBuilder CreateHostBuilder(string[] args) =>
    Host.CreateDefaultBuilder(args)
        .ConfigureWebHostDefaults(webBuilder =>
        {
            webBuilder.UseStartup<Startup>();
        });

private static async Task CreateRoleIfNotExists(RoleManager<
IdentityRole> roleManager, string roleName)
{
    if (!await roleManager.RoleExistsAsync(roleName))
    {
        await roleManager.CreateAsync(new IdentityRole(roleName));
    }
}

private static async Task AssignRoleToUser(UserManager<Identity
User> userManager, string userEmail, string roleName)
{
    var user = await userManager.FindByEmailAsync(userEmail);

    if (userEmail != null)
    {
        await userManager.AddToRoleAsync(user, roleName);
    }
}

private static async Task AddAppRoles(IServiceProvider
serviceProvider)
{
    var roleManager = serviceProvider.GetRequiredService<RoleManager
    <IdentityRole>>();
    var userManager = serviceProvider.GetRequiredService<UserManager
    <IdentityUser>>();

    string viewOnlyRoleName = Roles.ViewOnlyRoleName;
    string adminRoleName = Roles.AdminRoleName;
```

```
            await CreateRoleIfNotExists(roleManager, adminRoleName).
            ConfigureAwait(false);
            await CreateRoleIfNotExists(roleManager, viewOnlyRoleName).
            ConfigureAwait(false);

            var viewOnlyUserEmail = "viewonly@test.com";
            var adminUserEmail = "admin@test.com";

            await AssignRoleToUser(userManager, viewOnlyUserEmail,
            viewOnlyRoleName).ConfigureAwait(false);
            await AssignRoleToUser(userManager, adminUserEmail,
            adminRoleName).ConfigureAwait(false);
        }
    }
}
```

Next, I change the Main method to be async. Then I create a scope and call a new method I added named AddAppRoles, which does the work of adding and assigning the roles to our test users:

```
using (var scope = webHost.Services.CreateScope())
{
    await AddAppRoles(scope.ServiceProvider);
}
```

Then the web host is started asynchronously:

```
await webHost.RunAsync();
```

I found out about this technique from Andrew Lock's blog post at `https://andrewlock.net/running-async-tasks-on-app-startup-in-asp-net-core-part-1/`.

In the AddAppRoles() method, we use the RoleManager and UserManager API to check if the roles exist first and create them if they don't. Then I check to see if the users exist one by one and assign the correct roles accordingly.

Enforce Authorization

Now it is time to lock down our app. The first thing we will do is only allow access to the Contacts page if the user has either the "View Only" or the "Admin" permissions.

Authorize the Contacts Menu Item

We are going to use the SignInManager and UserManager API to make sure the user is logged in either in the "View Only" or "Admin" role to gain access to the "Contacts" and "Report" menu items. To do this, open up the View/Shared/_Layout.cshtml file and update it to match Listing 21-2.

Listing 21-2. Updated Layout with Menu-Level Authorization

```
@using Microsoft.AspNetCore.Identity

@inject SignInManager<IdentityUser> SignInManager
@inject UserManager<IdentityUser> UserManager

@{
    var userId = UserManager.GetUserId(User);
    var user = await UserManager.FindByIdAsync(userId);
}

<!DOCTYPE html>
<html lang="en">
<head>
    <meta charset="utf-8" />
    <meta name="viewport" content="width=device-width, initial-scale=1.0" />
    <title>@ViewData["Title"] - EFCore5WebApp</title>
    <link rel="stylesheet" href="~/lib/bootstrap/dist/css/bootstrap.min.css" />
    <link rel="stylesheet" href="~/css/site.css" />
</head>

<body>
    <header>
        <nav class="navbar navbar-expand-sm navbar-toggleable-sm navbar-
        light bg-white border-bottom box-shadow mb-3">
            <div class="container">
                <a class="navbar-brand" asp-area="" asp-controller="Home"
                asp-action="Index">EFCore5WebApp</a>
                <button class="navbar-toggler" type="button" data-
                toggle="collapse" data-target=".navbar-collapse" aria-
                controls="navbarSupportedContent"
```

```
                aria-expanded="false" aria-label="Toggle navigation">
            <span class="navbar-toggler-icon"></span>
        </button>
        <div class="navbar-collapse collapse d-sm-inline-flex flex-
        sm-row-reverse">
            <partial name="_LoginPartial" />
            <ul class="navbar-nav flex-grow-1">
                <li class="nav-item">
                    <a class="nav-link text-dark" asp-area="" asp-
                    controller="Home" asp-action="Index">Home</a>
                </li>
                <li class="nav-item">
                    <a class="nav-link text-dark" asp-area=""
                    asp-controller="Home" asp-action=
                    "Privacy">Privacy</a>
                </li>
                @if (SignInManager.IsSignedIn(User) && (await
                UserManager.IsInRoleAsync(user, "View Only") ||
                await UserManager.IsInRoleAsync(user, "Admin")))
                {
                    <li class="nav-item">
                        <a class="nav-link text-dark" asp-page=
                        "/Contacts/Index">Contacts</a>
                    </li>
                }

                <li class="nav-item">
                    <a class="nav-link text-dark" asp-page=
                    "/Reports/PeopleReport">Report</a>
                </li>
            </ul>
        </div>
    </div>
  </nav>
</header>
```

```
    <div class="container">
        <main role="main" class="pb-3">
            @RenderBody()
        </main>
    </div>

    <footer class="border-top footer text-muted">
        <div class="container">
            &copy; 2020 - EFCore5WebApp - <a asp-area=""
            asp-controller="Home" asp-action="Privacy">Privacy</a>
        </div>
    </footer>
    <script src="~/lib/jquery/dist/jquery.min.js"></script>
    <script src="~/lib/bootstrap/dist/js/bootstrap.bundle.min.js"></script>
    <script src="~/js/site.js" asp-append-version="true"></script>
    @await RenderSectionAsync("Scripts", required: false)
</body>
</html>
```

You can see I use the IsSignedIn() method of SignInManager to make sure the user is logged in first. Then if the user is logged in, I use the IsInRoleAsync() method on the UserManager class to make sure the user is either in the "View Only" or the "Admin" role to show the "Contacts" and "Report" menu items.

Secure Razor Pages

Next, we are going to secure our Contacts List, Create, Edit, and Delete forms to enforce authorization checks. A view-only user will be able to view records, whereas an admin will be able to do everything.

Page Access Roles

In order to remove magic strings from our application for page-level access, we are going to create a static class that will have two properties named "AllAccess" and "AdminOnly" that will be used per page. The "AllAccess" property is a list of all roles that can view and edit contacts, and "AdminOnly" will only contain the "Admin" role. Create a new class named PageAccessRoles that matches Listing 21-3 that follows.

Listing 21-3. PageAccessRoles Class

```
namespace EFCore5WebApp
{
    public static class PageAccessRoles
    {
        public const string AllAccess = "View Only, Admin";
        public const string AdminOnly = "Admin";
    }
}
```

Base Secured Page Model

In order to consolidate our common page model authorization code, we are going to create a base class that inherits from PageModel that sets properties in the page model that say what access the user has on the page. Create a new class named "SecuredPageModel" and make it match Listing 21-4.

Listing 21-4. SecuredPageModel Base Class

```
using Microsoft.AspNetCore.Identity;
using Microsoft.AspNetCore.Mvc.Filters;
using Microsoft.AspNetCore.Mvc.RazorPages;
using System.Threading.Tasks;

namespace EFCore5WebApp
{
    public class SecuredPageModel : PageModel, IAsyncPageFilter
    {
        private readonly EFCOre5WebApp.DAL.AppDbContext _context;
        private SignInManager<IdentityUser> _signInManager;
        private UserManager<IdentityUser> _userManager;
        public bool IsAdminUser { get; set; }
        public bool IsViewOnlyUser { get; set; }
        public bool IsAllAllowedUser => IsAdminUser || IsViewOnlyUser;
```

```
        public SecuredPageModel(EFCOre5WebApp.DAL.AppDbContext context,
        SignInManager<IdentityUser> signInManager,
            UserManager<IdentityUser> userManager)
        {
            _context = context;
            _signInManager = signInManager;
            _userManager = userManager;
        }

        public override async Task OnPageHandlerExecutionAsync(PageHandler
        ExecutingContext context, PageHandlerExecutionDelegate next)
        {
            var userId = _userManager.GetUserId(User);
            var user = await _userManager.FindByIdAsync(userId);
            bool isSignedIn = _signInManager.IsSignedIn(User);
            IsAdminUser = isSignedIn && await _userManager.
            IsInRoleAsync(user, Roles.AdminRoleName);
            IsViewOnlyUser = isSignedIn && await _userManager.
            IsInRoleAsync(user, Roles.ViewOnlyRoleName);

            await next.Invoke();
        }
    }
}
```

We are using the OnPageHandlerExecutionAsync() method to run some common code that sets properties that will be available when the view code binds to its page model. The IsAdminUser property is set to true when the user is an admin-only user. The IsViewOnlyUser property is set to true when the user only has the "View Only" role. The IsAllAllowedUser property is a calculated property that returns true if the user has either the "Admin" or "View Only" role.

Secure the Contacts Index Page

We will first secure the main Contacts Razor Page named "Index". To do this, we use the [Authorize()] attribute on the class passing in the list of allowed roles like this:

```
[Authorize(Roles = PageAccessRoles.AllAccess)]
After that we inherit our class from SecuredPageModel:
public class IndexModel : SecuredPageModel
```

Your updated IndexModel class should now look like Listing 21-5.

Listing 21-5. Secured Contacts Index Razor Page Controller

```
using System.Collections.Generic;
using System.Threading.Tasks;
using Microsoft.EntityFrameworkCore;
using EFCore5WebApp.Core.Entities;
using Microsoft.AspNetCore.Authorization;
using Microsoft.AspNetCore.Identity;

namespace EFCore5WebApp.Pages.Contacts
{
    [Authorize(Roles = PageAccessRoles.AllAccess)]
    public class IndexModel : SecuredPageModel
    {
        private readonly EFCOre5WebApp.DAL.AppDbContext _context;

        public IndexModel(EFCOre5WebApp.DAL.AppDbContext context,
        SignInManager<IdentityUser> signInManager,
            UserManager<IdentityUser> userManager) : base(context,
            signInManager, userManager)
        {
            _context = context;
        }

        public IList<Person> Person { get;set; }
```

```
        public async Task OnGetAsync()
        {
            Person = await _context.Persons.ToListAsync();
        }
    }
}
```

The grid on the Index page contains links to the Edit, Details, and Delete pages. We will now secure those pages so the user must have the "Admin" role to view the Edit and Delete pages, and they can view the Details link if they have the "View Only" or the "Admin" role. To do this, update the Index.cshtml Razor Page view to match Listing 21-6.

Listing 21-6. Secured Contacts Index Razor View

```
@page
@using Microsoft.AspNetCore.Identity
@model EFCore5WebApp.Pages.Contacts.IndexModel

@{
    ViewData["Title"] = "Index";
    Layout = "~/Views/Shared/_Layout.cshtml";
}

@addTagHelper *, Microsoft.AspNetCore.Mvc.TagHelpers

<h1>Index</h1>

<p>
    <a asp-page="Create">Create New</a>
</p>
<table class="table">
    <thead>
        <tr>
            <th>
                @Html.DisplayNameFor(model => model.Person[0].FirstName)
            </th>
            <th>
                @Html.DisplayNameFor(model => model.Person[0].LastName)
            </th>
```

```
                <th>
                    @Html.DisplayNameFor(model => model.Person[0].EmailAddress)
                </th>
                <th>
                    @Html.DisplayNameFor(model => model.Person[0].CreatedOn)
                </th>
                <th>
                    @Html.DisplayNameFor(model => model.Person[0].Age)
                </th>
                <th></th>
            </tr>
        </thead>
        <tbody>
            @foreach (var item in Model.Person)
            {
                <tr>
                    <td>
                        @Html.DisplayFor(modelItem => item.FirstName)
                    </td>
                    <td>
                        @Html.DisplayFor(modelItem => item.LastName)
                    </td>
                    <td>
                        @Html.DisplayFor(modelItem => item.EmailAddress)
                    </td>
                    <td>
                        @Html.DisplayFor(modelItem => item.CreatedOn)
                    </td>
                    <td>
                        @Html.DisplayFor(modelItem => item.Age)
                    </td>
                    <td>
```

```
                @if (Model.IsAdminUser)
                {
                    <a asp-page="./Edit" asp-route-id="@item.Id">Edit
                    </a> <span>|</span>
                }
                @if (Model.IsAdminUser)
                {
                    <a asp-page="./Edit" asp-route-id="@item.Id">Edit
                    </a> <span>|</span>
                }
                @if (Model.IsAllAllowedUser)
                {
                    <a asp-page="./Details" asp-route-id="@item.Id">
                    Details</a> <span>|</span>
                }
                @if (Model.IsAdminUser)
                {
                    <a asp-page="./Delete" asp-route-id="@item.Id">
                    Delete</a>
                }
            </td>
        </tr>
    }
  </tbody>
</table>
```

Secure the Contact Details Page

We will now enforce the same authorization on the Contact Details Razor page controller as seen in Listing 21-7. This authorization code will prevent an unauthorized user from creating, editing, or deleting contact records. This extra level of security is needed if a user knows the URL for the page even if they don't have the link for the page displayed to them on the website.

Listing 21-7. Secured Contact Details Page Controller

```
using System.Threading.Tasks;
using Microsoft.AspNetCore.Mvc;
using Microsoft.EntityFrameworkCore;
using EFCore5WebApp.Core.Entities;
using Microsoft.AspNetCore.Authorization;
using Microsoft.AspNetCore.Identity;

namespace EFCore5WebApp.Pages.Contacts
{

    [Authorize(Roles = PageAccessRoles.AllAccess)]
    public class DetailsModel : SecuredPageModel
    {
        private readonly EFCOre5WebApp.DAL.AppDbContext _context;

        public DetailsModel(EFCOre5WebApp.DAL.AppDbContext context,
        SignInManager<IdentityUser> signInManager,
            UserManager<IdentityUser> userManager) : base(context,
            signInManager, userManager)
        {
            _context = context;
        }

        public Person Person { get; set; }

        public async Task<IActionResult> OnGetAsync(int? id)
        {
            if (id == null)
            {
                return NotFound();
            }

            Person = await _context.Persons.Include(nameof(Person.
            Addresses)).FirstOrDefaultAsync(m => m.Id == id);
```

```
            if (Person == null)
            {
                return NotFound();
            }
            return Page();
        }
    }
}
```

The Details page contains a link to the Edit page, so we want to hide that link if the user does not have the "Admin" role. To accomplish this, update the Details.cshtml to match Listing 21-8.

Listing 21-8. Secured Details Page

```
@page
@using Microsoft.AspNetCore.Identity
@model EFCore5WebApp.Pages.Contacts.DetailsModel

@inject SignInManager<IdentityUser> SignInManager
@inject UserManager<IdentityUser> UserManager

@{
    ViewData["Title"] = "Details";
    Layout = "~/Views/Shared/_Layout.cshtml";
}

<h1>Details</h1>

<div>
    <h4>Person</h4>
    <hr />
    <dl class="row">
        <dt class="col-sm-2">
            @Html.DisplayNameFor(model => model.Person.FirstName)
        </dt>
        <dd class="col-sm-10">
            @Html.DisplayFor(model => model.Person.FirstName)
        </dd>
```

```
        <dt class="col-sm-2">
            @Html.DisplayNameFor(model => model.Person.LastName)
        </dt>
        <dd class="col-sm-10">
            @Html.DisplayFor(model => model.Person.LastName)
        </dd>
        <dt class="col-sm-2">
            @Html.DisplayNameFor(model => model.Person.EmailAddress)
        </dt>
        <dd class="col-sm-10">
            @Html.DisplayFor(model => model.Person.EmailAddress)
        </dd>
        <dt class="col-sm-2">
            @Html.DisplayNameFor(model => model.Person.CreatedOn)
        </dt>
        <dd class="col-sm-10">
            @Html.DisplayFor(model => model.Person.CreatedOn)
        </dd>
        <dt class="col-sm-2">
            @Html.DisplayNameFor(model => model.Person.Age)
        </dt>
        <dd class="col-sm-10">
            @Html.DisplayFor(model => model.Person.Age)
        </dd>
    </dl>
    <table class="table">
        <thead>
            <tr>
                <th>
                    @Html.DisplayNameFor(model => model.Person.Addresses.
                    First().AddressLine1)
                </th>
                <th>
                    @Html.DisplayNameFor(model => model.Person.Addresses.
                    First().AddressLine2)
                </th>
```

```
            <th>
                @Html.DisplayNameFor(model => model.Person.Addresses.
                First().City)
            </th>
            <th>
                @Html.DisplayNameFor(model => model.Person.Addresses.
                First().State)
            </th>
            <th>
                @Html.DisplayNameFor(model => model.Person.Addresses.
                First().Country)
            </th>
            <th>
                @Html.DisplayNameFor(model => model.Person.Addresses.
                First().ZipCode)
            </th>
            <th></th>
        </tr>
    </thead>
    <tbody>
        @foreach (var item in Model.Person.Addresses)
        {
            <tr>
                <td>
                    @Html.DisplayFor(modelItem => item.AddressLine1)
                </td>
                <td>
                    @Html.DisplayFor(modelItem => item.AddressLine2)
                </td>
                <td>
                    @Html.DisplayFor(modelItem => item.City)
                </td>
                <td>
                    @Html.DisplayFor(modelItem => item.State)
                </td>
```

```
                    <td>
                        @Html.DisplayFor(modelItem => item.Country)
                    </td>
                    <td>
                        @Html.DisplayFor(modelItem => item.ZipCode)
                    </td>
                </tr>
            }
        </tbody>
    </table>

</div>
<div>
    @if (Model.IsAdminUser)
    {
        <a asp-page="./Edit" asp-route-id="@Model.Person.Id">Edit</a>
    }
    |<a asp-page="./Index">Back to List</a>
</div>
```

Secure the Create Contact Page

Now we will secure the Create Contact Razor page controller to only allow the "Admin" role to view it as seen in Listing 21-9.

Listing 21-9. Secured Create Contact Page Controller

```
using System;
using System.Collections.Generic;
using System.Linq;
using System.Threading.Tasks;
using Microsoft.AspNetCore.Mvc;
using Microsoft.AspNetCore.Mvc.Rendering;
using EFCore5WebApp.Core.Entities;
using Microsoft.AspNetCore.Authorization;
using Microsoft.AspNetCore.Identity;
```

```
namespace EFCore5WebApp.Pages.Contacts
{
    [Authorize(Roles =PageAccessRoles.AdminOnly)]
    public class CreateModel : SecuredPageModel
    {
        private readonly EFCOre5WebApp.DAL.AppDbContext _context;

        [BindProperty(SupportsGet = true)]
        public List<SelectListItem> States { get; set; }

        [BindProperty(SupportsGet = true)]
        public List<SelectListItem> Countries { get; set; }

        public CreateModel(EFCOre5WebApp.DAL.AppDbContext context,
        SignInManager<IdentityUser> signInManager,
            UserManager<IdentityUser> userManager) : base(context,
            signInManager, userManager)
        {
            _context = context;
        }

        public IActionResult OnGet()
        {
            Person.Addresses.Add(new Address());

            States = _context.LookUps.Where(x => x.LookUpType ==
            LookUpType.State).Select(x => new SelectListItem { Text =
            x.Description, Value = x.Code }).ToList();
            Countries = _context.LookUps.Where(x => x.LookUpType ==
            LookUpType.Country).Select(x => new SelectListItem { Text =
            x.Description, Value = x.Code }).ToList();

            States.Insert(0, new SelectListItem { Text = "Select an item",
            Value = string.Empty });
            Countries.Insert(0, new SelectListItem { Text = "Select an
            item", Value = string.Empty });

            return Page();
        }
```

```
        [BindProperty(SupportsGet = true)]
        public Person Person { get; set; }

        // To protect from overposting attacks, see https://aka.ms/
        RazorPagesCRUD
        public async Task<IActionResult> OnPostAsync()
        {
            if (!ModelState.IsValid)
            {
                return Page();
            }

            Person.CreatedOn = DateTime.Now;
            _context.Persons.Add(Person);
            await _context.SaveChangesAsync();

            return RedirectToPage("./Index");
        }
    }
}
```

Secured Contact Edit Page

Next, we will secure the Contact Edit page to only allow access to the "Admin" role as seen in Listing 21-10.

Listing 21-10. Secured Contact Edit Page

```
using System.Collections.Generic;
using System.Linq;
using System.Threading.Tasks;
using Microsoft.AspNetCore.Mvc;
using Microsoft.AspNetCore.Mvc.RazorPages;
using Microsoft.AspNetCore.Mvc.Rendering;
using Microsoft.EntityFrameworkCore;
using EFCore5WebApp.Core.Entities;
using Microsoft.AspNetCore.Authorization;
using Microsoft.AspNetCore.Identity;
```

```
namespace EFCore5WebApp.Pages.Contacts
{
    [Authorize(Roles = PageAccessRoles.AdminOnly)]
    public class EditModel : PageModel
    {
        private readonly EFCOre5WebApp.DAL.AppDbContext _context;

        [BindProperty(SupportsGet = true)]
        public List<SelectListItem> States { get; set; }

        [BindProperty(SupportsGet = true)]
        public List<SelectListItem> Countries { get; set; }

        public EditModel(EFCOre5WebApp.DAL.AppDbContext context,
        SignInManager<IdentityUser> signInManager,
            UserManager<IdentityUser> userManager) : base(context,
            signInManager, userManager)
        {
            _context = context;
        }

        [BindProperty]
        public Person Person { get; set; }

        public async Task<IActionResult> OnGetAsync(int? id)
        {
            if (id == null)
            {
                return NotFound();
            }

            Person = await _context.Persons.Include("Addresses").
            FirstOrDefaultAsync(m => m.Id == id);

            if (Person == null)
            {
                return NotFound();
            }
```

```
            States = _context.LookUps.Where(x => x.LookUpType ==
            LookUpType.State).Select(x => new SelectListItem { Text =
            x.Description, Value = x.Code }).ToList();
            Countries = _context.LookUps.Where(x => x.LookUpType ==
            LookUpType.Country).Select(x => new SelectListItem { Text =
            x.Description, Value = x.Code }).ToList();

            States.Insert(0, new SelectListItem { Text = "Select an item",
            Value = string.Empty });
            Countries.Insert(0, new SelectListItem { Text = "Select an
            item", Value = string.Empty });

            return Page();
        }

        // To protect from overposting attacks, enable the specific
        properties you want to bind to.
        // For more details, see https://aka.ms/RazorPagesCRUD.
        public async Task<IActionResult> OnPostAsync()
        {
            if (!ModelState.IsValid)
            {
                return Page();
            }

            _context.Attach(Person).State = EntityState.Modified;

            try
            {
                await _context.SaveChangesAsync();
            }
            catch (DbUpdateConcurrencyException)
            {
                if (!PersonExists(Person.Id))
                {
                    return NotFound();
                }
```

```
                else
                {
                    throw;
                }
            }

            return RedirectToPage("./Index");
        }

        private bool PersonExists(int id)
        {
            return _context.Persons.Any(e => e.Id == id);
        }
    }
}
```

Secured Contact Delete Page

Lastly, we will secure the Contact Delete page to only allow access to the "Admin" role as seen in Listing 21-11.

Listing 21-11. Secured Contact Delete Page

```
using System.Threading.Tasks;
using Microsoft.AspNetCore.Mvc;
using Microsoft.AspNetCore.Mvc.RazorPages;
using Microsoft.EntityFrameworkCore;
using EFCore5WebApp.Core.Entities;
using Microsoft.AspNetCore.Authorization;
using Microsoft.AspNetCore.Identity;

namespace EFCore5WebApp.Pages.Contacts
{
    [Authorize(Roles = PageAccessRoles.AdminOnly)]
    public class DeleteModel : PageModel
    {
        private readonly EFCOre5WebApp.DAL.AppDbContext _context;
```

```
        public DeleteModel(EFCOre5WebApp.DAL.AppDbContext context,
        SignInManager<IdentityUser> signInManager,
           UserManager<IdentityUser> userManager) : base(context,
           signInManager, userManager)
        {
            _context = context;
        }

        [BindProperty]
        public Person Person { get; set; }

        public async Task<IActionResult> OnGetAsync(int? id)
        {
            if (id == null)
            {
                return NotFound();
            }

            Person = await _context.Persons.Include(nameof(Person.
            Addresses)).FirstOrDefaultAsync(m => m.Id == id);

            if (Person == null)
            {
                return NotFound();
            }
            return Page();
        }

        public async Task<IActionResult> OnPostAsync(int? id)
        {
            if (id == null)
            {
                return NotFound();
            }

            Person = await _context.Persons.Include(nameof(Person.
            Addresses)).SingleOrDefaultAsync(x => x.Id == id);
```

```
            if (Person != null)
            {
                _context.Persons.Remove(Person);
                await _context.SaveChangesAsync();
            }

            return RedirectToPage("./Index");
        }
    }
}
```

Summary

In this chapter, I covered how to enable and enforce role-based security in an ASP.NET Core app. Then I covered how to use the RoleManager and UserManager API to create and assign roles to users. Lastly, we went through the contact pages and enforced role-based security on the Razor page controllers and views as well as the main menu-level access. In the next chapter, I will go over some resources that you can use to continue learning about Entity Framework Core 5 in general and techniques for further use in ASP.NET Core.

PART V

Learning More

CHAPTER 22

Delving Deeper

In this chapter, I will point you to some resources that will help you learn more about the fine details of Entity Framework Core 5 and ASP.NET Core MVC.

You can find a list of what's new in Entity Framework Core 5 from Microsoft online at `https://docs.microsoft.com/en-us/ef/core/what-is-new/ef-core-5.0/whatsnew`.

You can find Microsoft's list of breaking changes in Entity Framework Core 5 at `https://docs.microsoft.com/en-us/ef/core/what-is-new/ef-core-5.0/breaking-changes`. This will be useful if you are upgrading from a prior version of Entity Framework Core in your project.

You can find Microsoft's official Entity Framework Core documentation online at `https://docs.microsoft.com/en-us/ef/core/`. This site covers many facets of Entity Framework Core, both old and new.

If you would like to really hone your Razor Pages skills, then Learn Razor Pages is a great resource, which is online at `www.learnrazorpages.com/`.

If you would like to learn more about ASP.NET Core, then look no further than Microsoft's official documentation at `https://docs.microsoft.com/en-us/aspnet/core/?view=aspnetcore-3.1`.

You can get the latest version of .NET 5 at `https://dotnet.microsoft.com/download/dotnet/5.0` and the official .NET Framework documentation at `https://docs.microsoft.com/en-us/dotnet/`.

Also look out for a new Entity Framework Core 5 expert-level book soon.

E. Vogel, *Beginning Entity Framework Core 5*, https://doi.org/10.1007/978-1-4842-6882-7_22

CHAPTER 23

Conclusion

Thank you for reading my book. I hope you enjoyed reading it as much as I enjoyed writing it. Throughout your journey, you have learned the basics of Entity Framework Core 5.

We started our journey by learning how to install and set up Entity Framework Core 5 with Visual Studio. After that, we went over how to create your first EF Core data model and how to seed it with some data.

Once we laid the foundation, we learned the core features of any Entity Framework Core 5 project including how to create, read, update, and delete data. After that, we learned about navigation properties and how to structure related data in our data model.

After we learned the core functionality of EF Core 5, we picked up some more advanced data modeling techniques. These techniques included aggregations, stored procedures, and migrations. With these techniques, we can structure our data in a way that is easy to report upon.

For our final path in our journey, we learned about how to effectively use EF Core 5 on the Web with ASP.NET Core MVC. We first covered how to register and log in new users. Then we learned how to scaffold our Create, Read, Update, and Delete (CRUD) Razor Pages. After the scaffolding was in place, we then dived deeper into how to perform these operations effectively on the Web.

After that, we learned how to put our understanding of group by and aggregations into practice to create a basic HTML report that grouped contact records by their state of residence.

For the last step, we learned how to implement role-based security for our CRUD web app. It took some hard work, but in the end, we have a web app that is very similar to what you will encounter in the real world.

Thank you so much for reading my book. You can find the final code for the book online at `https://github.com/Apress/beg-entity-framework-core-5`. Any updates to the book text from the time of publication can be found online at `https://www.apress.com/in`. Good luck on your journeys with Entity Framework Core 5, and look out for Apress's future expert book on Entity Framework Core 5.

E. Vogel, *Beginning Entity Framework Core 5*, https://doi.org/10.1007/978-1-4842-6882-7_23

Index

E. Vogel, *Beginning Entity Framework Core 5*, https://doi.org/10.1007/978-1-4842-6882-7

D

E

F

G

H

I, J, K

L

T

U

V

W, X, Y, Z

Printed in the United States
by Baker & Taylor Publisher Services